ACTION

ACTION
A Guide for Actors

Sabin Epstein

McFarland & Company, Inc., Publishers
Jefferson, North Carolina

Sweat by Lynn Nottage, Act II, Scene 3, pp. 79–83.
From *Sweat* by Lynn Nottage. Copyright © by Lynn Nottage.
Published by Theatre Communications Group.
Used by permission of Theatre Communications Group.

"Act II, scene IV" from *Tartuffe* by Molière,
translated into English verse by Richard Wilbur.
English translation copyright © 1963, 1962, 1961
and renewed 1991, 1990 and 1989 by Richard Wilbur.
Reprinted by permission of Mariner Books,
an imprint of HarperCollins Publishers LLC.
All rights reserved.

ISBN (print) 978-1-4766-8896-1
ISBN (ebook) 978-1-4766-4778-4

Library of Congress and British Library
cataloguing data are available

Library of Congress Control Number 2023001115

© 2023 Sabin Epstein. All rights reserved

*No part of this book may be reproduced or transmitted in any form
or by any means, electronic or mechanical, including photocopying
or recording, or by any information storage and retrieval system,
without permission in writing from the publisher.*

Front cover photograph © 2023 Shutterstock

Printed in the United States of America

*McFarland & Company, Inc., Publishers
Box 611, Jefferson, North Carolina 28640
www.mcfarlandpub.com*

Table of Contents

Acknowledgments — vii
Preface — 1
Introduction — 3

One. Basic Concepts — 13
Two. Communication — 31
Three. Verse — 45
Four. The Sonnet: The Argument — 60
Five. The Soliloquy: Transformation — 73
Six. The Scene: The Loop, Part I — 94
Seven. The Scene: The Loop, Part II — 107
Eight. Molière: Status — 124
Nine. Congreve: Extended Character — 155
Ten. Ibsen: Opposites — 182
Eleven. Shaw: The Basic 8 — 209
Twelve. Nottage: Releases — 230

Appendix: Additional Plays and Playwrights — 251
Glossary — 253
Sources and Resources — 257
Index of Games and Exercises — 259

Tourist to a New Yorker:
"How do I get to Carnegie Hall?"

New Yorker to the Tourist:
"Practice, practice, practice."

Acknowledgments

I'd like to recognize my incomparable mentor, Edward Hastings, as well as Allen Fletcher and William Ball, inspiring teachers and directors at the American Conservatory Theatre in San Francisco, Rick Seer for his support while at the Old Globe/University of San Diego MFA Program, and colleagues Michael Cobb, Robert Davidson, Larry Hecht, Ashley Temple, and Daniel Renner, of the National Theatre Conservatory in Denver, for their collaboration and artistry.

Thank you as well to Richard Alleman, Allen Baker, Isabelle Clark, Dr. Andrew Hartley, Deborah Hecht, Kush Modgil, Anthony Newfield, Andrew Schwartz, Gail Shapiro, Kelly Siracusa, Lindsay Rae Taylor, and Lara Teeter, for their encouragement while preparing this text. And to Jan Gist, Theresa Dudeck, and Keith Johnstone for their generosity in supporting this project.

Special thanks to Dr. Tom Markus, for his invaluable insights about arranging and organizing this material, to Anne Penner, Karen Robinson, Pierre Bouchard, Steven Marzolf and Dr. Clare Hammoor for their feedback, insight and suggestions while developing this manuscript.

A very special note of gratitude to the late John Harrop, without whom this book would not have been written.

Preface

In 1998, I was working with a group of advanced acting students in Los Angeles; they were wonderfully adept at stripping away the artifice of acting, yet they couldn't play an *action* to save their lives. Although they were very busy *feeling,* they weren't very busy *doing.*

Yes, they were earnest, eager, and committed to the art as well as the craft of acting, yet their training had not provided them with any practical instruction in the basics of communication—both verbal and non-verbal—nor helped them to develop a methodology to rehearse and work on their own. I soon realized there are many actors, whatever their age or experience, who were in the same boat.

I also discovered that with a bit of practice, patience and persistence, these challenges could be overcome. The result? Trained actors who could play any type of text, from the classics to sitcoms, with confidence, imagination, a reliable process and a palpable sense of joy in performance.

This book is a distillation of the work begun in those early days of 1998, and I'm delighted to share this work with you now.

Introduction

Action: A Guide for Actors, with its emphasis on rehearsing the rehearsal—learning *how* to work as well as *what* to work—is an amalgamation of seemingly disparate techniques combined to create a fresh perspective, a fresh way of looking at communication, creativity and story-telling, as well as a fresh way of thinking about actor training, rehearsals and rehearsing.

This process transcends race, gender, political, social or sexual orientation. It is applicable to all plays, accessible to all players.

Action: A Guide for Actors has been tested and retested in a variety of venues, from 6th grade acting classes to BA, BFA, and MFA acting programs, from elite conservatory training programs to community theatres, with beginners as well as with seasoned professionals working on both stage and screen.

The material in this book has been taught as a full-year acting class, as a one-semester course focusing on selected aspects of the training, and in separate workshops focusing on a single writer—classical *or* contemporary—with an ever-evolving process.

In each and every instance, the process has worked because it's accessible, applicable, approachable, understandable, relatable, challenging, fresh, flexible and new.

RTN

If there's one defining theory underlying all of *Action: A Guide for Actors*, it's this: all scenes are organized around the concept of RTN: Relationships Transforming Now. The entire premise of this book is built on the belief that when you invest in playing *action*, not emotion, the process of relationships transforming becomes intensely interesting to watch, intensely interesting to experience—viscerally as well as emotionally—and intensely interesting to play. This process of transformation, with a clear beginning, middle and end, defines, shapes and guides the work to come.

Vocabulary

Just as there are only so many roads into Rome, there are only so many different ways to describe objectives, obstacles, given circumstances—the basic vocabulary for the process of acting as codified by Constantin Stanislavski in the late nineteenth and early twentieth centuries.

If we acknowledge and accept the fact that almost all trainers/teachers/coaches are trying to move us to the same point of understanding, using their own unique vocabularies, we must also acknowledge and accept the fact that sometimes one instructor will speak in a vocabulary that resonates with us, so that we suddenly "get it," whereas before we didn't.

Whatever the cause, we thank our lucky stars when we seemingly chance upon those moments, when we hear and see what the instructor's saying and the thought drops into the body: it's no longer a concept, it's an experience. We can then think of it as our own.

Perhaps, at some point in our lives, we'll pass it along to someone else, someone who's struggling with understanding and experiencing that very same concept. They'll hear us and "get it."

Experiential Vocabulary

Throughout this book, we'll be using a very specific, somewhat esoteric vocabulary to describe playing action: The Loop, The Bounce, status, mask/modeling, the Basic 8, and releases. Don't worry about learning or remembering all the names—they'll become clearer to you with time and experience. Also, no one else needs to understand this vocabulary but you and your partner(s).

This vocabulary is a way to communicate in a shared language based on shared experiences. It may not make much sense at first, but give it some time and see how it expands in meaning as you move through the process.

The Design of the Training Sequence

As you work your way through this text, you'll begin to see the overall design of the training sequence: we start with basics and gradually, exponentially and very carefully develop an ever-evolving and ever-expanding vocabulary, and an ever-evolving, ever-expanding technique, one that will enable you to unlock any text and play it with authority, surety and passion. Your technique—and the freedom of play that the mastery of technique affords—becomes more sophisticated as you move from chapter to chapter, author to author, scene to scene.

Heightened Language

Throughout, we'll be working with texts of "heightened language"—i.e., with language expressing intense or passionate emotions with intense and passionate images as well as intense or passionate thoughts. These texts are linguistically rich, psychologically complex and artistically challenging.

Each section includes suggestions for additional scene work organized around the same principle but sourced from more contemporary plays. There's an appendix at the end of the book with additional plays for you to consider for scene work.

If you prefer to start with modern plays and work your way toward more heightened language, begin *Action: A Guide for Actors* with the first three chapters, which detail the basic principles of communication, language and operative speech.

Once you've absorbed these principles, move into contemporary monologue or scene work, gradually adding the tools found in each successive chapter. This way you'll work in a parallel manner, developing skills by playing with slightly less challenging language.

Test the process—it works with all material, at all levels of experience.

The Process Itself

If art imitates life, then perhaps the opposite is also true: life imitates art. So, we'll start the process in Chapter One by examining the basic building blocks of acting and playing. You'll be introduced to the theories underlying our point of view about training and you'll begin to build an experiential vocabulary by playing a series of games involving the basics of action.

Since we see language as the foundation of our work, we'll examine the various components of verbal, vocal and visceral communication in Chapter Two. We'll also review the basics of grammar, language and rhetoric—the tools you'll need to approach that greatest of all writers of heightened language, William Shakespeare.

Chapter Three explores the technical elements you'll need in order to identify the clues hidden in Shakespeare's language, and we'll suggest ways you can translate what you read on the page into what you say—and play—on the stage.

Throughout, we'll stress playing text-based objectives, text-based obstacles and text-based given circumstances—the building blocks of Stanislavski's acting system.

In Chapter Four, we'll work with one of Shakespeare's sonnets, exercising the ability to play with technical accuracy while delving into the objectives and given circumstances motivating "the argument" of the text.

In Chapter Five, we'll advance the work by exploring a soliloquy, working on the structure of the speech to build the argument as well as its contradictory emotional content.

In Chapters Six and Seven, we'll bring all of this inner and outer work together by working the Richard/Lady Anne scene—Act I, scene two—from *King Richard III*.

Organization

From this point forward, the chapters are organized in distinct sections: there'll always be a discussion of the text in question and/or the concepts involved in acting and playing said text; a section applying those concepts, through analysis, as we work through a reading of a scene from the text, and a final section introducing rehearsal tools to be used in tandem with the step-by-step guide for rehearsing the rehearsal of the text.

Each successive chapter involves a different playwright, progressing historically from the 17th to the 21st century, embracing a wide variety of styles, concepts and tools for you to explore.

Introduction 7

The tools in Chapters Ten, Eleven and Twelve might just as well be exchanged for the tools in Chapters Six, Seven, Eight and Nine. However, we've organized the progression of the tools to correspond to what we see as the unique demands of playing each scene.

Modeling

Throughout, we'll model textual "detective work"—i.e., how to read, analyze and develop an interpretation of the text from an actor's point of view. What you'll be reading here is *our* interpretation of the text, how we see and understand it. We do this in order for you to learn what questions to ask while you read, analyze and develop *your* interpretation of the text.

Our focusing on text work is designed to eliminate the guessing, the "it seems to me…" school of acting and rehearsing. We want you to base your work on facts found in—and to make choices informed by—the text, not in spite of it.

You may choose to work and rehearse the scene we model, or you may choose to work a different scene—preferably one from the same play or by the same playwright. And, as we said earlier, there are suggestions for more contemporary plays suggested at the end of each chapter. The choice is yours.

Self-Direction

The exercises and games are tools for you to use to strengthen your imagination while exploring the material. They'll guide you and then help you refine your choices. Once we start working with a text, you'll be working without a director. As trained actors, you'll be expected to bring ideas into the rehearsal room—to be an active participant in the creative process—rather than a marionette, executing what you've been told to do. Now's the time to start flexing those creative muscles.

Step by Step

Once we start *rehearsing the rehearsal*, we'll divide the text into three "acts"—a technique developed by the actor and acting teacher Michael Chekhov for identifying the beginning, middle and end of the action within a text. We do this with solo as well as partnered texts. We intentionally divide texts into acts to focus on the moment-to-moment—the M2M—playing of action.

By focusing on M2M—the moment-to-moment—playing, you will train yourself to be specific, to hunt out the small, quiet, hidden moments in the text, those moments of stillness, of silences, giving a scene its unique nuance and flavor.

Prep Time

The prep work—the "detective work"—needs to be done on your own, before rehearsals begin. As with everything in life, what you put into the work is what you take out of it. The more investigating you can do by researching and parsing the text *before* rehearsal begins, the richer the rehearsal experience will be. And, the more time you can invest in rehearsing, the faster you'll progress.

Table Work

After the prep work, you will move to the "table work"—where you and your partner sit opposite one another, reading and beginning to act the scene. You'll repeat the table read *three* times. In fact, you will repeat each step of the rehearsal process *three* times. We'll guide you through the process, step by step.

First Showing

Your first showing—for your instructor and fellow students—will be your work on Act I of your scene, be it four lines or four pages long. You'll have rehearsed Act I approximately three times in rehearsal. When you show the work, you will receive feedback and notes from your instructor. Your classmates may also be invited to offer feedback.

Feedback

As an observer of the work, when asked to comment, always start with "this worked for me," or "this didn't work for me." You'll learn as much by watching as you will by doing. And having to articulate your thoughts and observations will help clarify your own process. Remember, it's called feedback, not directing.

Introduction

The feedback from your coach will be positive and encouraging, acknowledging the work you've done up to this point in the process as well as pointing the way for your work in the next steps in the process.

Take in and consider the feedback—i.e., what's working, what isn't, what needs adjusting or re-thinking. You're "inside" the scene—you can only go by what it feels like to you. The feedback is offered from an invested but objective point-of-view and, therefore, is valuable for its objectivity.

Being in "the hot seat" after a scene is always challenging. You may be asked questions you aren't readily able to answer; it's always easier to answer those questions when you're watching and *outside* the scene rather than having just been *in* the scene. As an observer, be patient and understanding during the feedback.

2nd and 3rd Showings

The second presentation involves showing Acts One & Two of your scene. The third (and final) time you show the work, you will work the entire scene, focusing on the full 180 degrees, or the "arc" of the scene. There will be feedback after every showing.

Rehearsing the rehearsal is not something to do by rote. It changes with each scene, with each rehearsal. Though you'll be using the same steps of the rehearsal process—The Template—you may be using more of one step than another, depending on your understanding of the needs of the character and your desire to expand or increase the quality of play in the scene itself.

Perfection

Although you want to play well, to do it "right," sometimes, in order to do it right, you first have to do it wrong. You may have to eliminate choices and reprioritize your options—by keeping, fixing, cutting or changing what you do—in order to arrive at what works best. This is a normal part of the rehearsal process.

Everyone works and grows at their own rate, their own speed. There's no predicting when you'll stumble into *insight,* that wonderful process of integrating physical experience with intellectual understanding. Sometimes the understanding happens long after the experience.

Remember, mastery of technique evolves over a long period of time. Usually, it's imperceptible. Suddenly, you're able to do things you've been struggling with; you don't know how or when you've changed, you just know you have. Your awareness—your perception—develops as your technique improves; as your technique improves, so does your awareness, your perception. You see more because suddenly there's more to see.

The first half of this book focuses primarily on **acting:** *what* you do and *why* you do it. As you become more proficient in engaging in action, the second half of this book shifts focus to the **playing** of action: *who* you are as the character and *how* you do what you do. There'll be some overlap between the two sections, but this is the primary design of the book.

Tools

As mentioned earlier, each scene you work will introduce a new tool or a new game or games to be used in rehearsal. It's not a question of being dutiful with the tools or games—use them when they're needed, don't use them when they're not. The tools are just that: tools.

The Games

The exercises and games are inspired by (and culled from) many different sources:

- from Viola Spolin, author of *Improvisations for the Theatre,* we incorporate her approach to improvisation and theatre games with written texts;
- from master acting teacher Earl Gister, we use the approach to action he taught at the Yale School of Drama—what we call The Loop;
- and from Rudolf Laban, an Austrian-Hungarian pioneer in movement analysis and action description, we work with what we call The Basic 8, a technical yet highly practical approach to what Stanislavski called "the spine" of a character.

Keith Johnstone

Most significantly, throughout this book, we'll be working with tools and games devised by Keith Johnstone, the founder of Theatre Sports and author of *Impro,* a ground-breaking and eye-opening book about action, status, and spontaneity.

Improvising

At times, you'll be improvising what we call **all offer/all accept** scenes, in which you must *offer* something to stimulate and provoke your partner's imagination, and you must *accept* your partner's offer by saying "yes." This is the basis for **The Bounce,** the dynamic exchange of energy we look for when acting and playing.

Sources

We'll also be referencing work from *Shakespeare's Shapely Speech*, devised by Jan Gist, Head of Voice, Speech and Text at the Old Globe MFA Actor Training Program. We will incorporate thoughts about creativity, communication and process from Edward de Bono, a British cognitive theorist and author of *Lateral Thinking.*

We'll incorporate guidelines, insights and exercises in approaching text inspired by British master voice/speech/text teacher Cicely Berry, director John Barton and American director Barry Edelstein.

We will also reference psychotherapist Dr. David Richo's approach to five basic developmental needs we see as underlying objectives.

In addition, we'll refer to thoughts, games, and insights from colleagues Larry Hecht, Ashlee Temple, Michael Cobb, Allison Watrous and Timothy McCracken, all of the National Theatre Conservatory.

Playing the Games

Many of the games may be familiar to you. If so, *please* seize the opportunity to explore them in greater depth, making your playing more specific, more exact, more moment-to-moment. If the games and exercises are new to you, *please* dive in with a sense of adventure and possibility. Be open to the new.

The important thing to gather from these sources and resources is the diversity, the breadth of influences and the wide range of thoughts and theories running throughout this book. We've borrowed from them, we acknowledge them and we encourage you to study each and every one of them in depth. There's a bibliography at the end of the book—Sources and Resources—to guide you in exploring the sources.

Action: A Guide for Actors evolved, slowly, over time, from all these sources, and from many, many more. From the "old," something "new"—or at least something "new-ish"—has been created.

What's Next

In the first chapter, we'll begin to examine the concepts and principles informing our approach to acting and the playing of objectives through actions, not emotions. We'll begin to develop a practical vocabulary for playing action—one involving The Bounce and The Loop.

One

BASIC CONCEPTS

Let's start by playing a game. After you've played, we'll take some time to discuss the game, its various component parts and see how they all work together.

Tell a Story

*In this game, you start with your own story and then trade stories with a partner. Trading stories means you have to tell the story **as if** it happened to you. Build your story based on the facts you hear. Fill in the rest of the details by inventing what you don't know. You'll have heard enough of the story, through its repetition, to grasp its essential meaning.*

*Once you own your partner's story, create a back story—a **subtext**— about your relationship with your partner, i.e., who you are to one another, why it's important to say what you have to say to this person now and what you want to change in the relationship by telling this story. Remember: the story has to have a purpose, a reason for being told.*

When you finally trade stories for the last time, you won't be telling your own story, you'll be telling your story as it's been reinvented by your partner. You will have moved from nonfiction—your story—to fiction— the new story.

Your task is to discover the new truth of the story, play it with conviction, authority, and authenticity, and make your partner believe this story really happened to you. That's why it's called acting.

Your instructor will call out directions and guide you as needed.

Action

Start by choosing a partner.

1. Sit facing your partner.
2. Tell a story—an anecdote, something that actually happened to you.
3. Let's add an obstacle to the playing: talk simultaneously.
4. Tell the same story to a new partner in one minute.
5. Stand.
6. With a different partner, physicalize the story—use your hands, body language, whatever you need to illustrate and act out the story.
7. With a different partner, tell the story with gestures but without words.
8. With a different partner, tell the story in words without movement.
9. Return to your original partner.
10. Concentrate on receiving your partner's story, even though you're still talking simultaneously.
11. Trade stories.
12. Own your new story.
13. Add a physical life—with gestures and movement—to your new story.
14. Tell the entire story in thirty seconds.
15. Tell the entire story in fifteen seconds.
16. Use just three sentences: one for the beginning, one for the middle, and one for the end of the story.
17. In five seconds, reduce the story to three key words. Use gestures.
18. Reduce the story to one sound containing the essence of each key word.
19. Repeat the sound, adding movement to it.
20. Exchange sounds with your partner, returning to your original story.
21. Extend the essential sound and gesture you've been given into three key words suggesting the beginning, middle and end of your new story.

22. Extend the three key words into three key sentences.
23. Tell your story in thirty seconds, with the three sentences forming the beginning, middle, and end of your story.
24. Repeat your story, never breaking eye contact with your partner.
25. One at a time, tell your story to each other.
26. Endow your partner, creating a relationship.
27. Give yourself a reason for telling the story, one that affects and changes your relationship with your partner.
28. You must make your partner's story yours.

Take a moment and talk with your partner about the experience. Notice how the story became more specific with each telling, how the point of the story became clearer and more economical with each telling, and how you wanted your partner to react as you told your story for the last time.

In essence, you were rehearsing the rehearsal, i.e., repeating the process over and over again until the action became more focused, direct, purposeful and powerful. The focus was always on making your partner react, not on how you were feeling.

Part A: Acting

Stories

Stories are about relationships changing. Something's wrong/off/askew at the beginning of the story and something's righted by the end of the story: strangers become lovers, lovers become estranged, everyone lives, someone dies. Sometimes, after trying as hard as they might, the relationship itself doesn't change but the *character* does. Whatever the outcome, the character is always in motion, and that motion—that *action*—is the story itself.

The Act of Theatre

An audience enters the theatre hoping to lose themselves in a well told (and, in some cases, oft told) story. They want to experience a tale of transformation and change, one told with clarity, immediacy, passion. Your job, as the actor, is to discover what the story you're telling is really about, determine how your character fits into and participates in the story and then immerse the audience as deeply as possible in the story by engaging in high stakes action.

The Art of Acting

Acting is predicated on the belief that *non-fictional behavior* happens within a *fictional* context, i.e., real communication happens between people in a make-believe world. What we witness, as an audience, is *behavior* transforming as well as *relationships* transforming. Behavior is what we *do* 24/7. It's not what we *feel*, it's what we *do*. Feeling is the result of the doing.

Action

Acting is a psychological and physical process—there's an internal want and an outer, physical expression of that want: an action. For example, imagine you're preparing to go on a first date with someone you've admired from a distance. You're in your room. What do you do? You try on a new outfit, you style your hair, you brush your teeth, you polish your shoes. Why? Because you *want* your date to like you. To do so, you have to make a good first impression.

A Goal

Though the outcome of the date is unknown, you have a goal in mind as you prepare: the date will either bring you two closer together or further apart. Whatever happens, by engaging in action—going out together—you're about to change the status quo of the relationship.

The 3 R's

As we've said before, all scenes, all plays, are about **Relationships Transforming** in the present, in the **Now**.

We're always in relationship with three things:

- with *ourselves,* as experienced in the inner monologue, the self-talk we hear in our heads every moment of our lives;

- with our *environment*—be it the room we've been sent to as punishment, or the social, political and cultural world we live in now, or the one we aspire to live in. The environment is part of the external, physical world;
- and, finally, with *people* and *objects* in our environment.

Text, Context, Subtext

The actor's roadmap for the RTN—the Relationship Transforming Now—is found in the **text:** the spoken word.

However, text does not exist in a vacuum; it exists within a **context:** the way things are—the facts—before the action begins. Stanislavski called these facts the "given circumstances."

Context conditions, tones, affects *how* you act, what you can and cannot do *when* you act, and the way in which you can and cannot behave *while* you act. *Context = the rules of the game.*

These rules must be agreed upon by all players in order to be in the same world, i.e., if I think we're playing checkers and you think we're playing chess, chances are we're going to have a problem.

A shared *personal* context establishes the history between the characters—the backstory—and, with it, the level and degree of tension existing in the relationship before the action begins.

Finally, the text is a reflection of the **subtext**—the inner psychological wants, needs, and desires compelling you, the character, to act. Subtext gives text and context forward momentum.

Acting is what a character does in a scene. Playing is how the actor does it.

The Building Blocks

Here are the building blocks, the individual components you'll need as you begin to discover and play action. We're introducing all of them now, and will focus on them individually as the work progresses.

Objectives

The desire—the "want for change" is what we call an **objective**.
There are many different ways to name, define or state an objective:

sometimes an objective is called *an intention*, sometimes *a want*. Each definition has a slightly different flavor, but they're all describing the same thing: the psychological wants and needs we use to propel us in time as we *plan* what we intend to do, or as we *justify* what we've done. An objective is always present in whatever we do.

Sometimes you may start the hunt for the objective by saying, "I want you to understand," or "I want to convince you." That's fine, as a starting point. Then ask yourself: what would change or what would happen, what would I get or receive if my partner understood or was convinced? Keep asking that question—what would happen if—until you discover what you really want, which is usually something visceral, immediate, tangible, and/or something to transform the relationship, and then rename the objective to include that want.

For example, transform "I want you to understand" to "I need you to make me feel" (happy, sad, grateful), or "I want to convince you that I love you" to "I want you to embrace me."

Use the verbs "understand" or "convince" to lead you into what you want your partner to do to you, how you want them to make you feel—and then focus on that new information as your objective.

Objectives are always stated in the form of infinitive verbs attached to the phrase, "I want you to…," such as "I want you to make me smile," or "I want you to forgive me." Objectives are positive, immediate, and obtainable.

Action

Action does not always involve physical activity. Sometimes you're waiting for an important phone call, or you're thinking about your life and how it might change. In both instances, the *outer* action is about stillness and the *inner* action is in turmoil as you think, plan, contemplate your options.

Action is always focused on affecting and changing someone—yourself and/or someone else. The character always transforms in the process. However, characters do not always get what they want.

But characters are always engaged in the pursuit of the objective. Larry Hecht, Head of Acting at the National Theatre Conservatory, calls acting "the passionate pursuit of the objective."

The 5 A's

In his book *How to Be an Adult*, psychologist Dr. David Richo identifies five basic human developmental and emotional *needs*: attention, affection, acceptance, allowance, and appreciation. If these needs were not fulfilled in childhood, we spend the rest of our lives searching for them.

Each of these 5 A's can be used as *generic* objectives—umbrellas hovering over the interior life of the character. They become the secret motivation informing every *specific* action the character undertakes.

For example, a brash, argumentative misanthrope may be acting out her need for attention, while a rebellious teenager may be acting out his need for acceptance. More specifically, Willie Loman in *Death of a Salesman* needs acceptance and allowance, a purpose, a meaning in his life. "Attention must be paid," says his wife, Linda. What does he do? He strives to become visible, to feel potent, vibrant once again. Even more specifically, he wants to continue with his job, to be the breadwinner, to have the respect of his children.

Or: Blanche Dubois in *A Streetcar Named Desire* craves attention, affection, beauty, intimacy. Even more specifically: a home of her own, financial security, escape from the realities of her all too real world of physical and emotional deprivation.

Obstacles

Sometimes what we *feel* propels us into action: we're angry, so we lash out, we're lonely, so we reach out to someone. Most often what we feel is a reaction to what's been said or done to us. Feelings can *motivate* us, or they can be an impediment—an **obstacle**—to what we do.

Inner Obstacles

Characters have ingrained beliefs and patterns of behavior, just as we do. These patterns and beliefs are the **inner obstacles** for the character: they inhibit the passionate pursuit of the objective and must be overcome in order for the character to reach their desired end.

As an example: imagine you're playing Pryor Walter in the first scene between Louis Ironson and Pryor in Tony Kushner's *Angels in America*. Pryor ends the scene by telling Louis he's been diagnosed with AIDS. Pryor knows Louis has an intense fear of death and a history of abandoning people in trouble, which are obstacles in their relationship.

Pryor may be angry, afraid, insecure—his inner obstacles—as he starts the scene, but he *has* to tell Louis about his diagnosis. He uses a series of tactics: to tease, cajole, argue, shame, blame, commiserate, humor Louis—to change Louis' behavior—until the moment when he feels the truth can be spoken.

Punchlines

When you tell a story, what's most important, the set-up or the **punchline**? If you don't have the set-up, there's no pay-off; if you don't know the punchline, there's no direction, no focus to the set-up. Once you know the punchline, you can shape the playing—the telling of the story, and the moment when the relationship transforms—to have maximum impact.

Reaching the punchline is the objective in every thought, speech, scene, play. Sometimes it's overt, sometimes covert. But it's always there, at the end of every thought, speech, scene, play.

Tactics

Imagine you're standing at a door, arguing with a friend: you either want to leave—in which case, why don't you?—or perhaps you want your friend to *make* you stay. Standing at the door threatening to leave becomes a **tactic.**

When you don't get what you want, you have to adjust, shift course, try something new, to get what you want. Think of a small child wanting its mother's attention: the child will repeatedly call out to its mother, then cry, then have a tantrum, then tug on its mother's clothes, or lie down on the floor. The child doesn't give up. It keeps inventing new ways to demand attention until it gets what it wants. A change in tactic involves a change in action.

Mono-Action

If your tactics *don't* shift in a scene, you'll end up playing one action over and over again. We call this **mono-acting**. Initially, the action may be interesting, but if it doesn't change, it becomes tiresome, then tedious, then boring.

Super-Objectives

The beat-to-beat, moment-to-moment, scene-to-scene objectives are held together by the "**super objective**," i.e., the **meta-punchline** at the end of the play. This meta-punchline is the magnet giving the action forwardness, flow, direction, momentum. Whereas objectives involve transforming someone else, the super-objective is almost always about transforming the character itself.

Playing Objectives

In order to effectively transform a relationship, we have to be attuned to how the communication between us is constantly being cued through spatial relationships and body language. We're continually reading these non-verbal signals for *new information* about who we are to one another.

Margaret Wheatly, an expert in organizational behavior and author of *Leadership and the New Science,* defines communication as the exchange of information, be it spoken or unspoken (i.e., written). Information, she says, is in constant motion. It's the currency we all trade in. We thrive on new information. And it has to be new to hold our attention.

The Two Hemispheres

We process information physiologically through two unique, distinct, yet inter-connected, inter-dependent channels, because our brains are divided into two spheres:

The left hemisphere, controlling the right side of our body, is in charge of speech, memory, articulation, comprehension, as well as arithmetic, analytical and conceptual skills. For most people, it's the more dominate hemisphere.

The right hemisphere, controlling the left side of our body, is in charge of holistic, intuitive, and spatial perception. It usually plays a secondary role in perception, but a primary one in creativity.

As an experiment, imagine your telephone's ringing. Pick it up.

Yes, actually pick up the imaginary phone. Which ear you do you hold the phone to—right or left? Switch the phone to the other side. Notice what that feels like. Return the phone to your preferred side of listening.

If you listen with the left ear, you're connecting more directly with the right side of your brain; if with the right, to the left side of your brain. If you're taking a business call, you might want to access the logical, arithmetical functions of your brain—right ear, left side, analytical thinking. If you're on a personal call, you might wish to access the more intuitive, non-verbal side—left ear, right brain, empathic thinking.

Once you become accustomed to the newness of the difference—a *change* usually effected and effective if you practice it at least *three times*—you'll begin to see how your physical behavior affects your inner state of being.

So, simple changes in physical behavior provoke changes in the inner experience. There's no separation between the two; they're all one.

Drills

Acting is like learning to play the piano: you drill the fingers to hit the keys to make sounds, until you realize that if you hit certain keys in a certain pattern you can make music. The music happens in the space between the notes.

Once you've made that connection, i.e., gone from the outer (hitting the keys) to the inner (making music), you can then work from the inner to the outer, i.e., play music to *express* feeling.

If you focus on the outer—what you do—you're able to repeat it. If you focus on the inner—what you feel—your playing will be inconsistent, random, haphazard.

Actor and therapist Susan Kelijian suggested we think of the training process like learning to drive a car. At first, you're aware of all the various components involved: starting the engine, putting the car in gear, driving and maneuvering in traffic, coordinating eyes, hands, feet (if you're driving a manual transmission). You're operating the vehicle with full conscious attention. Gradually, with time and practice, you think less and respond more intuitively to each challenge and obstacle in front of you, until, eventually, you're able to relax and actually enjoy driving.

And so it is with acting. At first, you'll be conscious of all the individual aspects: engaging in action with objectives, obstacles, and given circumstances, until gradually, with time and practice, you absorb the concepts, refine your technique, and actually enjoy the freedom and process of playing.

The Loop

Communication involves an exchange of information, which, in turn, produces a reaction in the listener, which, in turn, provokes a reaction, some form of response, in the original sender. This pattern—action, reaction, action again—is the basis of what we call **The Loop:**

I say something to you to provoke a response; you respond, and your response is my provocation. You provoke me, I provoke you.

The Loop is simple in theory, challenging in praxis. Based on the work of Earl Gister, the late Head of Acting at Yale University, in theory it goes something like this:

- I'm feeling (sad, unhappy, angry, frustrated—you fill in the blank).
- I want to feel something else, something I'm not feeling now (again, fill in the blank).
- Who can make me feel that way? The person I'm with right now.
- What would that person have to do to me to make me feel better?
- What do I have to do to that person to provoke that person into doing something to me to make me feel better?

Here's a simple game (devised by Keith Johnstone) to illustrate how this works:

When playing this game, or any game, you'll need someone to call out the directions and, if necessary, keep track of the time. The designated leader—be it a teacher or a member of the group—guides the playing and monitors the progress of the game.

Remember When...

As the game unfolds, you'll gather more information about the relationship. As you do, focus on your partner and how you want your partner to feel. Your partner's reaction—or lack thereof—is the provocation for your action. You'll discover your objective, to make your partner respond as you'd like them to—and why—as the game unfolds.

1. Working with a partner, agree to look through an imaginary photo album.
2. Your partner points to a picture and says: "Remember when…" (fill in the blank, i.e., the house burned down? You painted the cat blue? The car broke down in the middle of the night?).
3. You respond by saying: "Yes, and…" (fill in the blank, i.e., the fire department never showed up … I got blamed for destroying the furniture when the cat ran into the house and ruined the new white carpet … we had to walk 15 miles in the dark on a moonless night).

Simple, yes? Build the conversation back and forth, together creating the memories evoked by those imaginary photographs.

And then you…

1. Now, for the fun of it, add one more condition to the game: after every *offer*, every "Remember When…," *accept* the offer by saying "Yes, and *then you…*."
2. Elaborate as much as you want about what happened.
3. Then make a new offer by saying, "And then you…" telling your partner what they did.
4. Your partner *must* accept the offer and eventually make a new offer with "And then You…."
5. Continue playing until the pattern of offer/accept feels easy, natural, and spontaneous.

Notice how the narrative—the story—moves forward just by simply offering and accepting. Notice as well what happens when you're provoked into reacting. The provocation has physical impact—it lands within you.

6. Now add an objective: to make your partner feel guilty, ashamed, beguiled, charmed, alarmed.

7. Pursue the objective until you get your desired response, or change your tactics until you arrive at the "punchline" with a new response.

The focus, at all times, is on your partner, *not* on yourself. Gauge the effectiveness of your playing by the reactions you see, hear, and sense in your partner.

Q of P

To act, you must provoke your partner, who we'll call "the Other." The provocation is what you do. We call it action. How you do it is what we call play. How well you do it is what we'll call the **Quality of Play**, or **Q of P**.

Part B: Playing

Imagine you're a musician, a pianist. You're learning a new piece of music. You learn the piece note by note, studying the relationship of one note to the next to the next. You're aware of whole notes, half notes, quarter notes, eighth notes, rests, as well as the dynamic notations. Every time you play the piece, you play it note by note; the notes are your *text*, your pathway into the heart and soul of the music.

Playing it note by note does not mean you have to play it the same way every time you play; in fact, the way you play it Tuesday will be a little different because you've learned something by playing it Monday. The way you play it Wednesday will be slightly different again because you've learned something from Tuesday's performance.

Actors have to play the *text* note by note; they have to honor the intent of the playwright, as they understand it, as well as the intent of the director and the intent of the production.

How actors play, however, will be slightly different from night to night, for play involves spontaneity, an exchange of energy—what we'll call **The Bounce**—between scene partners and the audience. This is how the material lives, breathes.

Bounce

Let's play a few games to experience "bounce" and put what we've been talking about into practice. Follow the rules of each game and play the game full-out, i.e., create objectives, obstacles, and given circumstances, and infuse the game with ever deepening stakes. As you become more engaged in the playing, you'll begin to experience actual **bounce**, that sensation of energy moving between all of you as you commit ever more deeply to the playing.

Your instructor or group leader will call out the directions as you play. Here's the first step in the game:

Changing Tempo

This is a group exercise. You must all collaborate if you are to change the tempo in tandem. You'll feel uncomfortable with the walk until you begin to add a context—given circumstances—to condition the playing. When you invest in the context, making it both tangible and physical, it becomes much easier to engage in the playing.

1. Move around the room in your own tempo and rhythm. Establish a consistent tempo for your walk.
2. Continually change the direction of your walk. The shape of the movement pattern should be unpredictable.
3. Create an imaginary "where" for yourself—where you're walking. Be specific about the time of day, the quality of the light, the temperature, the smells, the textures of the environment. Let the where arise from the quality of your movement.
4. Justify being in the where.
5. Include people around you as part of the where. Be specific about your relationship with the others in your space. Know who they are to you, who you are to them.
6. Without leading and without following, work together to slow down the walking tempo. Justify the change in the tempo by changing your relationship with the people around you.
7. If the givens—the context—stop feeding your imagination, change them.

One. Basic Concepts

8. Walk without making noise. Justify the need for absolute silence.
9. Walk without touching anyone. Justify No Touch.
10. Keep your focus at eye level at all times.
11. Once the tempo's extremely sustained, reverse the process, increasing the tempo together until it's extremely quick.

Move from this game directly into Cross Thru.

Cross Thru

This game involves both offensive and defensive playing. Focus on increasing the quality of your play by creating challenges—obstacles—to engage your imagination. The tempo should accelerate throughout the playing.

1. Move rapidly around the room. Always move through the center of the space.
2. Do not touch one another when moving. Justify your tempo. Justify No Touch.
3. Gradually shrink the size of the playing area. Let the boundaries close in. Continue to move through the center of the space. Continue to justify No Touch.
4. As the playing area contracts, increase your tempo. Continue No Touch. Continue to justify the action.
5. Freeze. Release.

In Changing Tempo, you worked to *slow* the tempo down—that's part of the forward motion of the game. In Cross Thru, you worked to *accelerate* the tempo. There should never be a moment when you're idling—marking—the action.

No Touch is an obstacle—it increases the level of difficulty in the playing, especially as the space contracts. Create a penalty for making physical contact. Notice how the penalty affects the quality of your play.

In Nine

*This is a "framing" game. The counts are like giant parentheses—they "frame" the action. Anticipation—**jumping** into the future—is* *another liability when playing this game. It takes you out of the moment. Do not move until you hear the first count. You may need to repeat threes, twos, and ones until everyone moves at the same time.*

1. Lie on the floor on your back, with your eyes closed.
2. Rise to a standing position in nine counts. Use all nine counts.
3. Lie down in nine counts. Use all nine counts.
4. Repeat, reducing one count at a time, until you rise in one count.

Every action exists in its own time and space. It has a beginning, a middle, and an end. The frame ensures you won't begin the new action until you've completed the old action. It's a way of giving every action enough time and space to breathe, to resonate.

Squat 10

*In this game, the playing is both offensive and defensive. There's **no way** you can win; winning has no value or meaning in this game. The value of the game is in the playing of it and playing well.*

There's no way you can control the playing of any of the other players. Adjust/adapt as the moment requires. Do not cue one another with sound. You must play in silence throughout.

Squat No. 1

1. Form a circle.
2. Move through the center of the circle without touching one another.
3. If someone touches you, or if you touch someone, squat down to the floor, silently count to ten, then resume moving to the other side of the circle.
4. Once you're safely through the circle, turn around and repeat the activity. The playing's continuous.
5. Turn around, with your back to the center of the circle. Play backwards.
6. Do not look behind you while moving.

Squat No. 2

1. Repeat Squat No. 1.
2. This time, you may not touch anyone while moving.
3. You have a secret. The secret explains why No Touch is imperative.
4. Change your secret whenever it stops charging your imagination.

Squat No. 3

1. Repeat Squat No. 2.
2. Increase the intensity of the secret.
3. Close your eyes. Play blind.

The quality of the play changes dramatically between rounds one, two, and three.

In round No. 1, there isn't a reason for doing anything. Your focus is random. You don't have a context for playing the game. You're just following the rules. Notice how once you add a context, in round two, the quality of playing improves. No Touch gives you a purpose, a reason, an intent to inform your playing: to make it to the other side of the circle intact. You automatically start to play with a subtext; you have relationships with those around you: they're potential threats to your safety.

Because there are consequences to your action—**stakes**—playing carefully becomes mandatory, as a matter of survival. You can feel the tension in the circle; the playing becomes more dangerous. And more interesting.

Blindness, in round 3, increases the danger quotient with a physical *obstacle*. By removing two senses, sight and touch, you compensate by using your other three. The atmosphere feels more electric. You play much more slowly, more carefully, with greater focus and deliberation.

Further reading: Edward de Bono, *Lateral Thinking*; **Theresa Dudeck**, *Keith Johnstone: A Critical Biography*; **Keith Johnstone**, *Impro*; **Uta Hagen**, *Respect for Acting*; **Viola Spolin**, *Improvisations for the Theater*; **and Constantin Stanislavski**, *The Actor Prepares*.

What's Next

In the next chapter, we're going to look more deeply at the process of communication and how we can use it as the foundation for acting and playing.

Two

COMMUNICATION

Part A

Just as musicians play with notes, dancers with steps, painters with shapes and colors, so actors play with language—with a text—with its thoughts, its meanings, its sounds, with the way it's spoken, the way it *might* be heard. Text exists to either reveal or conceal who and how we are.

If language is thought in action, as British Master Teacher for the RSC Cicely Berry contends, then learning to read, decode, and activate Text is at the heart of the training process. When you know what you're thinking, you know (or have strong suspicions about) what you're doing.

Text, Context, Subtext

Text does not exist in isolation. It's always conditioned by **context,** Stanislavski's "given circumstances"—the social, ethical, and cultural codes of behavior embedded in time, place, and culture, as well as the personal moral and behavioral codes of conduct influencing and shaping every character. Context encircles the text.

Interweaving and uniting text and context, **subtext** is the unseen psychological, social, autobiographical, and emotional factors propelling the actor—and the character—into action. It's the unspoken but always present need to continue until peace or resolution is found.

Being in a state of **doing**—rather than a state of **being**—is the key that frees the actor's impulse to play. You do something to someone; they do something to you. The relationship changes. Simple.

In and of themselves, text, context and subtext are interesting concepts. But, as actors, we're concerned with practicalities, i.e., how we put these concepts into *action* and how we use action itself as the vehicle for change and transformation. Let's start at the beginning.

How We Communicate

In a study conducted at UCLA in 1967, researchers found that words alone carry only seven percent of communication; we'll call this the **verbal** action.

Thirty-eight percent of meaning is communicated through the use of the voice—we'll call this the **vocal** action, while fifty-five percent of communication is nonverbal and is *actioned*; we'll call this the **visceral** action.

The Verbal

Words describe: things, events, people, actions. When combined, words create images or *word pictures*, i.e., … dishes in the sink, clouds drifting above. Sometimes we choose our words very carefully—when we're breaking up with a loved one, when we have good or bad news to deliver, and sometimes we don't—when we're offended, emotional, caught off-guard. Then the words come spewing out.

The Vocal

There are three non-verbal but *vocal* aspects of communication that affect how we *listen*, the first of which is **pitch**. Most of us think of a high-pitched voice negatively; when a high-pitched voice is combined with nasality, we think of it as the worst non-verbal quality imaginable, whereas we think of a speaker who's either too loud or too soft as merely unpleasant.

The second non-verbal yet vocal aspect of communication is **stress**. We use either a higher pitch and/or louder volume to create **stress and emphasis** when we speak. The higher the pitch and the louder the volume, the greater the stress. There's usually *one* stress peak in every sentence, most likely toward the end of the sentence.

And then there is the **pause**.

Approximately 40–50 percent of all spontaneous speech is made up of pauses. A **filled** pause is one in which we use "oh" or "ummm" to fill the silence. **Cognitive pauses** give us time to plan what we're going to say, whereas **social pauses**—i.e., pausing in the middle of a sentence, avoiding eye contact—tells the listener, "Don't speak, I'm busy thinking."

Interpretation

Words themselves are open to any form of interpretation. They rely on *context* to give the words meaning. Whereas the verbal—the words—come from the head/mind, the vocal and visceral come from the heart and the gut: they're spontaneous, usually unedited, uncontrolled. They express the meaning of the words we've chosen to use. As an experiment:

1. Find a partner and say these three words out loud: *I love you.*
2. Now say it again, in a different way, and then again, in another way.
3. Each time you speak, by varying the way you speak, you create different meaning, different impact.
4. Combine the words with body language—either direct contact, with hips facing hips, or indirect contact, hips turned out from one another, and you'll begin to experience the disparity between what you say and what your body's saying and doing.

The Visceral

Hedwig Lewis, author of *Body Language: A Guide for Professionals*, and an expert in all forms of communication, tells us nonverbal messages serve four functions: they *emphasize* by re-enforcing words through actions; they *regulate* and *control* action (such as the nod in agreement); they *repeat,* which displays affect or emotion; and they *substitute,* by using *gesture* to communicate.

Syntax

Verbal language is either written or spoken. Nonverbal language deals with signals and gestures. It streams continuously. There's a design to verbal communication: we call it **syntax.** And there's a design to nonverbal communication: it's observed in patterns of **congruence** and **incongruence**.

Congruency

Congruency refers to the matching of gesture with gestures as well as matching with the verbal sentences they accompany. You nod your head up and down when you say "Yes" or shake it from side to side when you say "No."

Now imagine you're *saying* "Yes" but shaking your head from side to side rather than nodding it up and down. The word says "Yes," but the gesture says "No." Does the gesture enforce the spoken message or contradict it? If it contradicts, it's **incongruent.** Most importantly, for our purposes, audiences always sense the *incongruent* gesture.

In a scene, when you say to your partner "I love you" and move in to embrace one another, if only your upper torso makes contact and your pelvis is miles away from your partner, the audience knows you're lying. Something feels "off." The audience may not be able to articulate or describe what's "off," but they know it because they see/sense/feel it. This is because we trust what we see/sense/feel *more* than what we hear. The nonverbal signal carries about five times as much impact as the verbal.

Actioned Feedback

Lewis defines **feedback** as the constant in communication because it's *actioned*: it streams before our eyes and ears in response to the information we send. The face is our most important channel for expressing emotions: gestures, postures and body movements are the other channels, but less informative. Our hands and feet reveal the emotion we try to conceal with our face.

Fine Tuning

Without non-verbal feedback from your partner, you won't get the necessary information you need to **fine tune** your playing. Imagine starting to confide a deep, dark secret to a friend and your friend barely blinks, let alone reacts in any visible way. Do you continue, or do you change your tactics until you get the desired response? How do you know what to do, how to play the moment, unless you have visual feedback from your partner? Here's how:

Synchronicity

When talking, people tend to change their posture, to move their bodies and their features in a rhythm that matches the rhythm of their own speech. This is called **synchronization.**

Testing Synchronicity

There are two ways to test synchrony: try *not* to move while listening or try *to* move *out of sync* with the speaker. The listener's movements are completely dependent on the speaker's body language, which is, in turn, dependent on the speaker's words. In short: *a feedback loop*.

If you aren't really listening, you won't be body synching, which is crucial information when you're trying to provoke your partner, create impact, play an action, or create a reaction.

We understand this information intuitively. In training, we elevate this intuitive understanding, make it conscious, drill it, rehearse it until we have access to it, until it becomes a tool for deliberate, creative expression.

Moving on:

Part B

Sentences

Thought groups are usually clustered together in groups of seven to nine words. These thought groups are *sentences*. We always listen first for the verb—we want to know what's happening—and then we listen for the noun, to find out who it's happening to. Verbs and nouns usually carry the stress within the sentence because they carry the meaning.

FYI: the average rate of speed when talking—the rate of utterance—is between 150–200 words per minute. Yet we have the mental capacity to comprehend somewhere between 600–700 words per minute.

The Notes

As we suggested earlier, think of language and a text as our "notes," our music. Before we can play a song—any song, any *style* of song—we have to know/learn the notes, which, for us, means we need to know the technical elements of language before we can make music.

So let's review the notes we learned when we were younger and then play some "scales," i.e., practice texts, before we begin to make music, first with a sonnet, then a soliloquy, then a scene.

At Its Most Basic

A syllable is a single unit of sound. All words consist of one or more syllables. A syllable is produced by a single element, usually a vowel, sometimes a diphthong, which is a vowel flanked on either side by one or more consonants.

Words are signifiers; they appeal to the intellect, forming, when combined, pictures and images to convey meaning. They also have a *felt* quality, appealing to the listener's emotions.

Three ways to use sound to hook the ear into feeling, or sensing, the visceral quality of thought, image, and action are:

Alliteration, which happens when we repeat **consonant** sounds within words in a line or lines of verse. Alliteration might also include repeating an initial sound and an interior sound, like: blue berry.

There's also **assonance,** when we repeat **vowel** sounds *within* words in a line or lines of verse. The repetition creates *near* rhyme: a tintinnabular suspicion, for example.

And finally, there's **onomatopoeia,** which is when we use a word with both its sound as well as its sense to represent what it defines: bees buzz, cows moo, birds chirp, thunder rumbles.

Punctuation carries as much significance as the word itself. Think of punctuation as a form of musical notation identifying rests, silences, mergers and shifts of direction in thought. For instance,

commas (,) indicate a short pause;
semicolons (;) indicate a slightly longer pause;
colons (:) tell us something is to follow;
periods (.) tell us when a thought has been completed;

a **question mark** (?) indicates a direct question;

an **exclamation point** (!) signals a strong feeling;

the **dash** (—) alerts us to a sudden or sharp change of thought;

the hyphen (-) joins parts of words or expressions;

apostrophes (') are used to form possessives, plurals, or indicate contractions;

quotation marks ("") tell us when words or dialogue come from a different source;

parentheses () highlight thoughts loosely related to the rest of the thought; and

an **ellipsis** (…) is used to clue us to material missing from a thought.

The Eight Parts

Language breaks down into eight component parts. Each has its own function:

1) **Adjectives** are words that describe, usually nouns or pronouns: *small, pretty.*
2) **Adverbs** are words describing verbs, and they often end in *ly: quickly, thoughtfully.*
3) **Conjunctions** are words that join: *and, but, if, or.*
4) **Interjections** are words that exclaim: *Hey!, Oh!, Wow!*
5) **Nouns** are words that name: *plate, cat, house.*
6) **Prepositions** are words that glue: *above, below, under.*
7) **Pronouns** are words substituting for other words: *her, him, their.*
8) **Verbs** are words that do or are: *to swim, to breathe, to live, to die.*

Words are often grouped together to create extended thoughts or images:

A **clause** is a word group expressing a single thought; clauses contain a conjugated verb.

An **independent clause** is a word group or thought complete unto itself: "The assistants did the research and the manager wrote the report."

A **dependent clause** needs another thought to complete it: "…that try men's souls."

A group of words expressing a single thought *without* a conjugated verb is a **phrase:** "The White House, home *of the president,* is closely guarded."

Parentheticals amplify or explain; they're usually digressive statements, complete unto themselves, quite often set off by commas: "The committee's decision, *to say the least,* sparked considerable debate."

These component parts combine to create longer, more extended, more complex units of thought: sentences.

Sentences give us information:

Who (the subject) is found in nouns and pronouns (substituting for nouns): *the cat.*

Did what (the action), which is signified by a verb: *ignored.*

To whom (the object), which is, again, found in nouns or pronouns (substituting for nouns): *the mouse.*

We also want to know **when**, or the time of the action, i.e., past, present or future: *the cat ignored the mouse last night.*

Pay special attention to the tenses of the verbs. Deborah Hecht, a text teacher at The Juilliard School, believes verb tenses provide enormous information about the state of mind, the progression of the arc of the scene, and the intent of the speaker.

How many people (quantity) are involved (first, second and/or third), singular or plural: *eight people.*

Who **owns** or **has** (possessives): again, nouns or pronouns: *previously owned the cat.*

How, describing people, places and things (adjectives and adverbs): *eight people previously owned the cat, one at a time.*

Where, in relationship to (using prepositions and conjunctions, words that glue): *Eight people previously owned the cat, one at a time and now, with you, it has its ninth life.*

When using or listening to verbal communication, remember: the word by itself does not convey a precise meaning. It needs to be *attached* to a context or it lacks a definite message.

Here are 8 language strategies devised to reveal, conceal, describe or persuade the listener:

1) **Aphorisms** are descriptions in a few telling words: "lost time is never found again." (Benjamin Franklin)
2) **Epigrams** are clever, pointed statements, often using antithesis: "crying is the refuge of plain women, but the ruin of pretty ones." (Oscar Wilde)
3) **Euphemisms** substitute a softer word for a harsher one: *pre-owned vehicles* for used cars.
4) An **innuendo** is a disparaging remark, often sexual, used to undercut by allusion. While shopping, a man might say, "Nice set of melons" about a female customer.
5) An **ironic** comment is an expression contrary to its common meaning: "Yet Brutus says he was ambitious; and Brutus is an honorable man." (Julius Caesar)
6) **Metaphors** imply comparisons: "life's but a walking shadow, a poor player, that struts and frets his hour upon the stage." (Shakespeare)
7) While a **paradox** is a statement challenging common sense but containing truth: "what a pity that youth must be wasted on the young." (GB Shaw)
8) A **simile** is an explicit comparison between two things, and uses the words *as* or *like*: "reason is to faith as the eye to the telescope." (D. Hume)

Operative Words and Images

Operative words and images carry the information of the text; they reveal thought, action, meaning, and intent. They should grab our attention, leading us from one thought to the next. **Inoperative words** do nothing but confuse the listener; they make you work harder to hold the listener's attention.

Knowing and using the rules of operative words and images will be the foundation for our work with prose.

Here are the seven major rules of operative words and images:

1. Verbs of being ("am," "are," "is") are never operative. The operative words are those that explain the kind or quality of being. "I am <u>happy</u>." "He is my <u>brother</u>."
2. Avoid stressing pronouns ("he," "she," "it," etc.) whenever it's possible to do so. Whenever there is any alternative that makes sense, use it. This includes possessive pronouns ("his," "hers," etc.).
3. Possessive nouns are never less important than the words they possess (i.e., "My *father's house*").
4. Articles ("a," "an," and "the"), prepositions ("to," "from," "on," "in," etc.), and conjunctions ("and," "but," and "or") are rarely operative. They contain no images but serve to show the relationship between images. Find the words with images.
5. Adjectives and adverbs are treated as part of the noun or the verb they modify. The key operative word is the noun or verb, with the adjective or adverb incorporated in the image as a modifier.
6. An image that is repeated is not operative. What's operative is any new quality that's added in the repetition. This is called repetitive contrast. Stress the *new* information.
7. Do not stress the negative. "No" and "not" are almost never operative. The operative word is, instead, the word that is being negated. "<u>Go</u> not till you hear from me." "I <u>love</u> thee not; therefore, <u>pursue</u> me not."

Test It

Here's a very simple, quick way to discover how pervasive inoperative speech is in our culture, and with it, a way to begin to attune your ear to the value of operative speech:

When watching television or streaming programs or listening to a podcast, pay special attention to the voice-overs in advertising: "**I'd** like **you** to come down to **our** store and buy **our** mattresses." Notice how all the inoperative pronouns are stressed: **I'd** like **you** to come down to **our** store and buy **our** mattresses. Repeat the phrase. Stress the verbs and nouns. See how the message changes: I'd **like** you to **come down** to our **store** and **buy** our **mattresses**. We could even simplify that message to: **buy our mattresses**.

While the first, inoperative version may grab your attention by stressing the pronouns, it really doesn't contain any information—information being the name of the game.

PVTF

Jan Gist, head of voice, speech and text at the Old Globe/University of San Diego MFA program, stresses the following four major qualities of vocal presentation to create dynamic vocal emphasis:

Pitch—high to low tones,
Volume—loud to soft,
Tempo—quick to slow,
Force—strong to light.

To be effective with operative speech, we want to be as economical and efficient as possible, stressing only those words and images carrying information. Think of operatives as words in a text message: you'll be charged $10 per word, so, be brief, get to the point, score your point, move on to your next point.

The Skeleton

How do you use the principles of operative speech? You need to train your eye (recognizing operative speech on the page) and ear (hearing it in the course of playing, feeling it when it's not happening), so you can course correct in the moment.

Determine the skeleton of a written text—the way the thought moves—by underlining. Check the line for primary and secondary stresses; mark them with double underlines.

Mark pauses with a caret: ^
Mark major breaks in phrasing with a double vertical line: //
Mark minor breaks in phrasing with a single vertical line: /
Mark a new breath with a small circle. O
Mark rising inflections with a rising curve: ⌣
Mark falling inflections with a downward curve. ⌢

Mark sustained inflections with a horizontal line: —

Mark image groups (nouns/adjectives, verbs/adverbs) with a parenthesis ().

Shapes of Thought

If language is thought in action, consider what Gist calls "the **shapes of thought.**" These *shapes* are patterns of action, meant to appeal to the logical mind of the listener:

When **comparing and contrasting**, weigh one idea against another. Both have more meaning in relationship to the other than if they stood alone.

When you **connect the parts,** phrase words to bring words and images together, rather than isolating or separating them.

Lists involve two or more items. They can be simple individual items, complex phrases within a sentence, a list of sentences, or lists inside of other lists (study the lyrics of songs by Stephen Sondheim to see variety in list making). Lists are often in order of importance, from least to most important. A list can appear in any part of a sentence. Wherever it is, it works as a build unto itself, or builds to the next point following it. Express each individual item and drive forward through to the end of the entire thought. Don't over individualize, losing the items inter-relationship, or race to the end, losing individual ideas.

With **long sentences,** drive to the end of the thought; don't get lost in the middle. Work with the *structure* within the sentence, such as lists, complex comparisons, repetitions, and parenthesis. Be final at the end of the thought/sentence.

With **questions, commands and statements,** really ask the question, insist on your demands being met, and want every statement fulfilled. If you speak a question as a command, or make a statement into a question, you're changing the nature and intent of the writing.

There can be many different interpretations of questions, commands and statements. A question might be an innuendo or a direct investigation; a command might be a demand or a suggestion; a statement might be complete within itself or it might have a command within it.

Therefore, **intonations** are helpful to differentiate these forms. Up endings usually ask, down endings usually command or finalize statements, and sustained endings and circumflexes help connect phrases or suggest additional ideas.

To build a speech or scene, **crescendo,** *growing* in intensity by incrementally raising pitch, volume or tempo.

If you **decrescendo,** build on or gain intensity by *dropping* pitch, becoming quieter, going slower.

Think of both crescendo and decrescendo as a ladder you take step by step. These steps are the ideas, building either up or down.

If/then—"If" is a step up, "then" the fulfillment of the "if." Find the relationship of these parts to the whole thought by weighing them one against the another. Often the "then" is assumed. Sometimes "if/then" develops into "if/then/therefore" or "if and...." Express the whole structure by partnering or comparing all the parts to each other.

With **repetitions and banter,** Gist suggests you find the new idea connected to the repeated word.

Banter is the extension of repetition into sophisticated word play. It's a kind of "one-upmanship." The first speaker offers X, the 2nd speaker acknowledges X and raises with Y. Sometimes the X is repeated, sometimes it's understood and the speaker moves on to Y without it. There's usually a sense of bouncing words and ideas back and forth (**ping ponging**). Give equal attention to the set up and the punch/pay off.

Self-banter involves characters using this word play within their own lines, one-upping themselves.

And, last but not least, here are eight important rhetorical elements:

Alliteration (consonants), Assonance (vowels),
   Onomatopoeia (sounds)
Rhythm
Pauses
Antithesis
Rhyme
Irony
Puns
Repetition

Recommended listening to attune the ear to recognize and hear operative speech in both prose and verse: Dr. Martin Luther King, Jr., "I Have a Dream"; John F. Kennedy, "1960 Inaugural Address"; Representative Barbara Jordan, "1976 Democratic Convention Keynote Address"; John Gielgud, *Ages of Man*, and Dame Edith Evans as Lady Bracknell in *The Importance of Being Earnest*.

What's Next

Armed with all this information, in the next chapter we're going to prepare for playing Shakespeare by looking at the components of verse.

Three

VERSE

Part A

Rather than working exclusively with games and improvisation, we're now about to turn our attention to the demands of a formal, structured text. The text we'll be working with is a song of your own choosing—a song you're familiar with, a song you like. You'll need to know the lyrics of the song. You won't be singing; you will be speaking the lyrics. We'll use the text of the song to prepare us for the challenges—and the rewards—of working with Shakespeare.

Text

Text is the alpha and omega of the actor's craft. It's the baseline, always present, always the source of discovery. Throughout the rehearsal process, you will return to the text over and over again, hunting for clues to inform and confirm your choices. Remember, a text has both visceral as well as intellectual appeal. It gets us feeling just as it gets us thinking.

Words and Music

Playwrights are like that special breed of composers who write both words and music. In a song, the words supply meaning; the music supplies the heart and soul—the emotion—of the experience.

As actors, we parse and analyze the *text* for its meaning, and we do the same, through the *rhythm* and *tempo* of the text, to locate its heart and soul. The writer always provides the What. We have to discover the Why and the How.

A Bit More About Heightened Language

Imagine either the best or the worst news you could possibly receive. You're either elated or in deep despair, high as a kite or lower than a hole in the ground. The words you use to respond to this news spring from the depth of feeling you're experiencing. Diving into this well of feeling, your thinking moves from prosaic *everyday* language—**prose**—to something more elevated, perhaps more lyric, definitely filled with more images and word pictures: what we'll call **heightened language.**

When you're in a world of heightened language—be it in a play by Richard Brinsley Sheridan, George Bernard Shaw, Tom Stoppard, Sarah Ruhl, Tony Kushner, August Wilson, or Lynn Nottage—as well as a play by Shakespeare—you're in a world where language matters, where being able to express yourself with technical proficiency matters, where impact is based not on brute force but on subtlety, nuance, elegance of thinking and phrasing. And a passion for ideas.

On and Under the Line

Plays of heightened language ask you to "**play on the line**"—as if the thought is happening the very moment the character speaks. Pauses are usually written into the language, either with stage directions, or in the musical structure of the text—its **meter.** In plays of heightened language, pauses do not need to be added.

Adding pauses is what we might consider playing "**under-the-line.**" It's an attempt to sound natural, i.e., contemporary—as in the way characters talk on television or in the movies. Playing under-the-line undermines the intention of the writer. But we're getting ahead of ourselves.

Meter and Verse

In plays of heightened language—especially with Shakespeare and the other 17th century poets of the theatre—meter, the musical structure of language based on the interplay of stressed and unstressed syllables, reveals *how* the character is thinking, not necessarily *what* the character's thinking. Most often these plays are written in verse.

Verse, quite simply, is a term we use to describe writing which has a metrical *rhythm* to it. Verse typically has a *rhyme*, either *inside* the line or at the *end* of the line. When at the end of the line, the rhyme is usually meant to correspond to the word at the end of the next—or previous—line.

Blank verse is **poetry** written with regular metrical, but *un*rhymed lines.

The Trap

When speaking in verse, we never want to get caught playing the music; rather, we want to keep the focus on the lyrics, *informed* as they are by the music/meter.

A song is an example of heightened language. It exists in a *context*: it's usually about either wanting, starting or ending a relationship. In the song, something has happened, is happening, or is about to happen. That something—the **event** of the song—(someone's broken your heart or you've just met "the one")—causes a deep response in the person singing and an even deeper need to express that response through poetry.

The melody gives you information about your *emotional* state of being—the *subtext*—while the lyrics carry *information* about the changes you want to make, either in you or in the other person or in the person/people you're talking to about the relationship. Remember: it's always about the RTN, i.e., the Relationship Transforming Now.

When we listen to a song, especially for the first time, we usually attend to the lyrics and ride the melody. And usually, with the lyrics, we're anticipating the rhyme at the end of the phrase. The same is true when we listen to a play written in verse. Unless it's spoken well, we can get carried away by the "music"—the sing-song of the rhythm—and never attend to what the words are doing and saying.

In speaking and rehearsing verse, we'll start by investigating the relationship between words and music, looking to see how they influence one another. A little later we'll focus on how to use the lyrics to keep the story moving forward. To begin, we have to engage in some formal detective work, looking for clues about the meaning of the text, and how to speak it.

The Song Exercise

We'll be using a song you know as our first formal exercise in detective work. We're going to be looking for information about synchrony, congruence, and how the words (not the music) carry and drive the action of the song.

At the same time, we're going to focus on the "inner," i.e., the psychology of the speaker and how the meter—the music—carries the emotional impact of the lyrics. The lyrics are the sense, the story, while the music is the emotional subtext of the story.

Personalizing

You'll be re-contextualizing the given circumstances of the song, so you will have to start by understanding the context of the song as originally written. You'll then have to create a new context for the song from your own experience, **personalizing the text,** filling in the given circumstances to help make the lyrics alive, active, and meaningful for you.

Re-Looping

The song is not about how you feel—how you feel is merely the starting point. How you feel *now* is what you want to change. The song is about what you want the other person to feel so they will do to you what you want them to do to you so you can feel the way you want to feel. In short, The Loop.

Knowing this, you'll have to infuse the playing with a variety of *tactics,* until you either get what you want or you let go of that particular want and move on to another want.

The Song Exercise

1. Walk about the playing space reciting the lyrics of the song you've chosen.
2. Think about the meaning of the song and the meaning of the lyrics.
3. As you walk, try to focus exclusively on the lyrics and go for the sense of them—see if you can divorce the lyric from the melody/music.
4. Concentrate on the lyric and work *against* the melody—work for sense and not sentiment.

As you will discover, the song exercise is very challenging.

5. Find the operative word in each phrase.
6. Don't pause at the end of each line; pause at the end of each thought.
7. Keep the intention moving forward—find the set-up and look for the punchline at the end of each thought/action.
8. Now, one player will sit in a chair and we'll work through the song, focusing on lyric without playing the music
9. To help you as it becomes your turn, create a context for the song—a situation which makes sense of the lyric: who are you speaking to? Why? What has just happened that demands a response? Who are you to each other? What do you want to have happen to change the situation?
10. As the answers to these questions become clearer, let's shift the focus to the How—how are you going to affect your (imaginary) partner, i.e., the person you're speaking to. As the thought changes from phrase to phrase and line to line, change the pitch, volume, tempo, and force.
11. Finally, change your physical position: sit on an angle in the chair, stand and move behind the chair, kneel and speak to someone on a lower level—let each shift of posture and position reflect and express a change in the relationship between you and your imaginary partner.

A Few Thoughts About the Song Exercise

- WORK AGAINST THE RHYTHM

As you've discovered, it's very easy to get caught up in the melody and let it do all the work for you. In this exercise, we're consciously working *against* the melody to break the ear-worm connection between word and music. If you focus exclusively on the lyric, you will find the objective, and with the objective, the action you'll use to get what you want. Remember, the song is about RTN, a Relationship Transforming Now.

- OPERATIVES

Ultimately, the focus is on the thought contained in the lyric rather than the beat. Find the operative words and cluster the words together in *image groups:* **word pictures.**

If you drive the action forward with intention and immediacy, playing the *thought* through to the end of the sentence, rather than phrasing with the beat, the language transforms. Suddenly the listener hears, sees the images, and understands the text as it's tied to character, intention, action, inner conflict, and outer dynamic. In short, the text becomes active and alive.

- Rhyme

In the song exercise, you also had to decide if you deliberately want the words to rhyme. Does stressing the rhyme illuminate the thought or just draw attention to how clever your thinking is? As we'll see in Chapter Eight—Playing Molière (when you will play an entire scene with rhyming couplets), stressing the rhyme can obscure the meaning of the text. However, with a soliloquy or a scene in blank verse, an ending rhyme might be used *deliberately* to signal to the audience, "we're wrapping it all up now, let's move on."

- In Action

As the exercise progressed, notice what happened to the text: you moved from phrasing driven by the music to thinking and speaking driven by thought. The text itself guides the playing. The music may have told you how you felt, but the lyrics tell you how you're acting based on the feeling. If language really is thought in action, you've now consciously begun to make the act of thinking an action.

- Outside In

When you worked from the outside in—studying and parsing the text *first*, using detective work to hunt for clues about what you're doing—what you did gradually began to make sense. You "got it" through your body as well as your mind. Once you "got it," you moved from the inside out, using verbal and vocal technique to reveal rather than conceal the progression in your thinking.

Remember, when the thought changes, the action changes, and the action always changes because the thought has changed. Every change of thought can be signaled by a change in the PVTF—pitch, volume, tempo, force.

- Repetition

Repetition is now a major component in the "rehearsing the rehearsal" process. As you've just discovered, the more you repeat—

each time with a clear focus—the work becomes deeper and clearer. And, as it deepens, it's easier to personalize, to bring the text to you or to bring yourself to the text.

- MAGIC THREE

    In rehearsal, as a general principle, try to repeat the work *three times*. The first time involves discovery; the second, recreating the discovery; the third time, rediscovering the discovery anew. Test it out to see if this holds true for you. It's no wonder the French call rehearsal "la répétition."

Part B

Moving On

We're now going to shift the focus to the how's and why's of **blank verse**, which is written with metrical precision and *without* rhyme.

To understand and play with blank verse, let's get a feel for how meter works.

Counting Syllables

1. Working with a partner, select a topic or issue for discussion.
2. Each of you must speak in phrases containing only single syllable words: *once there was a cat*
3. As you become comfortable with phrases with only single syllable words, expand to phrases with two syllables: *the cat would eat*
4. Then three syllables: *the cat sat ... growing fat*
5. Then four: *the fat cat sat and saw a bat*
6. Then five, six, seven, eight, nine and ten syllable sentences.
7. Make sure the conversation is a true back and forth—don't make disjointed statements.

Variation: argue **pro and con**—one of you takes one side of an issue, the other takes the other side.

Metric Feet

While a one syllable phrase may be interesting as a way to release emotion, it doesn't really give us much information, and information is, after all, the name of the game. However, once you begin to work with two syllable phrases, the possibility of new information increases exponentially. As you slowly build your way up to ten syllables, the possibilities are endless.

Scansion

Just as we use the rules of operative speech as the tool to break the code of language in *prose*, we use scansion as the tool to break the code of language in *verse*, be it rhymed or unrhymed.

Basics

We use the term **scansion** to identify "foot divisions" and syllable lengths.

Think of verse as a form of hip-hop music and scansion as the way of analyzing the structure of the song, how it actually does what it does musically. In verse, the standard pattern, short vowel, long vowel—(unstressed, stressed)—de DUM—traditionally is seen as one beat, or one **foot**.

There are usually (but not always) two beats to a foot (occasionally three), and the standard line in Shakespeare is made up of five feet—that is, ten beats. (A line with just three feet is called a trimeter, with four a tetrameter, with five, a pentameter, while a line with six beats is called a hexameter, with seven a heptameter, and a line with eight feet is called an octameter. Longer lengths are possible, but rare.)

A stanza is a *group* of lines: two lines form a couplet, three a tricet, four a quatrain. When every line of a stanza is written in the same meter, we call the verse blank verse.

Patterns

As with hip-hop, the music of the text is created by either the repetition or the variation of stressed/unstressed vowels. For example, the de-DUM pattern is called an **iamb**. Strict iambic meter ends up sounding like de DUM de DUM de DUM de DUM de DUM: *Mary had a little lamb, its fleece was white as snow.* The stressed—emphasized—syllable is *on* the beat, while the unstressed syllable is *off* the beat.

As the standard pattern in Shakespearean verse, an iambic foot can be a single word or a combination of words. For instance, in the word Mary, the "Ma" is unstressed and the "ry is stressed," and in the phrase "was blue," the "was" is unstressed and "blue" stressed.

Mono

With iambic pentameter, we first look to find the *repetition* of the pattern—this establishes the base line, the melody: de DUM/de DUM/de DUM. Unfortunately, this is the sing-song pattern we associate with most verse. Because it's repeated so often, it gradually has a numbing effect on the ear, i.e., it becomes what we've called earlier *mono-active*: nothing changes. We tune out and don't attend to what's being said.

Clearly, as actors, our intent is not to let the audience drift while we speak; our job is to guide the audience's ear to the important words in the line/thought, and then keep the thought moving.

Skipping Stones

Speaking verse is like skipping stones at the water's edge: you want to skip the stones gently across the water, lightly emphasizing stressed words, then moving on until, touching down for a brief moment of contact, the thought reaches its conclusion—its punchline—at the end of the sentence.

Breaking the Pattern

The text becomes much more interesting when we discover the variations and deviations breaking the pattern, i.e., DUM de or DUM DUM or de de DUM. The variations *usually* (but not always) occur at the beginning or end of a line.

Here's one example of a variation at the beginning of a line from *King Richard III*: "Now is the winter of our discontent." The line opens with: DUM de/de DUM/de DUM/de Dum/de Dum. The variation calls attention to the word "now"—as in, this very second, even as we speak.

Or, this example from *King Lear*, Act V, scene iii: Albany says:

"Run, Run, O Run"—notice the intensity, the insistence, of those two repeated words, created just by varying the stresses in the rhythm with a long or sustained "O" to off-set "Run."

These variations tell us something new and unusual is happening in the mind of the speaker. Suddenly, our ear perks up to hear, and feel, the new information.

As actors speaking verse, we always ask ourselves: Why is the pattern broken and the thought different? What does this textual clue mean? Why is Shakespeare drawing attention to this particular word and that particular thought in this particular moment? *Always* stress the variation rather than the repetition of the pattern.

Variations

Here are the variations. Try to feel them as you read them (aloud, if possible) and experience the effect of the shifts in emphasis. Variations in two syllables:

- One stressed followed by an unstressed syllable—**DUM-de**—is called a **trochee** (Tiger, tiger [burning bright]).
- Two stressed syllables—DUM DUM—is called a **spondee** (handshake, Facebook).

Variations with three syllables:

- Long, short, long—**DUM de DUM** (elephant, typical)—is called a **dactyl**—(Now is the time [for all good men…]).
- Short, short, long—**de de DUM** (understand, manifest)—is called an **anapest** (*Not a creature* was stirring…).
- Short, long, short—**de DUM de**—is called an **amphibrach** (Amusing deception/ bird watching).

There's also this:

- Short, short—**de de** (it is, as is)—is called a **pyrrhic.** Pyrrhic feet contain no stresses.

Two other important musical notations used with scansion:

- A **feminine ending** is an ending with a short syllable. The short syllable is the clue to move directly to the next line; the thought is so full that it runs over the basic ten beats and asks you to connect

it to the next line. An example of a "feminine ending" (though it's always open to debate) would be, "To be, or not to be, that is the question." If you scan this line to be in regular iambic feet, the end of the word "question" counts out to eleven feet, telling you the thought is so rich, so full, that it has to spill over one smidge.
- **Caesura** means there's a pause or a suspension within a line for balance and emphasis: "It was the best of times, it was the worst of times." You can just feel the caesura, that little pause created with the comma to set-up the contrast between the phrases.

The Technical Work

To help you better *see* the shape and structure of blank verse, we need to determine the *skeleton* of the text—the way the thought moves—by underlining:

Check each line for primary and secondary stresses; mark them with double underlines: ＝
Mark pauses with a caret: ^
Mark major breaks in phrasing with a double vertical line: //
Mark minor breaks in phrasing with a single vertical line: /
Mark a new breath with a small circle. ○
Mark rising inflections with a rising curve: ⌣
Mark falling inflections with a downward curve. ⌢
Mark sustained inflections with a horizontal line: —
And mark image groups (nouns/adjectives, verbs/adverbs) with a parenthesis: ( )

The names of the variations are not as important as being able to recognize the sound and feel of them. These shifts carry the new information, and they need to be stressed through use of pitch, volume, tempo and force in order to draw the ear's attention to them.

A Reminder

Scansion is a technical tool you'll need to *know* and *use* when working with verse, especially blank verse. We're studying it now because we're about to work with Shakespearean verse in a sonnet.

Part C

Shakespeare's Verse

Shakespeare's verse is extremely musical. There's a pulse to it, a rhythm to it—it appeals to us viscerally through the confluence of its stresses, rhythms, assonances and alliterations, and it appeals to us philosophically through its metaphysics, and it appeals to us intellectually through Shakespeare's use of the shapes of thought and shapes of rhetoric.

The Rewards of the Work

As we approach playing blank verse, the verse itself may appear dense, but with a little detective work and a lot of scansion, the beauty of the sounds of the language will open up and you will have a chance to *bona fide* revel in it.

At the same time, in playing a text in blank verse, we'll be exploring and applying the basic tenets of Stanislavski's system—objectives, obstacles and given circumstances—to infuse the text with a dramatic pulse and meaning. Master this language and you can play any text, anytime, anywhere.

Your Job

Shakespeare has encoded the text with information about the mind and the thinking of the speaker. Your job, using the tools at hand, will be to discover and uncover these clues—and then create a context, with given circumstances, to inform and condition the playing. You will look for clues to transform the text into viable, textually supported, dramatically active and alive *action*.

Mix and Match

As a prelude to working with the sonnets, and as a way to bring this all together at this stage of the training process:

Write a Short Love Poem

Write the poem to someone you know, or to someone you'd like to know.

Create a context—given circumstances—providing information about the relationship.

Your beloved, or soon to be beloved, or hoping to be beloved, has done something, either good or bad, to you, and you're responding to that gesture.

Use the poem to express your feelings and, in so doing, impact your partner and transform the relationship.

The Poem's Perimeters

The poem must be in iambic pentameter, i.e., two syllables per foot, one weak, one strong—in any pattern or variation—five feet to the line; the lines should not rhyme.

Try to use the sounds of language—alliteration, assonance, onomatopoeia—to *express* your feelings and *impact* the object of your desire.

In order to choose the right words, you'll need to know how your beloved thinks and feels. Use the poem to make the other person feel the way you want them to feel so they can make you feel the way you want to feel.

See if you can use any of the rhetorical shapes we've already discussed in the previous chapter to appeal to your partner's thinking.

Try to make sure the poem has a beginning, middle, and end—a three-act structure. Make sure the beginning and the end of the poem are 180 apart. Vary your tactics.

The poem should be twelve lines long. You may choose to end the poem with a rhyme, if you so desire. Spend no more than six minutes writing the poem.

The Next Step

Once everyone's written their poems, trade poems with someone. Now you're going to do some detective work: scan the poem. Underline or circle the operative words—the words the scansion tells you to stress. See if there's any **antithesis**—a comparing of opposites—you may want to stress, and identify the rhetorical shapes you think the reader/listener should hear. Use the text to determine your objective: what you want from your beloved.

And see if you can find, *in* the text, the obstacle either within you or within your "beloved." This obstacle will make the pursuit of the objective more active and challenging. Spend no more than five minutes scanning and preparing the text.

The Final Step

Unlike the song exercise, where you had to invent a person to speak to, you've already chosen a partner—the person you've just traded poems with. Decide who is A and who is B.

1. If you're A, you're going to play this poem as if your partner is the beloved in the poem.
2. Create a subtext for the poem by personalizing it. Make it your own. Based on the text, and the clues you've uncovered with detective work, know who you're speaking to, why, what's just happened, and what you want to have happen.
3. Circle the operative words and/or operative images in each line. Devise a strategy to emphasize and stress them. Know why those words are important to you, and why they're important to your partner.
4. Heed the punctuation; it's your musical notation, signaling the movement shaping the thought. If there's a comma, use the slight pause—the caesura—to separate thoughts; if there's a question mark, really ask the question.
5. Can you begin to see the arc and progression—180—in the poem? Divide it into three acts—beginning, middle, end—and begin to see how the structure of the poem reveals the thoughts/thinking of you, the speaker.
6. Find the punchline at the end of the poem. Work backwards and decide how you're going to make the set-up have a clear beginning and middle as you sprint to the finish line.
7. Gauge how you play the poem based on the visceral/physical feedback you're receiving from your partner.
8. Play the poem as if it's your own story.
9. Once you've played the poem, B becomes the speaker and A listens.

Take a minute or two to talk with one another about the exercise. Discuss what worked, what didn't, and what you might do differently.

What You've Just Done

You've worked from the outside in and then from the inside out.

By using the basic tools of scansion, you've mined the text to discover clues about the relationship needing transformation. Now you're sharpening your eye and ear to recognize operatives, and you're using pitch, volume, tempo and force to physicalize and vocalize changes in tactics as you pursue your objective.

With both the song exercise and the love poem, you're becoming familiar with the preparatory and early steps in the rehearsal process.

For a broad spectrum of activities involving scansion and text, see *The Actor and his Text* **by Cicely Berry, and/or** *Playing Shakespeare* **by John Barton, both books considered classics, and the extremely detailed and useful** *Thinking Shakespeare* **by Barry Edelstein.**

What's Next

In the next chapter, we're going to apply what you've just done to an actual text, one of Shakespeare's sonnets. We'll investigate Sonnet 23 together, uncovering the structure—what we're going to call the **architecture**—of the text. You'll then use **The Template** we're developing to rehearse the rehearsal by working and playing a sonnet of *your own choosing*.

Four

THE SONNET: THE ARGUMENT

Every sonnet, soliloquy and scene in Shakespeare's canon is built around an "argument." We're not implying there's an *actual* physical fight on the page, but a metaphorical one, in which the tension of the argument is built on opposition, antithesis, comparisons and contrasts, examining an issue or theme first from one side, then from another.

Part A

Structure

The structure of the argument is very clear: there's an opening statement—the question or issue at hand, the topic the speaker will explore. It's usually a problem, practical or philosophical, needing a solution. The speaker then uses the text to explore or solve the problem.

In the case of a sonnet—a poem written in fourteen lines—the initial exploration happens during the first eight lines. The thought then turns, and, in the next four lines, the speaker examines another side of the issue—options. Finally, in the last two lines, the speaker reaches a conclusion—quite often a summation of the issue—in a rhyming couplet.

Context

In the Elizabethan era, the word "love" had diverse meanings—yes, it includes romantic and sexual love, but it could also describe deep and abiding friendship and in some instances, patronage between a benefactor and an artist.

Scholars think that Shakespeare's sonnets were written between 1592 and 1598. There are 154 sonnets that are usually divided into two groups: Sonnets 1–126 are believed to be written to a man, and Sonnets 127–154 are written to a woman, often referred to as "the dark lady of the sonnets."

In Sonnets 1–17, the writer praises his young friend's beauty, insisting that he marry and have children to extend and preserve this beauty beyond his eventual death.

In the next group of poems, the poet creates variations on the themes of love and beauty. Eventually the poet moves to a theme of betrayal, abandonment, and jealousy.

Further on (Sonnets 110–111), the poet fears his friend resents the public display of affection and attention. Eventually, in the final poems of this first sequence, there is a reconciliation and a return to mutual friendship.

Sonnets 127–154 focus on a woman with a dark complexion—one who is neither beautiful nor faithful to the poet. The poet sees himself as scorned and wronged, his love unrequited.

Let's test the sonnet structure to get a feel of how it works in our everyday lives:

Pro and Con

This activity involves both offensive and defensive playing. There's no way you can win. Your focus is on exploring both sides of an issue with equal fervor.

1. Working with a partner, decide on a topic you wish to explore.
2. Player A will argue the pro, Player B will argue the con.
3. After two minutes, switch sides—argue the other side of the issue/topic.
4. Summarize and reach a conclusion about the topic together.

Let's write one final poem to hone and develop skill in playing "the argument" before we deep-dive into scansion, structure, playing an objective, and creating context and subtext.

As we work through this exercise, we'll also be developing **The Template**—the step-by-step process we'll use in preparing a text in verse for rehearsal. Select a topic—an issue or problem you want to explore or resolve. It can be highly personal: your beloved is leaving you, or, should you quit your job? It can also be global, like how to solve climate change or fix a broken political system. The poem must be in iambic pentameter, i.e., two syllables per foot, five feet to the line; the lines should not rhyme.

In this phase of the exercise, you're working to change your relationship with yourself: you have a problem, you're uncomfortable with it, and you will feel better if you can resolve it.

1. State the problem in the first two lines of your poem.
2. Write a proposal for taking action in the next six lines.
3. Then counter, examining the other side of the issue in the next four lines.
4. Finally, resolve the problem in the last two lines.

Now, taking your time with the following steps in the process, let's assume that someone else can help you solve your problem.

5. Play your poem to a partner.
6. See if you can engage or enlist your partner to help you arrive at a solution to your problem.
7. Focus on how you want your partner to react.

Trade poems with your partner. Take two minutes to briefly scan your new poem:

Find the operative *words* and/or operative *images* in each line.
Using either pitch, volume, tempo or force, devise a way to emphasize and stress the operatives.
Know why those words are important to you, how you want them to affect your partner.
Know who you're speaking to, why you're speaking now, what's just happened, and what you want to happen.

Create a subtext for the poem, one that makes sense to you: what you want to change in the relationship, how you want your partner to react, what's at stake if you fail. Heed and observe the musical

notations—the punctuation. Have a beginning, middle and end to the argument. Drive to the punchline of each thought and of each proof in your argument. Experiment with using crescendo to build your argument. Play the poem as if it's your own story. And, finally, think of yourself as a lawyer doing your final summation to the jury.
Take two minutes to evaluate your work with your partner.

Putting It Together

Now, to better see the sonnet structure in a more formal context, we'll repeat **The Template,** step by step, using Sonnet 23 as our model:

First, read the sonnet straight through:

Sonnet 23

1. As an unperfect actor on the stage,
2. Who with his fear is put besides his part,
3. Or some fierce thing replete with too much rage,
4. Whose strength's abundance weakens his own heart;
5. So I, for fear of trust, forget to say
6. The perfect ceremony of love's rite,
7. And in mine own love's strength seem to decay,
8. O'ercharged with burdens of mine own love's might.
9. O let my books be then the eloquence
10. And dumb presagers of my speaking breast,
11. Who plead for love and look for recompense
12. More than that tongue that more hath more expressed.
13. O learn to read what silent love hath writ!
14. To hear with eyes belongs to love's fine wit.

Next, let's break it down, step by step:

Do the Math

Divide the text, line by line, into five feet, or units of thought/action, based on length of vowels—in other words, *scan* the text. Divide the sonnet into three acts: beginning, middle and end.

Scan the Sonnet

Knowing the basic pattern of verse is short/long—de DUM de DUM—scan the sonnet for the irregular patterns:

Line 1: the second foot is irregular—two stressed syllables—it's a spondee (DUM DUM)
Line 2: regular
Line 3: the second foot, fierce thing, is also a spondee (DUM DUM)
Line 4: the fifth foot, "own heart," is also a spondee (DUM DUM)
Line 5: regular
Line 6: the fifth foot, "love's rite," is also a spondee (DUM DUM)
Line 7: fourth foot, "seem to," is long, short (DUM de), so it's a trochee
Line 8: the most complex line of the sonnet: 3rd foot, "den of," is short, short (de de), or pyrrhic, while the 4th and 5th feet, "mine own love's might," are both spondees—long, long (DUM DUM)
Line 9: regular
Line 10: regular
Line 11: regular
Line 12: starts with a trochee, "More than," long, short (DUM de)
Line 13: regular
Line 14: regular

Use the scansion to find the irregular stresses in the lines and ask yourself: Why is the line irregular? Why that particular word? Why must it be stressed or emphasized? How do I want it to impact the listener?

More Clues: Punctuation

Check the punctuation at the end of each line—we're looking for **run-on lines** (line endings without punctuation, i.e., commas, semi-colons, or periods) telling you to continue the thought without pausing to take a breath. We're also looking for **end-stop lines** (lines punctuated with a period, comma, or semi-colon), telling you to pause, breathe or let the thought hang in the air and resolve itself before moving on.

Note that lines 5, 9 and 11 are run-ons—the thought moves directly from the end of one line to the start of the next, no pausing or resting (caesura) in between them, just one continuous motion/action.

Interpretation

Remember, unfortunately, there are no definitive answers. We're looking for *clues* within the text to guide you into choices about how to *play* the text.

Sentence Length

Remembering that the punchline exists at the end of a sentence, reread the sonnet to determine the length of the sentences. Note: the first eight lines are all one sentence. The next four lines are one sentence. The final couplet is one sentence. Try sustained and rising inflections at the ends of words to keep the momentum going.

The Architecture

This A/B/C form—A being the first eight lines (Act I), B the next four lines (Act II), and C, the final couplet, is consistent within all 154 sonnets.

In Sonnet 23, lines 1–8 are a straightforward apology, a plea for forgiveness; lines 1–2, the first couplet, states the problem: "as an unperfect actor." Lines 3–8 offer examples—proofs—of why I've failed to tell you of my feelings. They build the argument by elaborating a single image—the penitent, pleading for forgiveness, failing to speak of their love.

The argument turns at lines 9–12; the speaker changes direction, arguing that their books contain all the emotion not spoken. This is the pro/con development of the argument.

The last two lines, 13–14, a rhyming couplet, *conclude and resolve* the argument, imploring the listener to believe, to trust what's written rather than spoken, as proof of their love's pure and true devotion. We're working what Cicely Berry calls a **ladder**: from sound to sound, syllable to syllable, word to word, phrase to phrase, thought to thought, sentence to sentence.

Your Turn

Select a Shakespearean sonnet. Read it through. Read it a second time; look up any and every word you don't know or understand.

Note sentence length and the punchlines. Knowing the punchline, reread the text to follow the thought progression from set-up to punchline—the arc, the 180, of the transformation.

Divide each line into five feet, each foot consisting of two syllables. Scan the text to determine the length of the vowel sounds within each foot. Look for any patterns breaking the unstressed/stressed (iambic) rhythm of the meter.

Note the punctuation, especially commas, semi-colons and periods. Think of the punctuation as signals telling you when to step on the gas (run-on lines), when to pump the breaks (commas, semi-colons), and when to come to a complete stop (periods).

Underline adjective/nouns and adverb/verb groups and put the groups in ().

Next

Read the sonnet for the "argument" of the first eight lines, noting how the text drives to the punchline in this first phase of the argument. Note the "argument" of the next four lines—how it turns in focus yet how it too moves towards its punchline. Note the conclusion inherent in the final couplet—how it's the overall punchline, usually ending in a rhyme.

- ANSWER THESE QUESTIONS ABOUT THE CONTEXT

You'll find the answers to these questions in the sonnets preceding your sonnet:

Who are you speaking to?
What's the story of your relationship?
What are the circumstances surrounding your relationship in this moment?
What's just happened, compelling you to speak now?
What has your partner just said or done to you to trigger this response?

Four. The Sonnet: The Argument

- ANSWER THESE QUESTIONS ABOUT THE SUBTEXT

The answers to these questions will propel you into playing The Loop:

> What do you want to change in the relationship?
> Why do you want to change the relationship? What's missing in the relationship?
> What do you want to remedy or fix? Why do you need to change the relationship?
> How are you feeling now? How do you want to feel?
> What must you do to your partner to get them to do what you want them to do to make you feel the way you want to feel?
> How can you use the text—through pitch, volume, tempo, force—to make them feel that way?

Part C: Let's Start Playing

Your instructor will guide you through the process. To start:

1. Work with an *imaginary* partner.
2. Use scansion to identify the operatives, those words carrying the greatest, most profound impact. They give the text a direct charge, affecting and swaying the listener.
3. We could also ask: which words are the most "expensive" in terms of thought, effort, and energy? They need to be stressed. Which are the least important? These can be used to help support the more expensive ones.
4. Then, return to the text and, speaking quietly to yourself, note corresponding or repetitive sound patterns— overlapping or underscoring the "felt" or "sensed" visceral experience of the language: alliteration and assonance.
5. Look for and use the *long* vowel sounds you might extend or exaggerate to carry the *emotional impact* of your argument,
6. And, look for consonants that you might tap, or bite into, to clarify the sense and carry the *intellectual* meaning of your argument.

Paraphrasing

Paraphrase the text, thought by thought, making the writer's words your own. Can you parallel the text, precisely and exactly? Use paraphrasing to reveal the clarity of your own thinking in this situation. Then, alternate between the text as written and your paraphrasing.

When you feel absolutely confident about the meaning of what you're saying and its intent, drop the paraphrasing. Infuse the text with the same intent, immediacy and personalization you found with your own words.

Next, to experience the flow and visceral movement of the text, walk around the room, speaking the text aloud and **stomp** out the rhythm of the scansion. When there's a stressed syllable, stomp with more force, accenting the stressed beat. Continue stomping until you have the experienced/felt sense of where the stresses in the text exist, and how they resonate in your body. These are the words you would accent were you to engage directly with a partner in the argument.

Combine with Change of Direction

Add to the mix: every time the thought changes—either within a line or from line to line—change the direction you're walking in, i.e., turn to the left, to the right, turn around, proceed forward as the thought moves forward, swerve as the thought swerves. Physicalize the thought by experiencing the shifts of thought as actual dynamic shifts in space. And, finally, when you reach the last word at the end of a sentence, kick or throw an imaginary ball to your imaginary partner, punctuating the conclusion of the thought. Know what has just happened immediately before you speak; use this information as your "**trigger**" to launch your speech. Know what will happen immediately after you speak. Use this particular sonnet to bridge the movement between past and future.

Environment

Use the answer to these questions to help create a specific, physical and visceral context for the playing of the text:

Physically, where are you? Indoors? Outdoors?
Is there furniture?

What time of day?
What's the quality of the light in the space? The temperature?
What season is it? Is it dark, late at night? Snowing? A spring day?
What are you wearing?
Where are you standing or sitting in the space? Does that help or hinder you?
Is the meeting public or private?

Working with Subtext

Use the answers to these questions to support the objective you're about to pursue:

Who are you talking to and why?
What's your intent/objective in speaking these specific words, in this specific moment of your relationship?
What's at stake if your objective fails?
Are there cultural, social, political or religious differences between you?
What needs to shift, transform, change, specifically within the relationship, to bring it back into balance?
What sounds, words, images—tactics—will you use to affect your partner?
What do you know about your partner to make the use of these tactics imperative, vital, necessary for you, the speaker, to get what you want?
Most importantly, as the relationship changes between the first eight lines and the next four, and the final two, how do *you* transform and change in relationship to your partner?

Making the Argument

Emphasize and stress the operative words and images as your *agents* of transformation and change.

Send the operatives as a text message—only hit the key words containing key information. Repeat, using the full text. Emphasize the key information in the first eight lines, then the next four, then use the last two lines as the summation or conclusion of your argument.

Think of comparisons and contrasts as **balancing** separate, differing images, to make the argument as clear as possible. Also, think of a list as one long, sustained crescendo, building in pitch, volume, tempo, and force.

Tactics

Do you *give* power to your partner? After all, your fate is in their hands, or do you want to *make your partner feel* powerful? In so doing, you're playing a very different game. Do you begin by striking an arrogant, defensive tone, placing your partner in a combative position—again, as a tactic—so you can make your partner feel good when you switch positions in the final six lines? Try all three strategies—and whatever else you can invent within each line, or within the pairs of lines.

All you need remember is the golden rule: RTN—the relationship must transform now, in the course of the fourteen lines. It's your job to determine which is the best route to take to make that transformation happen.

As You Start to Play the Sonnet: The Loop

> How do you feel, now? How do you want to feel?
> What must your partner do to you to make you feel the way you want to feel?
> What must you do to your partner to get your partner to do to you what you want your partner to do to you in order to feel the way you want to feel?
> How do you feel at the end of the sonnet? What's changed?
> Using pitch, volume, tempo, and force as your primary agents of change, how can you change the relationship from line to line, or from thought unit to thought unit?

Seated on a chair, begin to speak. Use the trigger of the previous moment, as you imagine it, to help your launch.

1st Pass: Observe the punctuation—the slight pause/mini-beats/caesuras indicated by commas. Suspend and sustain the pitch, as indicated by dashes, use sustained and rising inflection with lists, punch and hit the operatives. Play through each thought, honoring run-on lines, until you reach the end of the thought and, then, observe the period/end of the sentence.

2nd Pass: Focus on changing your tactics—what you do to make your partner react—from thought to thought as the argument progresses.

3rd Pass: Focus on your imaginary partner's reactions; let those reactions trigger your shifts in tactics. Work slowly, methodically, through the text, moment to moment. Repeat until the patterns of action are clear to you.

Now, **remove the air**—get out the Hoover and vacuum those pesky pauses and, in so doing, find the momentum of the action and the argument.

Maintaining and refining all that's gone before, honor the twists and turns of the argument until you end the argument with your conclusion.

4th Pass: *Stand up* and repeat. Use your hands for emphasis, moving the argument into your entire body. As the thought changes, change physically: try shifting your weight from right to left or from left to right, and see if you can begin to feel the language viscerally living inside you. Use pitch, volume, tempo, and force as your primary tactical agents of change. Repeat until you feel the language and the sonnet begin to live inside you.

5th Pass: Repeat, standing, *without moving*. Keep the focus on your imaginary partner, and make your imaginary partner listen to you without being distracted by any bodily movement.

6th Pass: Work with an *actual* partner, and speak directly to your partner. Read your partner's reactions from moment to moment—the visceral, non-verbal feedback from their face and body. Adjust your playing accordingly.

If you're the partner, *don't* react physically. Make your partner work harder by being their obstacle. That's what obstacles do: they make you work harder and, in the process, define with greater clarity what you're doing and what the stakes are in the moment of playing. Reverse roles. Take a few minutes and evaluate the experience with your partner.

The Template

We've now begun to formally rehearse the rehearsal, working in a prescribed sequence. We're developing **The Template** to be used with all plays of heightened language, be they in verse or prose. Start with the technical detective work: scansion (when in verse), determining the skeleton of the text, identifying operative words and images as well as using sound and word pictures and rhetorical shapes as tactics to build your argument and transform your relationship.

Then move on to the internal detective work, focusing on objectives, given circumstances and obstacles as your conduit, your pathways into action, i.e., the actual work of transforming the relationship.

Additional material: read and work poems by Emily Dickinson, Amanda Gorman, Langston Hughes, Christina Rosetti, Maya Angelou, William Blake, Wilfred Owen, Lewis Carroll or Jericho Brown.

What's Next

In the next chapter, we'll work The Template with a soliloquy. In working with a sonnet, *you* had to create the context; in working with a soliloquy, the context is *provided*. You will still do the same textual detective work and ask the same question, and you will still be asked to bring yourself to the text as well as the text to you.

Five

THE SOLILOQUY: TRANSFORMATION

Part A: Plot vs. Story

At their core, Shakespeare's stories examine a theme or issue. Sometimes the issue is left unresolved, sometimes it's wrapped up neatly with a nice little ribbon and the story has a tidy, happy ending.

The Plot

A plot is how events in a story unfold. Plot is not necessarily what a speech, scene, or play is *about*. Stories are always *about* something; they're never random.

For example, in our reading of the text, *King Lear* is about one man discovering his humanity, *Macbeth* is about the consequences of unchecked ambition, and *As You Like It* is about the healing power of love, in all its variegated forms.

The plots of these plays—of any play—charts how the themes and the topics under discussion reveal themselves due to the interaction and transformation of the characters. Lear could not discover his humanity without meeting Gloucester on the heath, Macbeth could not revel in unchecked ambition without his wife to egg him on, and Rosalind could not transcend her sense of isolation without meeting Orlando.

Characters never exist in a vacuum; they sometimes want to shake up and/or change the social and political order by becoming king (*Richard III*), by assassinating or murdering others (Iago in *Othello*, Brutus and Cassius in *Julius Caesar*), or by feeling empowered to be their true selves (Helena in *All's Well That Ends Well*, or the other Helena in *A Midsummer Night's Dream*).

Whether they succeed or fail, they transform their *own* self-image in the process of the doing.

The Audience

Even if an audience doesn't understand the meaning of every word spoken (and it's almost guaranteed they won't), if the thinking under and through the text is specific, if the arguments are laid out with clarity and precision, the audience will be able to follow you.

They probably won't know what you're doing technically, i.e., how you're using operatives, how you're using sustained and rising inflection to drive the text from set-up to punchline, how you're using comparisons, contrasts, alliteration. No, the audience won't know, and they shouldn't know, nor should they care about your technical expertise. They've come to the theatre to witness the twists and turns in the lives of the characters and to experience the characters' stories as dramatically, as intricately, as vividly as possible.

If you don't trust the audience's intelligence, you'll probably feel responsible for them "getting it." You will try to spell it out for them. This is called **indicating**. If you trust the audience's intelligence, you'll just play the scene. You do your job—let the audience do its job.

Soliloquy

Unlike a *monologue*, where a character has a long speech *to another character*—usually about the past—in a *soliloquy*, the character is *alone* on stage, voicing their inner thoughts. In a film, a soliloquy would be shot in a close-up of the character's face, with the text spoken in voice-over.

Surprise!

The structure of the soliloquy *usually* follows the traditional sonnet pattern: question/problem, examination of said question/problem from one side, then another, ending in some form of insight or resolution. There are exceptions, of course, but this is the traditional structure of the soliloquy.

From Inaction to Action

As we shall soon see, the character moves from confusion to a form of clarity, either about a situation or about the nature of the world or about life, love, or death.

Juliet, in Act IV, Scene iii, resolves, at the end of her "potion" speech, "Romeo, Romeo, Romeo, Here's drink. I drink to thee," and, after hesitating, drinks the Friar's sleeping potion. Hamlet, in Act II, Scene ii, recognizes "the play's the thing/Wherein I'll catch the conscience of the King," and plans the play within the play.

In each instance, the character starts the soliloquy in a state of inaction, and gradually, through investigation, examination and a series of proofs, arrives at a point of clarity and action. The transformation happens over the course of the speech's three acts and changes the character's relationship with themself (from inaction to action), and, in so doing, changes their relationship with their situation. In short, RTN—the Relationship Transforms Now.

- FOUR TYPES OF SOLILOQUIES

In *Acting with Style*, John Harrop identifies four basic types of soliloquies:

1) The introspective or contemplative soliloquy: when a character is trying to resolve an issue or reflect, philosophically, on a situation; the focus is inward (i.e., Hamlet's "to be or not to be" speech).
2) The actively reflective soliloquy: usually the "problem" is one of conscience or moral choice, and again, the focus tends to be inward (Macbeth: "If it were done when t'were done").
3) The direct address soliloquy: the audience becomes another character in the play, a silent partner in solving the problem; the focus is outward (Helena's "How happy some o'er others can be" from *A Midsummer Night's Dream*).
4) What Harrop calls "the objective correlative"—when the actor uses either an imagined or a tangible object (i.e., Yorick's skull or Macbeth's dagger) as the trigger and focus for reflection.

Modeling

As an example of the combined direct address and contemplative soliloquy, we're going to focus first on Viola's speech at the end of Act II, Scene ii from *Twelfth Night*.

We'll work in detail, gathering clues and information from the text to inform the *playing* of the soliloquy. We'll also be indulging in the kind of speculation you, as the actor, might relish as you prepare a role. Using the same tools at our disposal, we'll then analyze Edmund's first soliloquy in *King Lear*. Both soliloquies are models of the outer-inner, then inner-outer detective work we use as the major part of our template.

- A Word about the First Folio

The First Folio is a valuable resource, not necessarily as THE definitive text, but as a point of reference, especially in terms of punctuation and possible pronunciation.

The Folio was compiled by two actors in Shakespeare's company, John Heminge and Henry Condell, as a way of recording and preserving Shakespeare's plays. Plays were meant to be heard; our modern sense of theatrical spectacle did not exist at the turn of the 17th century. Actors were given their roles as "sides"; they didn't receive full scripts. They rehearsed once or twice, and that was that: perform, then on to the next play.

The First Folio is a compilation of texts as remembered by many of the actors who originated the roles. In some cases, spectators who could recall the texts, almost word for word, contributed to the folio as well. The punctuation approximates what the text sounded like to the ear. Perhaps the elongation of vowels as written in the First Folio might indicate which words were emphasized as operatives by actors. Three more folios were published between 1632 and 1685. They included additions and "corrections" of the First Folio. They're not considered reliable or primary textual resources.

Today, we have several different editions of Shakespeare's plays—all include annotations about the meaning of the words. If you compare and contrast the various editions—the Arden, Oxford, Riverside editions, for example—you'll discover a wide variety in the punctuation as well. Comparing and contrasting editions is a highly valuable and practical guide for determining the sense, and therefore the sensibility, of the text you're about to speak.

- ANOTHER NOTE

For our purposes, when working with Shakespeare, *any* soliloquy is valid as a jumping off point. Therefore, you can choose to play cross-gender: women can work on men's roles, men can work on women's roles. Focus on the language as a pathway into action; as long as you choose to play a character you love, all's acceptable.

- VERY PRACTICAL QUESTION

Because the character is alone on stage, the first question to ask is: who am I speaking to?

Sometimes a soliloquy combines different foci as the character moves through different stages of thinking/problem solving. Here are your four choices for points of focus: to the self, to an imagined other character, to an object (real or imagined), or to the audience.

In almost all instances, and whenever possible, we recommend using the audience as a scene partner. Why? Because, just as *you* might talk through a difficult moment with someone you trust or love, so the *character* needs to do the same. Personalize the relationship; make the audience someone you know, someone who'll listen and be there for you as you figure things out.

Part B: Working the Soliloquy

Here's our first speech: Viola, *Twelfth Night*, Act II, sc. ii.

Context

Viola is a twin, grieving the loss of her brother (not unlike Olivia, a countess, grieving the loss of her brother). Viola's been washed up on the coast of Illyria after a ship wreck. She's befriended by Antonio, a sea captain. She's now disguised as a young page, Cesario, in the service of Orsino, the Duke of Illyria. Orsino's in love with Olivia. However, Viola's crazy in love with Orsino, but cannot reveal herself. Olivia is crazy in love with Cesario/Viola. Viola now has a bit of a problem.

Malvolio runs Olivia's household. He's pretentious, and fancies Olivia for himself. This speech is triggered by Malvolio's dismissal of, and disdain for, Cesario. Malvolio has to play the messenger here, telling Cesario that Orsino doesn't stand a chance with Olivia. Malvolio sees Cesario as a potential rival for Olivia's affections. The speech starts as a response and in reaction to what's just happened, Olivia sending a ring to Cesario.

Viola

I left no ring with her: what means this lady?
Fortune forbid my outside have not charm'd her!
She made good view of me, indeed so much,
That methought her eyes had lost her tongue,
For she did speak in starts distractedly.
She loves me, sure; the cunning of her passion
Invites me in this churlish messenger.
None of my lord's ring? Why, he sent her none.
I am the man: if this be so, as 'tis,
Poor lady, she were better love a dream.
Disguise, I see thou art a wickedness,
Wherein the pregnant enemy does much.
How easy is it for proper false
In women's waxen hearts to set their forms!
Alas, our frailty is the cause, not we,
For such as we are made of, such we be.
How will this fadge? My master loves her dearly,
And I, poor monster, fond as much on him,
And she mistaken, seems to dote on me.
What will become of this? As I am man,
As my state is desperate for my master's love:
As I am woman (now alas the day!)
What thriftless sighs shall poor Olivia breathe?
O time, thou must untangle this, not I,
It is too hard a knot for me t'untie.

Let's divide the speech into three acts. We're going to number the lines to make them easier to reference.

In **Act I,** *Viola starts with direct address: she spells out her problem to us, the audience,* her *audience, her shrink, her best friend, her co-conspirator. She assesses the facts, realizing for the first time that Oliva's in love with her, or rather, Olivia's in love with Cesario, Orsino's page sent to woo her. Suddenly, who Viola is—and what she is—comes into question. The* * *indicates a line with an irregularity in the scansion:*

Five. The Soliloquy: Transformation 79

1) I left / no ring / with her: / what means / this la / dy?
2) *For / tune forbid / my out / side have / not charm'd / her!
3) She made / good view / of me, / in deed / so much,
4) That / me thought / her eyes / had lost her tongue,
5) For she / did speak / in starts / dis tract / ed ly.
6) *She loves / me, sure; / the cun / ning of / her pass / ion
7) *Inv ites / me in / this chur / lish mess / en ger.

In Act II, Viola turns inward, reflecting on the nature of love itself. She begins to see that love is different for men and women: women's roles are fixed, while men's can be fluid. She suddenly sees that she's in a unique position to see both sides of the equation.

8) *None of my / lord's ring?/ Why /he sent / her none.
9) I am / the man: / if this / be so / as 'tis.
10) *Poor la / dy, she / were bet / ter love / a dream.
11) Dis guise / I see / thou art / a wick/ ed ness,
12) Where in / the preg / nant en / e my / does much.
13) How ea / sy is / it for the pro / per false
*14) In wo / men's wax / en hearts / to set / their forms!
15) A las / our frail / ty is / the cause, / not we,
16) For such / as we / are made / of, such/ we be.

Knowing what she now knows about men, women, and love, in Act III, Viola's able to reassess her situation. It's still as impossible as it was before, but she has more clarity about it. She decides it's acceptable for her to do nothing. She'll let time resolve the situation.

17) *How will this / fadge? My / ma / ster loves /her dear ly,
18) *And I, / poor mon / ster, fond / as much / on him.
19) And she, / mis tak / en, seems / to dote / on me.
20) What will / be come / of this? / As I / am man,
21) *My state / is desper / ate for / my mas / ter's love:
22) As I / am wo / man (now / a las / the day!)
23) **What thrift / less sighs / shall poor / O liv / ia breath?
24) *O time, / thou must / untang / le this, / not I,
25) *It is / too hard / a knot / for me / t'un tie.

The Great Themes

For the Elizabethans, and especially for Shakespeare, time is one of the great themes for exploration, along with honor, worth, power, love, nature, and reality v. fiction. In this speech, Viola touches upon concepts about love as well as reality v. fiction, in addition to the workings of time. She begins in confusion and stasis, moves into discovery to "resolve'" the issue with the decision to let time unfold until there's a natural resolution to her dilemma.

Your task, as Viola, is to move from zero to 100 mph in 25 lines, from questionable self-doubt to resolved, resolute (in)action.

The Breakdown

The soliloquy consists of 25 lines: 18 lines are in regular iambic pentameter, 7 have variations; the 2nd, 7th, and 21st lines begin with trochees—DUM de—long short. And, as we said earlier, there are suggestions for more contemporary plays at the end of each chapter. The choice is yours. The 10th, 17th, 23rd and 25th lines contain spondees—DUM DUM—long, long; there are also two lines with feminine (run-on) endings needing to be elided with the start of the next lines (lines 1, 1, 17). Line 8 contains a double foot, with three stresses, and the 4th line contains an irregularity at the onset (that).

Make a Choice

There are no hard and fast rules as to what a spondee, trochee or dactyl *mean*—all we can do is note them, where they fall in the line, where the stress should go whilst speaking, and ask: why here? We do know with a feminine ending—a line with 11 beats—the thought is usually so rich, so full, so saturated with meaning, it extends beyond the norm; it runs-on to connect immediately with the beginning of the following line.

Sentence Lengths

Also, note the lengths of the sentences: they're not short, declarative statements. Rather, the first act begins with a question: "Why did Olivia send me this ring?," i.e., the "problem" of the speech. She then spends the next nine lines answering the question: "I am the man—she were better to love a dream." This is spoken in direct address—we, the audience, become her sounding board as she tries to figure out what to do.

Both Sides

Of course, the most delightful aspect of the speech is Viola being in a position to see both sides of the equation. She's a woman impersonating a man—and, as is common in "trouser" roles, this blurring of gender leads to insight and understanding of what the working man's world (forbidden fruit to an Elizabethan woman) is really like. At the same time, she's also a woman.

How does this insight affect her and her future actions? She's helplessly caught in a web of love and deception; she's prisoner to her feelings yet cannot act on them. Even in the best, most normal of circumstances, she could not become the wooer but must be wooed.

Boy Actors

To complicate the situation even further, and to add another level of deliciousness to the mix, the role of Viola would have been played originally by a young boy, as was the custom in Elizabethan theatre. We have a boy pretending to be a girl pretending to be a boy, deepening the layers of meaning in the speech and the basic conceit of the play: who is what they appear to be, especially in matters of love? How can we ever truly know the reality of what's in front of us?

The How To

We can understand, we can intellectualize the meaning of a speech or moment, but ultimately, we need to use detective work to uncover the clues embedded in the text—those clues designed to help us determine how to play the moment.

Use The Template to reveal metric patterns and irregularities, the structure of the argument, and the progression of thought. The scansion will prove that the operatives are verbs and nouns, with accompanying adverbs and adjectives forming word pictures. Scansion will also guide you to stress pronouns only in comparisons and to never stress the negative; stress what's being negated. Look for irregularities of rhythm/stress to determine when something unusual is happening.

To be redundant but thorough: make sure you understand the meaning of every word in the speech, as well as alternative meanings. Look for double meanings and puns. Divide the speech into three acts, with clear hinges, or transitions. See how the speech ends, then work backwards to set-up the punchline. Play the thought through to the end of each line and the end of each sentence. Play the lyrics, not the music. Language is thought in action: it's always moving forward.

Part C: A Different Approach

For a second, and very different example of how to use this template, let's look at Edmund's first speech in *King Lear*, Act I, sc. ii.

The Context

Edmund is the illegitimate son of Gloucester, advisor to King Lear, and brother to Edgar, Gloucester's legitimate son and, therefore, legitimate heir to his father's estate. Previously, the court had gathered to hear Lear announce his retirement and divide his kingdom between his three daughters. Although he's been residing in his father's house, Edmund is not officially recognized as Gloucester's son. This is his first appearance in the play.

*In **Act I**, as an outsider, one alienated from the general thrust of society, Edmund places his faith in the laws of nature, not man—mankind ignores, shuns, disregards him. He reasons he has every right to follow his inclination in overthrowing his brother, Edgar, in order to pursue his own interests; if society doesn't care for him, he'll care for himself. He still needs us, his audience, as a sounding board, to ensure his proofs, his justifications, are sound, and he makes a compact with nature to go for it.*

Edmund

1) Thou, Na / ture, art / my god / dess; to / thy law
2) My ser / vices / are bound. Wherefore / should I
3) Stand in / the plague / of cus / tom, and / permit

Five. The Soliloquy: Transformation   83

4) The cu / rios / ity of na / tions to / de / prive me,
5) For that / I am / some twelve / or four /teen moon /shines
6) Lag of / a broth / er?

In **Act II**, *Edmund's mind, his thoughts, his speech, are as broken, as disjointed, as the world is at the moment. He asks seven questions in Act II of the speech, then answers them with a series of proofs before arriving at a conclusion in a brief Act III, which is his own call to action.*

7) Why / bastard? / Where fore base?
8) When my / dimen sions are / as well / com pact,
9) My mind / as gen/ erous, and / my shape / as true
10) As hon / est mad/ ams issue? / Why brand / they us
11) With base? / With base / ness? Bas / tardy? / Base, base?
12) Who in/ the lus/ ty stealth / of na/ture take
13) More com / posi/ tion and / fierce qual / i ty
14) Than doth, / with in / a dull, / stale tir/ ed bed,
15) Go to / th' crea/ ting a / whole tribe / of fops,
16) Got 'tween / asleep / and wake?

What does Edmund do at the end of the speech in **Act III**? He puts his plan into action by using the letter to trick his father and upend his brother. If this is the punchline, the rest of the speech is the set-up.

Knowing you have to make a 180 arc, what could the starting point be? Perhaps inaction and indecision? If you start here, you have 23 lines to make the decision or to make us agree with your decision.

The letter gives you a focus to make the decision: to act or not to act? Immediate, tangible. It's a constant reminder of what's at hand, quite literally.

   Well then,
18) Le git / i mate Ed / gar, I / must have / your land:
19) Our fath/ er's love / is to the / bas tard /Edmund
20) As to the legit/ imate. Fine / word, / "legit imate."!
21) Well, my "legit / imate." If / this let / ter speed,
22) And my / in ven / tion thrive/ Ed mund / the base

23) Shall top / th' legit / imate—: / I grow, / I pros / per;
24) Now, gods / stand up / for bas / tards.

How the Text Works

Is this an easy decision for Edmund? Not in the least. Notice the number of feminine ending/run-on lines throughout the speech—one thought tumbles into the next. Nothing at first feels regular, even, controlled.

The Want

What does Edmund want? Consider this possibility: as we see it, Edmund's first two lines could be a negotiation with "Nature." I'm doing this—I'm pledging my faith and trust to you, "My Goddess." He ends the speech by imploring the Goddess Nature to "stand up for bastards." "I do this for you, you do this for me." Not only is this speech a spur into action, it's a contract signing, one with terms, conditions, and proofs.

The point is: as the actor playing Edmund, you have to go from inaction/indecision to action/decision. Is it best for you to remain introspective, figuring it out for yourself, or to engage us, the audience, in the process? If the latter, who, exactly, specifically, are we to you? What do you need from us? How do you proceed in order to satisfy that need? What, exactly, are you doing/playing?

Repetitive Sounds/Alliteration

Throughout the speech, note how the "b" sounds repeat and repeat and repeat. What are you going to do with them? They're there for a reason, so: how do you want us to react? Are they all the same—baseness, bastardy, base, base?—or are they each slightly different? Do you want us to laugh—are they riddled with sarcasm? Or, do you want us to shake our heads in dismay? Or, do you want us to boo you or cheer you on?

The Argument

What about the consistency of the argument, i.e., your dogged determination to justify what you may do? Edmund believes he has rightness on his side; it's the world that's a little cockeyed. Does he seduce us? Mock us? Expose our prejudices? Celebrate our good sense? Use us to prod himself into action?

Antithesis

We also have the balanced argument of bastard v. legitimate, as well as the quest for acceptance, attention, power, recognition. Edmund wants to be seen as an equal. We know, throughout the play that he's amoral, Machiavellian—that he believes his ends justify his means.

He's also irresistible to both Goneril and Regan, Lear's two older daughters. Where and what is the power of his attraction? Raw sexuality? Pure charisma? Wit, intelligence, charm? If all of the above, how can you, as Edmund, establish all of this in the soliloquy?

Edmund's a profoundly logical thinker: he can argue his case, he can justify his means, he can seduce through humor, wit, intelligence. All are operative factors in this speech, broken and chaotic as it is, broken and chaotic as his thinking is.

Edgar

And then there's the question of his brother, Edgar: in order for Edmund to advance in the world, he needs to eliminate his brother. The word "brother" starts with a "b," and it's linked to the repetition of "b's" throughout the speech.

Isn't Edgar Edmund's obstacle throughout the speech? Edgar = legitimate, politically correct, legally recognized, seen, acknowledged by society. Edmund = illegitimate, hidden, invisible—a man who has a strong desire, unspoken until now, to be very public, very seen, very visible.

In order for his plan to work, Edmund must "top the legitimate"— please note, the oblique or not so oblique sexual innuendo with "top the legitimate," i.e., Edmund places Edgar in a submissive sexual position so that he, Edmund, can dominate the situation.

Transformation

In order to succeed, Edmund must transform his relationship with his brother. This speech, this moment, initiates that action. And, by transforming his relationship with his brother (and by inference, with his father, Gloucester), Edmund transforms his own self-image, his stature in the world.

Using the Model

As you can see from the above examples, a thorough grounding in the text frees you to make informed choices as you start to work on playing a soliloquy of your own choosing. These models also include a great deal of speculation about possibilities. We'll be expanding this aspect of preparatory/detective work as we work with other texts. Speculation is meant to feed your imagination as you consider the practical choices you will have to make.

The point is: question, investigate, speculate, and, just as you would when buying clothes, try on all your options, and keep trying them on until you find the best fit.

Part D: A New Element

You'll be using your soliloquy as "clay": you're going to mold and shape the clay into a dramatic structure, a **score of action**.

Score of Action

The score of action is a repeatable sequence of physical movements corresponding to and reflecting the emotional as well as the psychological transformation happening within the character and within the character's relationship to others. Chances are, some of these physical moves may feel more "right" than others, and you'll hold on to them. There's a natural, organic progression in the rehearsal process: hold on to what works, discard what doesn't. Keep, fix, cut, change.

Shape

The totality of the physical, visceral movement, as well as the vocal movement, gives the speech or the scene what we'll call its **shape**. It may start fast and loud, then slow, then crescendo, then slowly resolve into silence, just as the character is excited, then contemplative, then inspired, then determined to move on.

Architecture

Ultimately, you will end up playing a *sequence* of physical and vocal actions. The shape is like architecture: it's a sequence of boundaries within which something happens. In rehearsal, you're constantly working to define and then refine the shape within its boundaries.

To start: Choose a soliloquy—one you love. Then read the play from start to finish in one sitting, if possible. Even when working on one speech, let alone an entire scene, *read the entire play*. Know what happens before your speech or scene and what happens after. Think about how your scene bridges past and future in the present moment.

Define and Paraphrase

Look up the meaning of every word you don't understand. Use the various editions of the text to discover potential new meanings of the words, meanings which might change the thought and intent of what you're saying/doing.

To personalize the text, paraphrase the text, thought by thought. Be accurate in tracing the progression of the argument. Then, scan the text for metrical irregularities to determine the stresses within the line. The stresses define the operative words. Shakespeare always points you to the operatives through the scansion.

Pin, Punch, Personalize

Having identified the operatives—what we'll call "**pinning**" the operatives—don't be afraid to **punch** them, i.e., make them as obvious, as dynamic as possible.

As the work progresses, you'll **personalize** them, i.e., rather than punching, lightly tap them, until eventually you can stress them with a slight change of inflection or the lift of an eyebrow.

Structure

Observe and honor all **punctuation**, just as you would honor the dynamic markings in a score of music. Use punctuation as markers for shifting vocal dynamics when the thought/action changes.

Now turn to the rhetorical devices: alliteration, assonances, antitheses—the tools you'll use to make your argument. Play the contrasts, comparisons and lists to create dynamic tension within the line.

Identify the "**punchline**" at the end of each sentence, then go back to the beginning of the sentence and consider the tactics you'll use to give the set-up momentum as you drive to the punchline.

Divide each speech into three acts by locating the "**hinges**" or changes of thought, i.e., the pros and the cons of the argument.

Part E: From Outer to Inner

This is all the outer work. Now it's time to speculate on the destination that the detective text work is leading you to: the objective.

Ask the basic questions: how do I feel now and how do I want to feel?

What needs to change within me, or within my situation, to make me feel better? In short, what's my problem and what are my options? And, how can I enlist you, my friends, to make me feel better?

The 180

To start, you have a problem to resolve or a moral or philosophical issue to contemplate. You're going to define the facts of your problem—here's the "pro" side of the argument, there's the "con" or other side of the argument—and, then, you'll arrive at a conclusion, a solution or resolution for the problem. This is the first part of **The Template** for your 180, the arc of the transformation.

After Defining It, Play It

You'll rehearse on your own, then show the work in class.

The Warm-Up: Begin your warm-up by working through the entire speech.

Start by walking in any direction. When the thought changes, change direction.

Recite the text in neutral; don't try to act it. Just say the words, repeating them until the sounds of the words begin to vibrate on the lips.

Extend and exaggerate the vowel sounds; clip and exaggerate the consonants. Make the contrasts between the vowels and consonants as strong as possible. See if, in extending and exaggerating the vowels, the sounds themselves help create or define the "meaning."

PVTF

Run through Act I of the speech changing pitch from thought to thought, then change volume, then tempo, then force. Let the changes be arbitrary.

Try to let the changes themselves suggest meaning; you're not trying to make "sense" of the material, you're just warming up, flexing the muscles.

Repeat, combining Acts I and II. Then repeat, combining all three acts.

Lean Into It

Next: engage your body. Metaphorically, lean into the experience of the text. Begin to infuse it with meaning, but play it melodramatically, "emoting," over-playing each moment. Send it out into space, as if you're filling a football stadium; you want to reach the very last person in the very last row of the arena. Repeat, until the size of the playing begins to feel easy, natural.

Now, do the opposite: stand still. No gestures. No arms or hands. Keep the face neutral. Pull everything in, making the playing small, contained, barely whispered, as if you're on camera in a very tight close-up.

Repeat, combining Acts I and II. Repeat, working through all three acts of your soliloquy.

Moving On

Now you're ready to rehearse with more intensity. Working just Act I of the soliloquy, start seated, in neutral. Barely whisper the text. Focus inward, speaking to and for yourself. No "acting." Simply the words.

Work through the act, thought by thought, moment to moment. Take your time. Observe the length of the sentences, the punctuation, the repetition of sound and image. Focus on lightly tapping the operatives. Remember, as in the work on the sonnet, you're playing the lyric, not the melody.

Focus

Do you prefer to play the entire act with an inward, contemplative focus, or with an entirely external focus? Experiment with shifting the focus from internal to external, or vice versa. Investigate which shifts or changes move you from Act I to Act II to Act III.

Try all possibilities in investigating the material. You're not looking to fix or set the material just yet. Rather, you want to discover the architecture of the thinking, the rises and falls of the action, and then, how you can give it a *shape* illuminating its meaning.

Repeat this process, working Acts I and II, focusing on the differences between the two acts. Then, repeat this process a third time, focusing on setting up and then arriving at the punchline.

- ADD: JUST THREE MOVES

When you feel ready, add this to the entire soliloquy: make no more than the following three physical moves—and only three—during the speech: you may stand up, you may sit down, you may kneel. That's it. You don't have to use all three, but you may not use more than three. You may start standing, you may start sitting, you may start kneeling.

Move during the hinge, i.e., when the thought, the direction of the argument, changes. Use the moves to mark out the shifts of thought— and thereby, the shifts of action. Try to keep all gestures to a minimum; make thinking—and by extension, the speaking of the thoughts—your main focus.

Eye Acting

Now we'll use more physical cues, garnered from *Neural Linguistic Programming*, created by Richard Bandler and John Grinder.

These two men observed that the eyes move subconsciously in six different directions as we're thinking: if the eyes move to the upper left while we're speaking, we're creating a thought or image; if they move to the upper right, were recalling/remembering an image; If the eyes shift to the center left, we're creating sound; if to center right, we're recalling a sound or audio sensation. Finally, if the eyes shift down to lower left, we're engaged in feeling/kinesthetic recall, and if they move to lower right, we're engaging in self-talk.

Consciously change the position and direction of your eyes as you move from one thought to another. See how this shift in focus affects you viscerally, intellectually, and emotionally.

Experiment. Play with changing the eye focus from act to act; then, try within each act. See how these simple eye movements help you shift from internal, contemplative action, pulling us in to you, or, with external focus, pushing us away from you. Either direction is a tactic you can use to solve your problem.

Try all possibilities in investigating the material. You're not looking to fix or set the material. That will happen through repetition as you rehearse. Rather, *now* in rehearsal, you want to discover the architecture of the thinking, the rises and falls of the action, how you can give it a shape illuminating its meaning.

Mix and Match

All of the above are exercises and suggestions for exploring and then making choices about the soliloquy. Now, let's put all the pieces together.

Finalize the physical score of action—the choices you've made about what you're going to do—and when—in space as you speak.

Try to limit your choices. Keep the focus on the words by limiting gesture.

Keep repeating and working the score of action until you feel it has a sense of flow, an internal logic, a sense of shape to it. This is what you'll show when it's time to show the work.

Time to Play

Speak directly to us, your audience, as you work through your problem.

Really talk *to* us, rather than *at* us. Check our reactions—this is the feedback loop; adjust your playing accordingly. Take us through the entire thought process, from problem to alternatives to solution. Spell it out.

Build the tension in the thinking by stressing contrasts, comparisons, and lists.

Play the thought all the way through to the end of the line. Observe *natural* pauses in the line, as indicated by punctuation, and don't break the thought with *unnatural, unscripted* pauses in order to make the speech sound "more natural."

Stress the operatives. We'll follow the logic of your thinking and, therefore, the logic of your argument, if you stress the operatives. Breathe at the end of the thought or phrase, using the caesura to help you take a catch breath. When you finish, hold the thought for a moment—let it hang, suspended, in the air.

Your instructor will give you feedback on the work—what worked, what could work better. Think of the feedback process as a form of gardening, giving you information about what needs more watering and what needs less, what needs to be pruned back or weeded, what can move into the sunlight to continue growing. This is vital information to inform your playing, especially as we move on to scene work.

Once Again:

If you can make this language clear and accessible—by knowing what you're saying, and therefore what you're doing, you can play any text—classical or contemporary—in any context, with any subtext. The rest is just icing on the cake.

This process takes time to ingest. We call this way of working the "foie gras school of acting": we're going to cram this information down your throat, over and over and over again, until you "get it" on a visceral level. The challenge in this way of working is to move from the head (intellectually understanding concepts) into the body (being able to work without overthinking). We want the material to "drop down and drop in" so the playing has spontaneity, surprise, unpredictability to it.

Note: this process is progressive. We're always building on what's come before, taking it one step further. Sometimes you'll focus first on context, sometimes on subtext; the point is to be fluid, yet proficient, with all the steps in the process. In this way of working, you won't be playing an entire scene in one go until you know how to play Act I, then Acts I and II, and then Acts I, II, and III. Baby steps all the way.

Additional soliloquies to experiment with: contemporary soliloquies *are challenging to find; most modern plays use monologues— one character speaking at length to another character—rather than one character, alone on stage, seeking a solution to a problem. However, here are a few examples found in song:* "Billy's Soliloquy" from

Five. The Soliloquy: Transformation

Carousel, "Rose's Turn" from *Gypsy* or George's song, "Finishing the Hat," from *Sunday in the Park with George.* **In these instances, characters define a problem, then work through it to arrive at a solution. Try speaking the text rather than singing.**

What's Next

In the next chapter, we'll be working the Richard/Lady Anne scene from *King Richard III.* We'll apply The Template to see what happens when we expand the playing to actually interact with a real scene partner.

Six

The Scene: The Loop, Part I

Part A: The Visceral

In the previous chapters, we've focused on the verbal and the vocal aspects of engaging in action by playing objectives. However, once you start rehearsing with a partner, you'll spend the majority of your time determining when and where to move, when and where to be still, when and where the relationship changes and how to best express these changes physically, *in space*. This is the *visceral* aspect of playing, and we're now going to focus our attention on this aspect before we move on into scene work.

The Body Never Lies

Words can deceive. We can trick ourselves into believing the words we're saying or hearing, but the body will always give us away when we lie. Subtle eye movements, like the expansion or contraction of the iris, give us away (which is why many negotiators prefer to wear dark glasses while negotiating—the involuntary eye movement, if detected, might reveal too much information to an opponent), or the withholding of the pelvis when embracing on stage reveals an actor's discomfort with physical intimacy, or the focus and direction of the pelvis or the feet (either engaging or evading your partner) tells the audience, subconsciously, where you'd like to be rather than where you are.

As we'll soon see, the body stores visceral information in muscle memory. Once released, you can use innate visceral sensibility to influence and impact your scene partner just by changing the spatial relationships.

Here's a simple exercise to test this theory: we'll play first, then, after you've played, we'll talk about some of the principles involved in non-verbal communication. As always, the instructor will give you directions:

The Dolly

1. Form two teams. Select a partner in the opposite team. Stand on opposite sides of the room, facing your partner.
2. Use your hands to form a frame, or viewfinder. Look at your partner through the frame.
3. Keeping your partner "in frame," move or "dolly in" towards one another.
4. Keeping your partner "in frame," dolly back away from one another, returning to your starting position.
5. Abandon the viewfinder. Focus on your partner.
6. Take two steps in towards one another.
7. Stand in a neutral position. Without adjusting or adapting, see if your distance in space suggests a relationship to you. Do you know who you are to one another? Note any images that come to mind.
8. Take three steps towards each other. Freeze.
9. Who are you to one another now? Does the relationship feel any different?
10. Take a half step toward each other. Stand nose to nose. Wrap your arms around one another. Who are you now? Take one step back from one another. Is the relationship the same, or has it changed?
11. Still maintaining visual contact, make a quarter turn to your right. Who are you now?
12. Very slowly, make a half turn to your left. Who are you to one another now?
13. Make another quarter turn to your right. Face one another. Take two steps back. Pause. Who are you now?
14. Take three steps back. Who are you now?
15. Still facing one another, move back to your original, starting position. Who are you now?
16. Release.

Take a moment or two to talk with your partner. Discuss what happened as the space between you changed, as you changed direction with one another and how the relationship changed as the space expanded or contracted.

Here are some of the principles involved in The Dolly:

- DIRECT AND INDIRECT

Playing with your chest and stomach unprotected leaves you open, vulnerable. One simple way to protect yourself is to cross your arms over your chest or use one arm to reach across and hold the other.

Staying open and unguarded means there's a *direct* flow of energy between the two of you, especially from the hips and pelvis. You give your partner your undivided physical attention.

Indirect space splits your focus. During your quarter turn away from one another, while still maintaining eye contact with your partner, your upper body was ready for one form of engagement while the lower part of your body, with pelvis turned away, signaled that you were uncomfortable and wanted to escape.

We describe this indirect form of physical contact as an open V, i.e., upper body direct, lower body indirect. You were sending mixed—*incongruent*—physical messages. No matter what you may say with words, your body is saying you don't want to be there. Correct this by turning your hips **in** to face your partner. Think of the pelvis as a *headlight*. Wherever the pelvis is focused, that's where the light's shining.

- TACTICS

Direct and indirect focus are *physical tactics*. Say "I love you" with words, but turn your headlights—hips—away from your partner (that pesky open V), and you've sent a clearly enigmatic message about your feelings. Or: lie, and make your partner believe the lie by turning your headlights onto them. If you shine the light exclusively on them—making them feel important, special—you're more than halfway home to getting what you want.

Knowing just this much about body language can change the intensity of your playing by attending to use and direction of those headlights. If you "cheat out" in the course of the scene (i.e., if you turn your hips/headlights away from your partner—into the V), you're sending a subconscious message that you're more interested in being seen by the audience than you are in engaging directly with your partner. The point is that, from now on, make informed choices about where and when to shine the headlights, where and when to move, to be still, to sit, to stand, to move towards or away from your partner.

Your right side, in classic body language, is traditionally considered the dominant, active side. It responds directly to commands from the left side of the brain—the logical, analytical, "controlling" side of the brain. Leading with your right suggests you're withholding and protecting your left. Your left side is traditionally considered the receptive side. The left side is closer to the heart, responding to commands from the right brain—the emotive, intuitive side of the brain. Speaking into someone's left ear is much more intimate and emotionally appealing than speaking into their right.

"Safe space" in life—the socially accepted distance between people—is usually measured as 18 inches. Closer than that implies a situation of intimacy; further than that, the implication is one of formality or unfamiliarity. As you've discovered, any position in space can unlock emotional as well as psychological associations. During a scene, adjust and adapt the "safe space" as necessary to make sure your body language is consistent—*congruent*—with the facts of the text, context, and subtext.

How to Use This Information

As we move into scene work, we'll be combining all three aspects of action—the verbal, the vocal and the visceral—to form a consistent and methodical sequence of steps: i.e., **The Template.**

You can use The Template with any scene to investigate the material, create a repeatable score of action and elevate the quality of play— the Q of P—as you pursue your objective.

Part B: Preparing for Scene Work

As you know, from this point forward in the training process, we'll be focusing on scenes. As a reminder, we're using *our* interpretation of each scene as a model for how we'd like *you* to read and examine a text, i.e., how to hunt for the information you will need as you prepare to act, and how the hunt itself can stimulate and feed your imagination throughout the rehearsal process.

After we've worked through our model of the text for this scene, you'll need to select a scene—**in blank verse**—to rehearse. Use the Rehearse-the-Rehearsal section as your guide through all the stages of the rehearsal process.

Out and In

You'll be rehearsing your scene *outside* of class, then showing your work *in* class for feedback from the instructor. Incorporate the feedback into your subsequent rehearsals. Each scene will be in rehearsal for approximately three weeks. And, as we've mentioned earlier, in the scene we're about to do from *King Richard III* and in the scenes to follow, you're *self-directing*, i.e., there's no one to tell you what to do—you and your partner will have to figure it out on your own.

As a general principle, we suggest working on scenes between *3–5 minutes* in length. This gives you the opportunity to use your rehearsal time with greater efficiency and focus. As you become more comfortable with the process, the scenes can expand in length. The sooner you are off book (i.e., have memorized the text), the sooner you can make sustained eye contact with your partner the sooner you can actually engage in the visceral experience of playing a scene. Usually, as you put the script down and start to play a scene, there's an awkward period of what we'll call "**teleprompter acting**": you see the words on the page whilst looking at your partner and you're suspended in a no-man's land of action/inaction, until the words are lodged firmly in your body. The remedy? Patience, practice, and persistence.

Since we're working each scene act by act, you only have to memorize the text for Act I of your scene to start. You will add the rest of the text in increments when you rehearse Acts I and II for the next showing, then Acts I, II, and III for the final showing. This makes memorizing a slow, easy process. But you have to be diligent and disciplined in learning the text *verbatim*.

That being said, let's experiment with all three aspects of action—verbal, vocal and visceral—as we move on to the scene itself:

Act I, scene ii, King Richard III

To begin: read the entire play, then reread your scene and start to gather information about the given circumstances that will color and condition your playing of the scene.

The Facts

Richard has set the stage for his rise to power and the throne. He has murdered King Henry VI and Henry's son, Edward. Anne, Edward's widow, is transporting Henry VI's body to its final resting place. As scripted, this scene takes place in a public space—a street— and the scene should be considered a public confrontation.

The Cuts

To conform to our recommended time limit, we've made a few cuts in this scene. We're starting our scene with the first direct exchange between Anne and Richard, after Anne's funeral oration. As is now our custom, we've divided the scene into three acts.

Act I *is fueled by a relentless barrage of compliments from Richard to Anne: she's an angel, divine, a fair creature, fairer than fair, a beauty beyond compare. In fact, his passion for her drove him to murder. She's the cause, the blame. Anne denigrates and derides Richard: he's the devil, a beast, an infection of a man, a hedgehog (the animal on his family crest). Like Richard, Anne does not relent in the face of opposition; in fact, she may be spurred on by his resistance—she may find the combat of wits, of insults, of rebuffs, exciting. Instead of relenting in the face of her resistance, Richard doubles the intensity of his attack. Anne's resistance is Richard's obstacle; Richard's persistence is hers.*

The calls and responses happen in exactly the same position in each line—the characters are mirroring one another, but in opposition. It's immediate. It's exact. It's deliberate. When played rapidly, it feels like a volley of words and thoughts, compliments answered by insults, push responding to pull. In short, The Bounce.

1) **Rich.** Sweet saint, for charity, be not so curst.
2) **Anne.** Foul devil, for God's sake hence, and trouble us not.
3) **Rich.** Lady, you know no rules of charity,
4)   Which renders good for bad, blessings for curses.
5) **Anne.** Villain, thou know'st no law of God nor man.
7)   No beast so fierce but knows some touch of pity.
8) **Rich.** But I know none, and therefor am no beast.
9) **Anne.** O wonderful, when devils tell the truth!

10) **Rich.** More wonderful, when angels are so angry.
11)   Vouchsafe, divine perfection of a woman,
12)   Of these supposed crimes, to give me leave,
13)   By circumstance, but to acquit myself.
14) **Anne.** Vouchsafe, diffus'd infection of a man,
15)   Of these known evils, but to give me leave,
16)   By circumstance, t'accuse thy cursed self.
17) **Rich.** Fairer than tongue can name thee, let me have
18)   Some patient leisure to excuse myself.
19) **Anne.** Fouler than heart can think thee, thou canst make
20)   No excuse current but to hang thyself.
21) **Rich.** By such despair I should accuse myself.
22) **Anne.** And by despairing shalt thou stand excus'd
23)   For doing worthy vengeance on thyself
24)   That didst unworthy slaughter upon others.
25) **Rich.** Say that I slew them not?
26) **Anne.** Then say they were not slain:
27)   But dead they are, and, devilish slave, by thee.
28) **Rich.** I did not kill your husband.
29) **Anne.** Why then he is alive.
30) **Rich.** Nay he is dead, and slain by Edward's hand.
31) **Anne.** In thy foul throat thou liest: Queen Margaret saw
32)   Thy murd'rous falchion smoking in his blood,
33)   The which thou once didst bend against her breast,
34)   But that thy brothers beat aside the point.
35) **Rich.** I was provoked by her sland'rous tongue,
36)   That laid their guilt upon my guiltless shoulders.
37) **Anne.** Thou wast provoked by thy bloody mind,
38)   That never dream'st on aught but butcheries.
39)   Did thou not kill this King?
40) **Rich.**   I grant ye, yea.
41) **Anne.** Does grant me, hedgehog! Then God grant me too
42)   Thou mayst be damned for that wicked deed.
43)   O he was gentle, mild, and virtuous.

44) **Rich.** The better for the King of Heaven that hath him.
45) **Anne.** He is in Heaven, where thou shalt never come.
46) **Rich.** Let him thank me that holp to send him thither,
47)   For he was fitter for that place than earth.
48) **Anne.** And thou unfit for any place but hell.
49) **Rich.** Yes, one place else, if you will hear me name it.
50) **Anne.** Some dungeon?
51) **Rich.** Your bed-chamber.
52) **Anne.** Ill rest betide the chamber where thou liest.
53) **Rich.** So will it, madam, till I lie with you.
54) **Anne.** I hope so!
55) **Rich.** I know so.

During **Act II**, *Richard launches into a full-on, full force, full-frontal assault: he tells Anne he's blinded by her beauty; her beauty compelled him to commit crimes; he's in love with her; if he's lying, she should kill him. As we see it, he's like a cobra looking to strike, every line chipping away at her defenses, appealing to her vanity. Anne refuses to relent.*

There are two sets of shared lines, lines 84, 85, 86, and again, lines 88, 89, 90. Psychologically, the characters appear to be drawn to one another. However, Anne spits at Richard after line 89, and this physical action changes the rhythm and dynamic of the scene. Although it's a shared line, we think Richard has to pause in order to recalibrate his approach ("Why dost thou spit at me?"). Her action demands a response, and Richard can break the rhythm of the shared line to signal a change of tactic.

His next move in the scene is the critical maneuver in transforming the relationship: he kneels before her, offering his sword. Richard's lines, 105–110, are one long sentence, in which he gives her the power of life and death.

Richard makes Anne believe he's acknowledging her power: she holds his life in sway. He's gambling with very high stakes; she's abandoned her curses—and her mourning—to engage directly with him on a more immediate, personal, visceral level. This is the climax and turning point in the scene, with Richard kneeling, Anne poised with the dagger at hand. By the end of Act II, they're a perfect match: two combatants, matador and bull, ready for the kill.

56)   But, gentle Lady **Anne**,
57)   To leave this keen encounter of our wits,
58)   And fall something into a slower method:
59)   Is not the causer of the timeless deaths
60)   Of these Plantagenets, Henry and Edward,
61)   As blameful as the executioner?
62) **Anne.** Thou wast the cause, and most accurs'd effect.
63) **Rich.** Your beauty was the cause of that effect:
64)   Your beauty, that did haunt me in my sleep
65)   To undertake the death of all the world,
66)   So I might live one hour in your sweet bosom.
67) **Anne.** If I thought that, I tell thee, homicide,
68)   These nails should rend that beauty from my cheeks.
69) **Rich.** These eyes could not endure that beauty's wrack;
70)   You should not blemish it if I stood by.
71)   As all the world is cheered by the sun,
72)   So I by that; it is my day, my life.
73) **Anne.** Black night o'ershade thy day, and death thy life.
74) **Rich.** Curse not thyself, fair creature; thou art both.
75) **Anne.** I would I were, to be reveng'd on thee.
76) **Rich.** It is a quarrel most unnatural,
77)   To be reveng'd on him that loveth thee.
78) **Anne.** It is a quarrel just and reasonable,
79)   To be reveng'd on him that kill'd my husband.
80) **Rich.** He that bereft thee, lady, of thy husband,
81)   Did it to help thee to a better husband.
82) **Anne.** His better doth not breathe upon the earth.
83) **Rich.** He lives that loves thee better than he could.
84) **Anne.** Name him.
85) **Rich.**   Plantagenet.
86) **Anne.**   Why that was he.
87) **Rich.** The selfsame name, but one of better nature,
88) **Anne.** Where is he?
89) **Rich.**   Here. *Spits at him.*

Six. The Scene: The Loop, Part I   103

90)   Why dost thou spit at me?
91) **Anne.** Would it were mortal poison, for thy sake.
92) **Rich.** Never came poison from so sweet a place.
93) **Anne.** Never hung poison on a fouler toad.
94)   Out of my sight! Thou dost infect mine eyes.
95) **Rich.** Thine eyes, sweet lady, have infected mine.
96) **Anne.** Would they were basilisks, to strike thee dead.
97) **Rich.** I would they were, that I might die at once;
98)   For now they kill me with a living death.
99)   I never sued to friend nor enemy:
100)   My tongue could never learn sweet smoothing word;
101)   But now thy beauty is propos'd my fee,
102)   My proud heart sues, and prompts my tongue to speak.
   She looks scornfully at him.
103)   Teach not thy lip such scorn; for it was made
104)   For kissing, lady, not for such contempt.
105)   If thy revengeful heart cannot forgive,
106)   Lo here I lend thee this sharp-pointed sword,
107)   Which if thou please to hide in this true breast
108)   And let the soul forth that adoreth thee,
109)   I lay it naked to the deadly stroke,
110)   And humbly beg the death upon my knee.
   He kneels and lays his breast open, she offers at (it) with his sword.
111)   Nay, do not pause, for I did kill King Henry—
112)   But 'twas thy beauty that provoked me.
113)   Nay, now dispatch: 'twas I that stabb'd young Edward—
114)   But 'twas thy heavenly face that set me on.
   She falls the sword.

There's a shared line at the top of **Act III** *(lines 119-120: "I have already/that was in thy rage"), followed soon thereafter with four short lines (lines 125-126: "I would I knew thy heart/T'is figured in my tongue") followed by one more shared line (lines 130-132: "I Bid me farewell/T'is more than you deserve"). Note the progression: the confrontational banter of Act I evolved into intense cat-and-mouse wooing in Act II, and now,* in Act III, it shifts into serious negotiation, a denouement and resolution of the action.

In our reading of the text, the shared and short lines here indicate a change of tactics for both characters. There's a tacit agreement the relationship has transformed and a recognition that now's the time to complete the negotiation.

115)   Take up the sword again, or take up me.
116) **Anne.** Arise, dissembler; though I wish thy death, *[He rises]*
117)   I will not be thy executioner.
118) **Rich.** Then bid me kill myself, and I will do it.
119) **Anne.** I have already.
120) **Rich.**   That was in thy rage:
121)   Speak again, and even with the word,
122)   This hand, which for thy love did kill thy love,
123)   Shall for thy love kill a far truer love:
124)   To both their deaths shalt thou be accessary.
125) **Anne.** I would I knew thy heart.
126) **Rich.** 'Tis figur'd in my tongue.
127) **Anne.** I fear me both are false.
128) **Rich.** Then never was man true.
129)   Vouchsafe to wear this ring.
130) **Anne:** To take is not to give.
131) **Rich.** Bid me farewell.
132) **Anne.** 'Tis more than you deserve;
133)   But since you teach me how to flatter you,
134)   Imagine I have said farewell already.

Part C: Moving On

Having read the scene for content, reread the scene slowly, looking for the clues embedded in the text. We've already modeled how to do this work; now you're going to do it on your own with your own scene.

The Template

> Look up any words you don't know; look for possible variations in meaning. Make sure you know, precisely, what you're saying, word for word, thought for thought.
>
> Scan the text, looking for irregularities, noting where they fall.
>
> Note the punctuation. If there's a question mark, ask the question; if there's a semi-colon, use sustained inflection to connect the thoughts. When the thought ends, use a downward inflection.
>
> Note the sentence lengths and drive the thought to the punchline at the end of each sentence and to the end of each of our three acts.
>
> Look for end-stop and run-on lines. Look for shared lines. This will give you information about the rhythm of the scene. Shared lines must be played quickly, as if they're one line. No pauses.
>
> Look for alliterations, assonance, repetitions, almost soundalikes.
>
> Look for irony, wit, intelligence, playfulness, the humor—dark or light—in the sounds of the words themselves.
>
> Look to vowels to elongate and to consonants to snap or bite into, punctuating the vocal aspect of the scene.

Remember—and this cannot be stressed enough—verbs modified by adverbs and nouns modified by adjectives are the operative words. They carry the message of the thought, the information of who does what to whom. "**Pin**" by underlining or circling the operative words to identify them, then "**punch**" them—using either volume or force—to emphasize them, and finally, "**personalize**" them, transforming the punch into a way of speaking more specifically designed to affect your partner.

To truly own the language, paraphrase the scene, beat by beat, starting with the first beat in the scene, then the second and then the third. As you become comfortable with the paraphrasing, begin to merge, mix and match the paraphrasing with the actual text, until you're comfortable with what you're saying throughout the entire scene.

What's Next

Once you've done this basic textual detective work, we'll begin, together in the next chapter, to speculate about the how's, the what's, the why's of what you're saying. We'll then move on to rehearsing the rehearsal, going from table read to the final showing.

Seven

THE SCENE: THE LOOP, PART II

Part A: Speculation

For the fun of it, let's speculate: see if any of these ideas excite your imagination about who you (i.e., the character) are, what you want and what you might do to secure the want. Your answers to these questions will color the tactics you use to affect your partner. *We're* working with Richard and Anne: *you* work with the characters in your scene.

What's It All About?

Based on our reading of the play and our understanding of the social, cultural and political context at the time the play was written, the play is not only about the quest for power but also the consequences of power. We see both the rise and the fall of Richard III.

Shakespeare seems fascinated with unbridled, unabashed and unleashed ambition, and the consequences thereof and therein: think *Coriolanus*, think *Julius Caesar*. Richard falls directly into this trajectory of fatally flawed men seeking political power.

- RICHARD

Who is Richard and what's at stake for him? As we see it: Richard believes himself deformed *physically* but he's out to prove he's not deformed *mentally*. He believes he's smarter, sexier, and cleverer than anyone surrounding him. He feels he's entitled to the throne. He wants us, his audience, to go along with him on the ride to the top. Seduction, for him, is an extreme sport. Like all narcissists, Richard believes the world revolves around him; he's the single occupant, the self-interested driving force in his universe.

For Richard, the end justifies the means: in marrying Anne, he consolidates and solidifies his political position, takes control of her lands, her estate, and in a sense, her very identity. In short, he's the perfect stage villain, but with a twist (no pun intended), for Shakespeare gives Richard psychological complexity: he develops a conscience, embracing remorse before his defeat and death.

- ANNE

What about Anne? What's at stake for her here? In the historical and social context of the time Shakespeare was writing this play, a widow and a woman of Anne's rank and social position had no value alone without a man. Therefore, as newly widowed, Anne needs to be allied to a man, for, in so doing, she'll be acknowledged, appreciated, accepted and able to maintain her self-image and her value as a beautiful, desirable woman.

As we see it, her weapons of choice are her attractiveness and her sexual appeal. Whereas Richard wants to *grab* power, Anne wants to *hold on* to power.

One Other Factor to Consider

How much of this scene is performative—i.e., how much is Richard playing the villain, then the seducer? How much of Anne's grief is real? Or is it a performance in front of an audience? It's possible they're both *performing* for one another, each wearing a mask: she, the grieving widow, he, the penitent murderer. Shakespeare's written the scene with on-lookers, i.e., the pallbearers. As actors, you will need to decide if you will consider the public nature of the exchange or not.

Because we know the scene will end with Anne succumbing and Richard succeeding (or is it the other way around?), we want to start Act 1 with as much psychological—and spatial—separation as possible to make the arc of the action—the 180—all the more challenging and exciting to play.

Part B: The Table Read

This is the first time you're meeting with your partner to work the scene. You'll read through the entire scene *three times*, each time with a slightly different focus. Test the information you've been gathering with your detective work to see how it affects your partner and how you can use it as preparation for actually getting up and moving in space in the next rehearsal.

1st Pass: Sitting in chairs, face one another, hips facing hips, looking at one another as best you can while you read the entire scene with the script in your hand. You may decide later you'd prefer to play some of the beats indirectly, but for now, play the scene with direct focus. Take your time. Be willing to abandon your predetermined choices if what you hear isn't being said the way you thought it should be.

Read the scene straight through, without stopping. After the read, talk about what worked and what didn't work, keeping in mind the structure of the scene, the nature of the argument and the rhetorical shapes within the scene: antitheses, comparisons and contrasts, lists, and the force and velocity of the argument.

2nd Pass: Sit on the edge of your chair. Even if it feels arbitrary, trick yourself by reacting physically: lean in, sit back, stay forward, stay back, turn to your right, to the left. What you *don't* want to do is remain static or stuck in neutral.

Only move to provoke your partner; only move to increase the connection between the two of you, and only move to clarify the structure of the action as the relationship transforms.

3rd Pass: Don't "act," or play what you think "should" be happening; respond to what's *actually* happening right in front of you. Your goal now is to really talk to one another through the heightened language, with clarity, directness, and precision.

Real Names

To help you really talk to one another, call each other by your real names throughout the scene. Yes, use your own names. This is a highly effective trick, devised by Larry Hecht, to help you engage in real conversation. Use this "trick" with any scene you work on until you feel you're actually talking to one another.

Evaluate

Discuss what's working, what's yet to work, and what you'd like to focus on next, individually and collectively, as you move on to rehearsing Act I of your scene.

Part C: Working Act I

Building on the information you've gathered from the table read, we're going to move from the page to the stage, and in this rehearsal, we will only work Act I. Before you can start to rehearse Act I, you must agree on the point of focus: consider what your character wants, why your character wants what he/she wants, and what the character will do to get it.

The Arc of Act I

Divide this act into three parts, so it has a beginning and a middle driving to a punchline at the end. This act, and each successive act, must have its own arc, its own point of transformation, creating the overall progression of the Relationship Transforming Now.

Start The Loop Now

Throughout this act—nay, throughout this scene and all scenes—your tactics must be focused on affecting the other character and thereby transforming yourself. Make the other character respond the way you want them to. If they don't, change tactics. The focus is never on yourself—it's *always* on the other person. The scene happens in the space between you. Note: your choices will *change* as you gather more and more information with each rehearsal.

A Different Setting

To assist in exploring the possibilities of this, or any, scene, set it in another time and place, one closer to your own experience. Perhaps this exchange takes place outside a funeral parlor or in a morgue, some place where the presence of death (and by implication, all that Richard has done and, most likely, will do) is palpable. Or set it at a police station—somewhere associated with crimes and criminals. Or…?

Also:

Create **parallel relationships** to personalize and make this relationship more immediate: in this scene, Anne's a wealthy young widow seeking *revenge* for her husband's murder, i.e., a woman suddenly in need of social and emotional comfort and support. Richard's a criminal who, thus far, considers himself above the law—an outsider out to wreak havoc on a non-accepting world. If this scenario suggests a *film noir* or a political thriller, don't be afraid to use it as a parallel universe and rehearsal tool to make the playing more immediate for yourselves.

As a Warm-Up: Improvise the entire scene in this *film noir* setting. Try, as best you can, to mirror the structure of the entire scene. If you're really daring, try improvising in blank verse: honor the shared lines, do not add pauses. Hold on to your discoveries, and to whatever else you think of when you're thinking of these characters, as we prepare to work Act I.

The Bounce, even at this stage of the rehearsal, should feel like a seesaw, rising and falling, ebbing and flowing as the action changes throughout the scene. If it helps viscerally, throw a ball back and forth to one another throughout Act I. Use the ball to physicalize the sensation of call and response. Vocally, stress the opposing words, setting them up for your partner—they have to be mirrored precisely in order to have impact.

Consonants

Also, pay special attention to the consonants within the act: they're there to give edge to the language, to be bitten into, to wound, to penetrate, to crash through the protective shield worn by the other character.

A few examples: use the fricative "F" sounds in "Fairer" and "Fouler" to make the ear hear the opposition and the tension in the volley between these two. Yes, it's the same sound, but it's being repeated for different purposes and intents—she to wound, he to woo.

Or, bite into the "T" sound in words like "liest," or the "D" sound in words like "Devil" or "blood." Keep them crisp, sharp, on the attack. Notice how they make you feel saying them and how they make your partner feel when used to provoke them.

One other feature of this first act: short lines. As we noted earlier, when beats are missing within a line, Shakespeare's writing in a pause, be it two, four, even six beats. You have to make a choice: do you play the pause before speaking the next line, during the line or after the line? Or, do you ignore the pause entirely, playing the two lines as a shared line?

Let's agree, for now, Act I ends at line 55 with Richard's "I know so." Note the short line preceding Anne's "I hope so!" Let the missing beats hang in the air, waiting for a response. Build the tension and suspense with this "hanging." When the response comes, allow the missing beats to hang in the air, *again,* until Richard responds. Use the missing beats to crescendo and build the tension in the encounter.

From Outer to Inner

We're now going to shift focus away from the outer—the language—and move on to the inner—the psychology motivating the language.

Think of objectives as if you're **selling a car**: imagine you're at a car lot. You're the buyer, your partner, the salesperson. Salesperson wants to make the sale; buyer wants the best deal possible.

The salesperson has to make the buyer agree it's the right vehicle for them. The salesperson might cite facts, quote statistics, or make an emotional appeal to the customer. If the salesperson doesn't make the sale, the bank will foreclose on their home. As the buyer, you want the best deal possible. You have limited funds. You want the most car your money can buy. If you don't have a new vehicle, you won't be able to keep your job.

In this scenario, the stakes are very high and you have to use whatever you can in order to negotiate. In fact, you'd use anything that'll work for you. You'd have to stick to your objectives: buying/selling the car.

We think this is a direct parallel for the argument of this scene: Richard wants to "sell the car"—he wants Anne to marry him. He uses every personal argument, every tactic in his arsenal to close the deal. Anne also wants to close the deal; she says, in Act IV, scene i, that she wanted to curse Richard and damn him for all eternity. Ironically, of course, the very curses she showers on him and his future bride here and now come back to haunt her, for she falls victim to his "honey words" and does, indeed, become his bride.

Before you can start to rehearse Act I, you must agree on the *givens:*

Environment

Scenes always take place in a real environment—even if the setting is abstract, *it's real to the characters.* It's where they live. It's fully dimensional. An environment is not a single table or two chairs in the middle of the playing space; you can't get away with that and think you're creating a true-to-life world when you're in a skeletal environment.

Action is usually not confined to one central playing space surrounded by dead space. Every square inch of the playing space needs to be filled with the potential for something interesting about to happen.

Time and Place

Consider the time of day, the weather. Early morning or late evening? Warm or cold? How many layers of clothing are you wearing? To avoid "air acting," use a real *rehearsal prop* for the dagger and have someone act as the corpse. You shortchange yourself if you don't give yourself every possible opportunity to engage your imagination by using real objects to ground you in the reality of your make-believe world.

Setting Up

One extra value of using an extensive physical environment in any scene: the actual setting up of the environment starts your mental and psychological preparation for the scene.

While you're moving furniture or placing props, you're transitioning from your everyday world into the world of the scene. If you use the time constructively, you've already started playing the scene.

Always take an extra moment to connect visually with your partner before you begin to work, and then, take a deep breath before you begin the scene. Once you've determined the physical setting, dive in.

1st Pass: Try not to lose the moment-to-moment specificity you had whilst seated during the table read. Focus this rehearsal on physicality: you'll need to experiment with where to stand, when to turn, when to cross to or from your partner, how near, how far, direct or indirect focus.

And, remember those headlights! The light always comes from the direction and position of your hips.

Use the coffin/bier as a lynchpin for the scene physically, working around or across it. Again, help yourself by placing yourself in a physical position to promote and visually underscore the progression of the relationship.

Starting Point

Remember, too: where you start the scene, creatively, emotionally, is not necessarily where the scene will end. It's merely a starting point. As the work progresses within the first rehearsal and with every successive rehearsal, the physical relationship *evolves*.

In our process, a rehearsal's not about setting physical positions early on, then repeating and polishing them for performance. No—the work is about keeping the playing fresh, spontaneous, specific, collaborative, working from moment to moment, even with a set physical score of action.

The Loop, Part I

In thinking about the playing of this scene—nay, in all scenes—the crucial question becomes: how do I want to make the other character feel?

We've said it before and we'll say it again: the focus is always on the other character, provoking a response from them, one which takes you a step further towards satisfying whatever it is your character wants but lacks: attention, affection, acceptance, allowance or approval.

So, yes, we're back to The Loop, since The Loop is the breath of a scene: it involves an outward release of energy as you provoke the other player and an intake of energy as you react or respond to the provocation coming your way.

Evaluate

What worked, what didn't work? What would you like to keep, fix, cut or change?

2nd Pass: Repeat Act I a second time. Adjust the playing. Experiment with changing pitch, volume, tempo or force as the thoughts change. If you played near one another, play this second pass further apart, or vice versa. When you move, you may move *before* the thought, *on* the thought, or *after* the thought. Those are your three choices.

Evaluate

After you've run the scene this second time, evaluate: is the work evolving, or are you merely idling (i.e., repeating choices you've already made), or throwing each choice away for the sake of the new?

Discuss any new discoveries you've made about the action, about the text, about the relationship, about what you might want to try the next time you play the scene. Work the act a third and final time in this rehearsal.

3rd Pass: Focus on the change and transformation of the relationship from the beginning of this act to its end. Working just Act I, the playing time is not terribly long; it's only 55 lines, so there's enough time to be thorough, detailed, and specific.

Do the opposite of what you've done before. Find new, possibly contrary ways to play the same beat. Deliberately do it "wrong," and see what happens. You're still seeking possibilities.

Evaluate

Listen to your body. If you, the actor, aren't comfortable, we, the audience, won't be comfortable. We'll sense something's off if you're not in the right physical relationship. We may not know why, but we'll know it.

Vocally, there's no need to shout or yell. Just *talk* to one another.

Anchors

Even if they're arbitrary at first, set some physical markers for yourself, i.e., at this point in the scene "I'm here" and then "I'm there." Use these **anchors** to mark the *physical progression* of the scene. They can change. You don't have to play choices as if they're set in Krazy Glue. Eventually, you'll create a consistent pattern of movement—a choreography and score of action based on organic discovery. Hold on to what's working, discard what isn't, then work to bridge the gap between those passages that are working and those that aren't. This is how you organically build the score of action.

Cardinal Rule

You're *never* physically violent, invasive or abusive. *Ever.* If there's violence in a scene, discuss it, work it through slowly and carefully. Safety first. Always. The same is true of moments of intimacy. Discuss the physical contact first—do not proceed until everyone is comfortable with the level of physical contact in the scene.

End this rehearsal after evaluating the progress of the work. You'll be bringing your work on Act I into class for feedback.

Showing the Work

When it's time to show the work, take your time setting up the environment, as you did in rehearsal. Use the time as part of your prep for the scene.

Have a focus—something you want to work on or explore this time through.

Take a moment before you start to visually connect with one another, then take a breath before you begin the scene.

Feedback

Keep in mind you're sharing the process and your progress with the process with others in the class/workshop. The first showing is not a final exam or a fixed presentation. It's an opportunity for an objective third eye—the instructor—to give you feedback on what's working, what isn't, what's clear, what isn't, and where to take the work next as you combine Acts I and II.

Remember, *keep* the choices that are working—this is how you build the score of action. Cut, fix or change the choices that aren't working. That's when you can explore new possibilities.

Part D: Working Acts I and II

Having received feedback on your work in Act I, you'll have a clearer sense of what your combined efforts are communicating to an audience. And you're beginning to discover, through the experiences of play and playing, the nature of the story you're telling.

Focus for This Rehearsal: Tempo

We'll start this rehearsal by using the text as we would a score of music: you're looking now for practical clues about how to play the action of Act II.

In our scene—the Richard/Lady Anne scene—we'll use the short lines as musical signatures: speed up here, increase the force (i.e., the intensity) of the action there. Look for the same clues in your scene.

- SILENCES

    If you sustain the pauses—the silences—you'll heighten their impact. In our scene, we want to feel the impact of the action living *in* the pause—the impact of Richard's argument, the surge in Anne's power. Through the text, Shakespeare is telling you: this is where the action changes. Your job in Act II is to make those changes viscerally palpable without disrupting the progression of the action.

    As a Warm-Up: Start this rehearsal by rereading Act I. Pay special attention to the escalating tension throughout the act. Think, now, of Act I as a litmus test: these two characters have been testing the water, taking the measure of their opponent.

    They start the scene in diametrically opposed positions, he wooing, she repelling his advances. The movement throughout the first act brings them closer together psychologically, if not physically.

Changing Tactics

As noted earlier, the trap in the scene—in all scenes—is to play the entire scene with the same intent, the same inflection, the same energy throughout. In short, *mono-action*. If you follow and respond to the *rhythms* of the text, you'll intuitively feel the shifts in tempo. These outer shifts are the expression of the inner movement within the character. Remember, the character is always in a state of transformation.

In order to fulfill the objective, the character must continually assess the impact of his/her actions based on the visceral feedback from the other character.

More is More

The more the action changes, the more there is to play in the scene. The more there is to play, the more engaging the scene becomes to play and to witness.

1st Pass: Use the last few lines of Act I as the trigger to launch into Act II.

Pay special attention to the meter and rhythm of the text. Increase—crescendo—the force, intensifying a point or two on the intensity scale from beat to beat. Don't be afraid to exaggerate the rhythms.

Try and speak the shared lines as one line—i.e., keep the cues tight. Really pause and suspend the pauses built into the text. Don't add any of your own; play the score as written. Use changes in pitch, volume, tempo and force to throw curve balls to one another.

Mark the psychological progression in the relationship by changing the spatial dynamics.

If the bier is an obstacle between the two of you, find the appropriate time to move away from the bier and face one another directly, headlight to headlight.

Once you've worked Act II, you may need to go back and adjust your choices in Act I.

Evaluate

After the first pass, evaluate the work, checking to see if there are any speed bumps, those thorny sections which don't quite feel right yet. Decide what you'd like to keep, fix, cut or change.

2nd Pass: Let's attend to the speed bumps: play those sections of the scene individually. If the exchange isn't working, nine times out of ten it's because you don't know who you are to one another in that particular moment. Keep the focus on provoking your partner and monitoring the visceral feedback you receive from them.

Just Once

Only raise your voice *once* in this act. Just *one* moment of explosion. The rest of the time, justify containing the energy: it could be the physical proximity to one another or the public nature of the exchange or the private nature of the exchange threatening to become public.

Evaluate

Evaluate the work. Discuss what you'd like to keep, fix, cut or change. Are you comfortable with the physical relationships, or do they need adjusting? Are you playing the length of the sentences, or breaking the thoughts with unnecessary—and unwarranted—pauses?

3rd Pass: Working Acts I and II together, attend to the crescendo at the end of Act I and the crescendo at the end of Act II. See if you can get the ebb and flow of the tension to play with those dynamics.

Play the scene in very dim light. Add night sounds, or early morning sounds, or the sound of water, i.e., the River Thames.

Try playing the scene in a very small, contained space, then in a very large space. Keep your headlights focused.

Take your time. When you're ready—when you feel confident in your choices—get out the Hoover and suck up the dead, unfilled air in the scene.

Play on the line, not under it. Gradually increase the tempo from Act I to Act II.

Variations

Play both acts as if you're playing in close-up for a camera: small, intimate, and whispered. Stand at opposite sides of your rehearsal space, back to the wall. Don't move. Focus on the vocal action. Do the opposite and play the scene without stillness, in constant movement.

Evaluate

Discuss what you've discovered by trying different given circumstances (i.e., playing in dim light, playing while being observed or unobserved) and see what it feels like to play both acts as one continuous movement.

Showing the Work

As you did when showing Act I, use the set-up as part of your prep. Focus on something you'd like to explore in this run: the difference between Acts I and II, the changing tactics, varying the pitch, volume, tempo, force—use this focus to engage your imagination before making eye contact with one another. Then take a deep breath before you begin to play the scene.

Feedback

After you've shared your work in class, and after the instructor has offered observations and comments, don't be afraid to ask questions about specific moments in the work. You don't have to solve *all* the problems on your own.

Part E: Preparing for Act III

Physical Relationship

Shifts in the physical relationship parallel shifts in the psychological relationship. In Act I, both characters are separated by the bier—the physical reminder of Richard's ruthless cruelty. It's a constant presence throughout the scene. He advances psychologically as well as physically towards Anne.

The Game

Richard ends Act II and begins Act III by kneeling to Anne, giving her power and sway over him—he's literally playing a game of life and death. Anne has also played Richard to this point in the scene: by hurling abusive insults, she's *captured* his attention. By never *relenting*, she holds his attention.

The Chase Ends

Both characters enter this scene not knowing the outcome. This is what makes the playing of the scene dangerous. The tension builds from beat to beat, act to act. Now, in Act III, you've *earned* the right, dramatically, to sustain and suspend the tension.

After giving her his dagger, as we see it, Anne could slowly lift it, taunting Richard. In turn, sensing her hesitation, Richard taunts and dares Anne: "Nay, do not pause." He senses his advantage, yet Anne does not drop the weapon. Try playing this beat without movement, just sustained eye contact. Richard, without ever breaking eye contact with Anne, uses the next four lines—two complete sentences—to push his luck even further with flattery.

When Anne drops the dagger, between lines 113–115, Richard needs to take in the moment to acknowledge the action. The balance has shifted, and the relationship's transforming.

Rehearsing Acts I, II, and III

As a Warm-Up: Wouldn't it be easier to play a scene if you know it's a seduction? Or a break-up? Or a reconciliation? Title the entire scene "The Wooing of Lady Anne," or, "The Taming of Richard." Then, title each act: "Act I: Open Combat," "Act II: Full Assault," "Act III: Negotiation." Whatever you determine the titles to be, you've given the scene definition, and with definition, a shape, a perimeter to work within.

Now, to warm up, speed through the lines of all three acts. Yes, speed through them—no pauses, no time to think.

1st Pass: On your feet, work the entire scene. When you reach Act III, allow yourself to improvise physically. You can always repeat Act III in isolation, but for this rehearsal you need to feel the set-up of the first two acts in order to play the punchline of the third act.

The Argument

In this first pass, stress the structure of the scene. You each have a problem: here's my side of the problem (you're the devil, rot in hell), and here's your side of the problem (you're an angel, make my world heaven), now let's negotiate a solution (here's my ring—to take is not to give).

Variations for 1st Pass

Agree to play the scene only using the operative words. Think of it as a streamlined text message—send only the essentials. Agree to never move your arms or hands and allow your voice to do all the work. Agree to move once during Act I, once during Act II, once during Act III. Each move must be meant to clarify or physicalize the state of the relationship in that moment.

Evaluate

Discuss what worked, what didn't work, and what you'd like to keep, fix, cut or change.

2nd Pass: Use the warm-up—the speed through—to test your ability to think on the line: play the first act slowly, carefully, moment-to-moment. Then, for Act II, increase the tempo 25 percent. Act III, increase the tempo another 25 percent.

Double check: are you playing the thought through to the end of the line? Are you breaking the thought—and therefore the line—with unscripted pauses attempting to "sound more natural"? Breathe at the caesuras—those little balance points in the line—and at end of each thought rather than at the end of each line.

Evaluate

Discuss what worked, what didn't work, and what you'd like to keep, fix, cut or change.

3rd Pass: Continue to refine your choices. Play the entire scene as if you're playing in close-up for a camera: small, intimate, whispered. Then, do the opposite and play the scene without stillness, in constant movement.

Notice, we're only working with external, technical adjustments—with tools—letting the outside trigger the inside and then adjusting the outside to reflect the changes happening spontaneously, organically, within.

Finally, integrate the information you've discovered and play the scene one final time. Surprise your partner with one different choice and see how the quality of play—and The Bounce—changes.

Evaluate

At the end of the third pass, evaluate what's working, what isn't working, and what you'd like to keep, fix, cut, or change. The scene should transform with each pass in every rehearsal. Are you actively engaged in deepening the need for the other character to give you what you're looking for in this moment? Is The Loop becoming clearer, stronger, more specific as you rehearse?

Showing the Work

Incorporating the notes you've received from your Instructor, choose a focus for this run: the arc of the set-up to punchline, or overcoming an obstacle you've discovered in your partner's responses, or deepening your sense of playing action. Use this focus to engage your imagination and curiosity as you make contact with one another.

As always, use physically setting the environment as part of your preparation for playing the scene. Take a moment to make contact with one another, then take a deep breath before you begin to play the scene.

Feedback

When you've finished playing the scene, stay open to the feedback rather than self-evaluating your work. Take in the information your instructor offers as best you can.

To test The Template, apply the same process working Act I sc. 3, the "ring scene," between Antonio and The Duchess in John Webster's *Duchess of Malfi,* **or the "farewell scene," Act V sc. 5, between Giovanni and Annabella in John Webster's** *'Tis Pity She's a Whore.*

For more modern plays in blank verse, *see King Charles III* **by Mike Bartlett,** *Murder in the Cathedral* **by T.S. Eliot,** *J.B.* **by Archibald MacLeish, or Yusef Komunyakka's adaptation of** *Gilgamesh.*

What's Next

Identify the challenges you want to address as we refine the process working on our next scene, from Molière's *Tartuffe,* as translated and adapted by Richard Wilbur.

Eight

MOLIÈRE: STATUS

Part A: Rhyming

Unlike the scene we worked from *King Richard III*, in which we focused on *one primary* element (The Loop), we're now going to use the Mariane/Valère lover's quarrel in Act II of Molière's *Tartuffe* (as translated and adapted by Richard Wilbur) to focus on *two* elements: your technical ability to use operatives to counteract melody in a rhyming verse play, and your ability to use status as a structural tool to give your playing unpredictability, forwardness and momentum. Let's start with the textual challenges.

Rhyming Alexandrine Couplets

Jean Baptiste Poquelin, better known as Molière, wrote *Tartuffe*, *The Misanthrope*, *The School for Wives,* and *The Learned Ladies* in Alexandrine couplets: each line has 6 feet, or 12 syllables, every two lines rhyme, and every two lines contain a complete thought. This form adhered to the rigid standards of the Académie Française, which regulated French grammar and language (and still does).

The Wilbur Adaptations

The Richard Wilbur translations/adaptations compress the Alexandrine 12-line structure into the more comfortable, familiar iambic pentameter. The lines are more regular in their rhetorical structure. Unlike Shakespeare, there are fewer variations in the meter; hence, the language of these rhyming couplets presents a different challenge: how to play the lyric without the melody becoming monotonous, i.e., the familiar and dreaded singsong of iambic pentameter (de Dum de Dum de Dum de Dum de Dum).

To play the melody or not to play the melody? That, indeed, is the question. The solution: as with our approach to rhyming couplets in blank verse: always play the lyric, not the melodic expression of the thought. The same is true with the Wilbur: go for meaning and substance to counteract melody, unless you, as the character, are deliberately making a point by rhyming.

Remember, too, as with Shakespeare and blank verse, verse is meant to be played on the line, not under it, meaning there are no internal pauses in the thought unless written as such.

Rhyming Images

To help prepare to play the *Tartuffe* scene, let's spend a bit of time *improvising* rhyming couplets. Like the song exercise you worked earlier, the focus is on the sense of the argument and pursuing the objective—in this case, winning an actual argument.

To start: choose a partner. Then, pick a topic—an event in the news, a movie, a piece of music—anything engaging your interest and imagination. Begin to describe this topic to your partner. Talk in four syllable sentences, rhyming every fourth syllable: *My cat is fat*. Obviously, this might be a little ridiculous at first, but the point is to become familiar with the *pattern of thinking* in rhyming images. Play for 90 seconds, then reverse. Your instructor will call out the time for you.

Increments

As you become more comfortable with the format, expand the structure to six syllables: *My cat is fat and sat.* Then eight: *My cat is fat and sat inside.* And finally, ten syllables: *My cat is fat and sat inside my hat.* Alternate back and forth with your partner. Keep the topics separate; this is not a conversation, merely a description.

Next: select a topic for the two of you to discuss in strict ten syllable sentences. Player A starts, expressing one complete thought in two ten-syllable rhyming lines. A: *When you awake, and dare to make a cake, you'll prove to one and all that you can bake.* Player B responds, agreeing or disagreeing, also using two ten-syllable rhyming lines, expressing a complete thought. B: *When I awake, and dare to bake a cake, I'll prove to you it's not a big mistake.*

Move the conversation back and forth between you. Adhere strictly to the form and structure of the exercise; strive to engage in intelligent, coherent conversation.

Variation #1: Player A starts the discussion with a rhyming ten-syllable thought. Player B completes the thought with a second rhyming ten-syllable sentence.

A: *Our love will live long past each little lie.* B: *Our love won't die until we say good-bye. Tell me you love me and I'll speak my truth.* A: *No words from me. I dare not be uncouth.* Complete each other's thoughts, creating a rhyming couplet in the process.

Variation #2: Player A starts the conversation with a rhyming ten-syllable thought; Player B adds to the thought with another rhyming ten-syllable sentence, completing the couplet, then adds to the thought with another ten syllables. Player B responds with a corresponding ten syllable line:

A: *Our love will live long past each little lie.* B: *Our love won't die until we say good-bye. Tell me you love me and I'll speak my truth.* A: *No words from me. I dare not be uncouth.* Continue moving back and forth, completing one another's rhymes.

Variation #3: alternate between speaking in rhyming couplets yourself or completing your partner's couplets. At all times, focus on discussing the topic at hand. Cite proofs to build your argument.

Rebuttals

As we'll see in our scene from *Tartuffe*, if you're clear about the topic of the argument, clear about your point of view, and if you're ready to make your case, you'll have to respond to your partner by *contradicting* their argument. In other words, you will have to *hear* the operatives in order to *respond* with appropriate operatives. You can be clever in using a self-conscious rhyme, but only for the sake of scoring the point or winning the argument.

Detective Work with Rhyming Couplets

Scan the text, underlining or circling the operative words, i.e., stress nouns and verbs; never stress pronouns except in comparisons; attend to the tenses of the verbs, find the balance point in the line—the caesura—and use it to clarify the point you're making; heed and follow the punctuation, and play the thought through to the end of the sentence. If you do so, the rhyming patterns in the Wilbur adaptations will recede in the ear over the course of time.

Part B: Status

Let's move on to explore a major *visceral* component in *every* relationship, and then we'll see how it works specifically in our scene from *Tartuffe*.

Positioning

Status is about *dominance* and *position* relative to—in relation to—one another. Every move we make, either physically or psychologically, defines our status in relationship to our partners. It's part of who we are, how and what we do. Status is neither good nor bad; it's just a fact of life.

Status is transformational and transitional, i.e., it's always changing, and it's always relative to the specifics of the context. Dramatically, every scene, no matter the play or the playwright, involves status.

A status shift is what happens between people during a scene. The structure of a scene is almost always about people jockeying for position with one another. Without this movement, the playing is mono-active. With it, the playing has endless possibilities. Status' presence is visceral—we feel it, we sense it in our everyday lives, we intuitively know when it's right, we intuitively know when it's wrong.

How This Works

In her book, *Body Politics*, Nancy M. Henley identifies the person with the highest status in a group as usually the most secure, relaxed, and open, physically, in space. In a party, the high-status person will often stand in the center of the room, letting the world come to them.

Stand in a crowded elevator: observe how the status shifts and changes at each floor as people enter and exit the space. Notice how we endow and "read" one another physically, adjusting accordingly.

Henley also notes that in the United States, gender biases permit two women to share intimate space, but not two men, although in Italy it's quite natural to see two men walking down the street, arms clasped or entwined. Women also tend to address one another with **closed space**—hip to hip—whereas men are more comfortable with open space—indirect lower bodies, forming a V.

The Gap

A status gap identifies the degree of psychological, emotional or social distance existing between you and your partner at any given moment in a scene. It may be influenced by social, cultural or economic circumstances—think: *Romeo and Juliet*, with wide differences between the Capulets and the Montagues—or *Pygmalion*, by George Bernard Shaw (and the basis of *My Fair Lady*), where the social gap is narrowed between Professor Higgins and Eliza Doolittle. Either way, a gap is always present. If the gap is wide, we call it a ***maxi-gap***. If the gap is narrow, we call it a ***mini-gap***. We can change the gap by becoming more familiar and intimate with one another, or by becoming more formal and distant from one another. Psychologically or emotionally, we either ***move in*** *towards* or we ***move out*** *away from* one another.

Status also exists within every group—we are, by nature, social animals. We're usually part of a pack of animals, sharing similar tastes, goals, points of view. We're always jockeying for position within the pack; it's inherent in our natures.

If you're in the Army, and you're a private, you need to know where you stand with the corporal, and if you're the corporal, where you stand with the sergeant, and if you're the sergeant, where you stand with the captain, the major, the lieutenant colonel, the general. You get the picture.

Status Shifts

The status shifts—widening, narrowing, and as we'll soon see, raising and lowering—are the musical notes in the structure of any scene you play; they're what you *do* to someone to make them react to you, as you try to get them to do what you want them to do to you so you can feel the way you want to feel. Status changes as a relationship transforms.

Our bodies subconsciously reveal information about who we are. Let's test this theory with "Status Bodies," adapted (as are all these status exercises) from *Impro* by Keith Johnstone. We've adapted his improvisational approach as a new tool, informing both the detective work and the playing of a scene. We'll play first, talk after.

Status Bodies

Eyes are the key to Status Bodies. Your instructor will call out instructions and guide you through this exercise.

1. Stand in a circle, feet as wide as your shoulders.
2. Keep your focus at eye level at all times.
3. Lengthen your spine, lift your chest.
4. Work with strong gestures. Everything you do is firm, specific, direct.
5. When you walk and move, cover a lot of space.
6. Walk round the room, meeting and greeting one another. You're at a high school reunion. Endow one another with names and a history.
7. Return to the circle.
8. Shift your focus to the floor. Let your focus dart, flicking up and down rapidly.
9. Contract the spine, shrink the chest. Everything in your body wants to sink or turn in on itself.
10. Move with small, quick steps. Everything you do is indirect.
11. Freeze. Standing with a partner, decide who's A and who is B.
12. A: work with strong body, direct gaze. B: work with quick body, indirect gaze.
13. Reverse roles.
14. Move at random about the room, changing from direct to indirect as you so desire.
15. Freeze. Release.

- THE HIGH AND THE LOW:

When you work with a strong body and steady gaze, you wear the mask of the *high-status body.* High-status bodies tend to radiate strength and energy. They're comfortable in space and appear comfortable with themselves. The direction and focus of the body is outward. Working with quick body and indirect gaze, you wear the mask of the *low-status body.* Low-status bodies tend to apologize. They appear uncomfortable with themselves in space. Every part of the body turns in and implodes. One of these body types will feel more comfortable than the other. Whichever body feels *least* comfortable is the type you need to focus on to develop more range and flexibility in moving between the two types. There'll be time to specialize later.

In our scene from *Tartuffe,* you'll be playing with high-status bodies—as we see it, they're the *cover* for low-status interiors.

Covers

A **cover** *hides* and *protects* the inner self from the world. When your inner self is low, as in low self-esteem, the cover might be brash, bold or aggressive, to protect you from being hurt by the people in your world. Or, if your inner self is high, the cover might be feigned timidity, a tactic you use to deceive and manipulate someone into doing your bidding.

The basic status moves are raising, lowering, see-sawing, swapping and trading positions. Raising and lowering, as well as widening or narrowing the gap, are specific to their context. They're always motivated by the objective. These moves determine the structure—the note-by-note psychological action—between the characters, i.e., what happens in the scene. Here's how we do it every day of our lives:

Compliments

1. Choose a partner.
2. Agree on a Where. Play an all offer/all accept scene with your partner.
3. Speak in your normal voice and use everyday speech.
4. Name each other. Define your relationship through your behavior as soon as possible.

Eight. Molière: Status

5. Accept every offer. Make as many offers as possible
6. Gradually compliment one another.
7. Let the compliments develop naturally in the course of the scene. Compliment one another as much as possible.

When you compliment your partner, you raise your partner's status. Or we use **insults**:

1. Choose a different partner.
2. Agree on a Where. Play an all offer/all accept scene with your partner.
3. Again, speak in your normal voice and use everyday speech.
4. Name each other. Define your relationship through your behavior as soon as you can.
5. Accept every offer. Make as many offers as possible.
6. Gradually, in the course of the scene, insult one another.
7. Continue to insult each other throughout the scene.

When you insult your partner, you lower your partner's status.

The See-Saw

Status is a seesaw: you counterbalance one another, adjusting and adapting as the relationship grows, changes, transforms. Our instinct is for movement and action in the relationship, i.e., more conflict, more shifts, more changes.

When you raise or lower your partner, i.e., when you compliment or insult your partner, you change the psychological climate between you. When the gap is wide, the raising and lowering is easier to see; when the gap is narrow, the adjustments are more intimate.

Throughout these games, we've adjusted Johnstone's improvisational template by suggesting you agree on a Where before you begin; if you're truly daring, follow the Johnstone model and start the scene without a defined Where and let it define itself as you play.

1. Choose a partner.
2. Agree on a Where.

3. You're going to play an all offer/all accept scene with your partner, i.e., you'll make as many offers as possible and your partner will accept every offer.
4. Name each other.
5. Raise and lower your partner's status throughout the course of the scene.
6. Do not predetermine who you are or what you'll do in the course of the scene.
7. Play the scene through to its logical conclusion.
8. When you raise or lower your partner, i.e., when you compliment or insult your partner, you change the psychological climate between you.
9. When the gap is wide, the raising and lowering is easier to see; when the gap is narrow, the adjustments are more intimate.
10. To make the playing more challenging as you improvise, try using rhyming couplets.

These status shifts are what playing is all about.

It Helps to Know Tartuffe

As we'll see in the Mariane/Valère scene, compliments and insults can exponentially intensify and accelerate as a scene progresses, until, exhausted, the characters reach a stalemate and the relationship appears to end—or they find a way to break through the stalemate and the relationship is renewed and continues.

The Power Dynamic

When we talk about status, we're describing dominance *patterns*, dominance *positions*, and *transactions* involving shifting, changing, and realigning relationships.

Master and servant are the names Johnstone uses to describe archetypical dominance positions in a relationship. He prefers these names/titles/descriptors because they are easily understood all over the world. We could call them parent/child, employer/employee, seller/buyer, high/low—name them what you will, they are always relative to context, and can change from moment to moment, as a relationship transforms.

It's All Relative

Don't be deceived into thinking master—let's say the boss—is always high, and servant—the assistant—is always low. In some relationships, though the boss is called the boss, the assistant is really the one calling the shots.

For example, in *Tartuffe*, Orgon is the head of the household and Dorine is Mariane's confidante, lady's maid, BFF. The master/servant positions appear to be fixed.

But since status is always relative to context: in Act II, Orgon is continually unhinged by Dorine—she gives him advice, she advocates on Mariane's behalf, she orchestrates and usurps Orgon's position as head of the household, all in the name of love. Dorine, in this scene, plays high, making Orgon play low, until he leaves, too unsettled to continue the exchange.

The Structural Shifts

Then Dorine continues in the high position with Mariane, urging her to take decisive action in protesting Orgon's wish for her to marry Tartuffe. The two jockey for position, arguing and counter-arguing, trying to arrive at a solution to the Tartuffe/marriage problem. Throughout the play, Molière questions and upends traditional roles as part of the comic effect. The house is in chaos, and so are all the relationships.

Getting Dressed

In our next game, even if you have to artificially induce it at first, play this game to change your partner's status, and thereby, in the see-saw of status, change your own. This game is designed to heighten the visceral experience of playing both status positions.

1. The master is getting dressed. The servant assists the master.
2. Master calls the servant by the servant's fictional name—Jeeves, Stella; the servant calls the master *Sir* or *Madam*.

3. All clothing and objects are imaginary.
4. Do not predetermine who is the master and who is the servant.
5. At the start of the game, take a moment to look at one another; read the body language, follow your impulse, and address your partner as if they're either the master or the servant.
6. Adjust physically to play your status in the relationship.
7. The status may shift and change as the scene progresses.
8. When the scene's done, change partners and begin again—new relationship, new status roles.

Status Transformations

A status transformation has a clear beginning, middle and end. You start in one position, either high or low, and gradually, together, find your way to the opposite positions. *In the first few beats of the next game, establish the context by offering and accepting information about the history of the relationship. Do not predetermine who's high, who's low; discover your position and relationship as you play. Once you begin the transformation, don't idle or stall. Keep the action moving forward.*

As with any transformation, play without "**jumps**," i.e., sudden big shifts. Rather, the transformation happens through a series of small offers and accepts. The process is gradual, in continual motion.

One final note: remember, you're playing these games as characters, not as yourselves, which is why you give one another fictional names at the start of the scene. It's not about you—it's about your character. Remember, too, these games are all in the name of fun.

Play the structure—complimenting and insulting—keeping the punchline of your new position in mind. Take your time and allow the scene to unfold. You have to do it together, or the game doesn't work.

1. Choose a new partner.
2. Agree on a Where.
3. Play an all offer/all accept scene.
4. Make as many offers as you can.
5. One of you begins the scene with *high* status, the other with *low* status.

6. In the course of the scene, exchange status positions.
7. Make the transformation as smooth, seamless, and as even as possible.

Next:

We're now ready to move on to Act II, scene iv of *Tartuffe*. We'll look at the scene from the outside, i.e., from the language, taking us to the inside—the psychological needs of the characters—and then move from those psychological needs back to the outside, to behavior and action as seen through the lens of status.

Modeling

As with our scene from *King Richard III*, and all the scenes to follow this reading of *Tartuffe,* we're modeling detective work: this, now, is our interpretation of how to read the text, looking for clues to inform the playing of the text. You will have to choose another scene as the focus of your work with rhyming couplets and status. We suggest a scene from another adaptation/translation by Richard Wilbur, but that's up to you. Use the Rehearsing the Rehearsal section, Part D, as your guide to working your scene.

Part C: Context

In our view, *Tartuffe* is a play about religious hypocrisy, loyalty, fallibility, and forgiveness.

The Story Thus Far

Orgon, head of the house and Mariane's father, is experiencing a mid-life crisis of social, cultural, and spiritual impotence. The remedy for his ennui? Tartuffe, his new "spiritual" mentor, his guru, his guide. Tartuffe and Tartuffe's accomplice, Laurent, have moved into Orgon's house and are gradually taking over; though he's duped Orgon, Tartuffe's not able to fool the rest of the family.

Tartuffe is a fraud. He feeds off the gullible. Everyone in the house, save Orgon, is on to him and his grift. Orgon's two children, Damis (rhymes with peace) and Mariane, are both in love: Mariane with

Valère, a young man-about-town; Damis, with Valère's sister. Orgon has just announced he wants Mariane to marry Tartuffe, a creature she despises.

The Characters

Mariane and Valère are fashionable young people. They live in a culture of appearances; conversation and, above all, style and manners are important to them. How they present themselves, how they stand, how they speak, how they are seen by others—all the physical attributes we ascribe to one another to demonstrate "good manners"—all this is of vital importance to them. They exemplify and embody the concerns and manners of their day, just as the behavior of children born of affluence embody the manners and concerns of our own day.

- MARIANE

Mariane appears to be her father's favored child. She's been raised to be "sweet and docile"; she complains to Dorine that it would be wrong to disobey her father's wishes and not marry Tartuffe. At the same time, she thinks Tartuffe's a poseur, a fraud. Which he is.

Perhaps her grandmother, Madame Pernelle, best describes Mariane: "And you, his sister, seem so pure, /So shy, so innocent, and so demure. /But you know what they say about still waters." Like everyone else in this world, Mariane is capable of duplicity.

- HER OPTIONS

Mariane's deceased mother, Orgon's first wife, left Mariane property, which might equate to independence (Mariane begs Orgon to "Give him [Tartuffe] your property, and mine too"). Her only other option, as she sees it, is to enter a convent, living the rest of her life alone rather than marrying a man she despises.

The challenge for the actor playing Mariane is to not confuse 21st-century social norms with 17th-, 18th-, 19th- or 20th-century social and gender norms. Yes, look at the play with a modern sensibility, since we're performing for a modern audience, but understand the play's original social context first and foremost. As is the case with most Western European plays before the late 20th century, female characters were always subject to the dictates of a male dominated society and culture.

- MARRIAGE

  In haute bourgeois families, as in aristocratic homes, marriages were about real estate mergers; property was what was important, not love. If the bride liked or was attracted to the groom, what a bonus! Marrying for love—a very middle-class idea—was not the norm. In this society, women, in order to survive, had to be clever; a woman needed to know how to move a man in a direction favorable to her without him suspecting he was being moved. This is how social equilibrium was maintained. It's all about knowing how to play the game without being *detected* playing the game.

- VALÈRE

  Valère's a gentleman, He fills his days with friends, gambling, and socializing. He comes from a socially acceptable family. Pre-Tartuffe, he seemed a good match for Mariane, one agreeable to Orgon. He can be quick tempered, loving, cutting, and agreeable as the moment demands. We know very little about him when he enters. This scene in Act II is his first appearance; he disappears until Act V, when he reveals himself to be a stalwart young gentleman capable of decisive action.

- TITLES

  To help in the playing of this scene, we'll give it a title, one that describes the quintessential action of the scene: The Lover's Quarrel. Then, we'll title each act. Act I, for example, might be called: Strategy, Act II: The Breakup, and Act III: False Starts.

  Use the title as a guide: Oh, it's a lover's quarrel—I know what that is—I can do that! Oh, it's a breakup—I know what that is—I can do that! Flesh out the specifics of its unique content, then play the scene to fulfill its title.

- FRENCH SCENES

  To better organize the structure of their plays, 17th century French playwrights divided each act into a series of scenes, each scene marked by either the entrance or the exit of a character. Hence the name "French scene."

  In our scene from Tartuffe, Dorine and Mariane are already on stage when Valère enters, marking his entrance the start of a new scene. Dorine withdraws at the top of the scene, leaving the lovers alone.

  Note: while we're working this scene exclusively, we need to be aware that the conflict inherent in the scene is the set up for the reconciliation at the end of scene v.

Tartuffe—Act II, scene iv—"The Lover's Quarrel"

In our reading of this French scene, the scene breaks down easily into three acts: the first act ends with Mariane's "it's for your sake I take it, Sir," the hinge being Dorine's interjection, "Let's see which fool will prove the stubborner." Act II, the longest of the three acts, ends with Valère's "Madame, farewell. Your wish shall be my law." The duet ends with Dorine's "If you ask me/Both of you are as mad as mad can be."

Of the first 25 lines in **Act I**, *23 are shared, meaning they're meant to be played with urgency. Mariane and Valère are on the same page: there's no time to waste if the news—Mariane wedding Tartuffe—is true. In Act I, the problem is identified, positions drawn. Valère wants Mariane to act, Mariane wants Valère to rescue her.*

VALÈRE.
 Madame, I've just received some wondrous news
 Regarding which I'd like to hear your views.

MARIANE.
 What news?

VALÈRE.
  You're marrying Tartuffe.

MARIANE.
    I find
 That father does have such a match in mind.

VALÈRE.
 Your father, Madam....

MARIANE.
   ...has just this minute said
 That it's Tartuffe he wishes me to wed.

VALÈRE.
 Can he be serious?

MARIANE.
   Oh, indeed he can;
 He's clearly set his heart upon the plan.

VALÈRE.
And what position do you propose to take, Madam?

MARIANE.
         Why—I don't know.

VALÈRE.
   For heaven's sake—
                   You don't know?

MARIANE.
                              No.

VALÈRE.
                         Well, well!

MARIANE.
                         Advise me, do.

VALÈRE.
   Marry the man. That's my advice to you.

MARIANE.
   That's your advice?

VALÈRE.
            Yes.

MARIANE.
                Truly?

VALÈRE.
                       Oh, absolutely.
You couldn't choose more wisely, more astutely.

MARIANE.
   Thanks for this counsel; I'll follow it, of course.

VALÈRE.
   Do, do; I'm sure 'twill cost you no remorse.

MARIANE.
   To give it didn't cause your heart to break,

VALÈRE.
   I gave it, Madame, only for your sake.

MARIANE.
   And it's for your sake that I take it, Sir.

The Breakup

*In the first 43 lines of **Act II**, there are only three sets of shared lines. The exchanges are longer, as each character digs into an entrenched position. We're not yet talking about the Why, but the What—what the characters are doing. Each offers proof to support their argument, which has strayed from impending marriage to character flaws in the other. The argument ends in a stalemate; neither character backs down.*

[Dorine, withdrawing to the rear of the stage]
Let's see which fool will prove the stubborner.

VALÈRE.
So! I am nothing to you, and it was flat
Deception when you...

MARIANE.
                              Please, enough of that.
You've told me plainly that I should agree
To wed the man my father's chosen for me,
And since you've deigned to counsel me so wisely,
I promise, Sir, to do as you advise me.

VALÈRE.
Ah, no, 'twas not by me that you were swayed.
No, your decision was already made;
Though now, to save appearances, you protest
That you're betraying me at my behest.

MARIANE.
Just as you say.

VALÈRE.
                Quite so. And now I see
That you were never truly in love with me.

MARIANE.
Alas, you're free to think so if you choose.

VALÈRE
I choose to think so, and here's a bit of news:
You've spurned my hand, but I know where to turn
For kinder treatment, as you shall quickly learn.

MARIANE.
I'm sure you do. Your noble qualities
Inspire affection...

VALÈRE.
                Forget my qualities, please.
They don't inspire you overmuch, I find.
But there's another lady I have in mind
Whose sweet and generous nature will not scorn
To compensate me for the loss I've borne.

MARIANE.
I'm no great loss, and I'm sure that you'll transfer
Your heart quite painlessly from me to her.

VALÈRE.
I'll do my best to take it in my stride.
The pain I feel at being cast aside
Time and forgetfulness may put an end to.
Or if I can't forget, I shall pretend to.
No self-respecting person is expected
To go on loving once he's been rejected.

MARIANE.
Now, that's a fine, high-minded sentiment.

VALÈRE.
One to which any sane man would ascent.
Would you prefer it if I pined away
In hopeless passion till my dying day?
Am I to yield you to a rival's arms
And not console myself with other charms?

MARIANE.
Go then: console yourself; don't hesitate.
I wish you to; indeed, I cannot wait.

VALÈRE.
You wish me to?

MARIANE.
                Yes.

VALÈRE.
                That's the final straw.
Madam, farewell. Your wish shall be my law.

False Starts

Act III consists as an alternating series of short sentences and shared lines, with the stage direction "coming back again" repeated four times. The shared lines once again suggest an immediacy, yet the context—an exit, and with it, an implied end of the relationship—might suggest tempo variations. We still want to honor the shared line, but there's an opportunity here to explore variations in pitch, volume, tempo, and force—especially since there's hesitancy and regret running as an undercurrent in this act.

[He starts to leave, and then returns: repeatedly]

MARIANE.
Splendid.

VALÈRE. [*coming back again*]
This breach, remember, is of your making;
It's you who've driven me to the step I'm taking.

MARIANE.
Of course.

VALÈRE. [*coming back again*]
Remember, too, that I am merely
Following your example.

MARIANE.
I see that clearly.

VALÈRE.
Enough. I'll go and do your bidding then.

MARIANE.
Good.

VALÈRE. [*coming back again*]
You shall never see my face again.

MARIANE.
Excellent.

VALÈRE. [*walking to the door, then turning about*]
Yes?

MARIANE.
What?

VALÈRE.
                What's that? What did you say?

MARIANE.
    Nothing. You're dreaming.

VALÈRE.
                            Ah. Well, I'm on my way.
    Farewell, *Madame*.

MARIANE.
                Farewell.

As you read the scene, begin to look for clues about how to play the text. Let's start by looking for the contradictions between the inner and the outer—or perhaps a better choice of words might be between the public and the private, or the formal and the informal personae of the characters.

Mariane's Cover

Mariane presents as meek, timid, and mild. A dutiful daughter. She's the "good girl," "Daddy's girl." She plays by the rules. She's expected to acquiesce to her father's desires. She's to be seen and not heard. She utters all of two words in the first scene of the play, and barely speaks in Molière's Act II, scene 1, when Orgon announces his intention to have her marry Tartuffe.

Yet, alone, with Dorine, a slightly different—and deeper—picture of Mariane emerges: conditioned to be obedient, there's the potential here for a stubborn, strong-willed persona to reveal itself.

Mariane's problem: as someone who's relied on others all her life to make important decisions, she must now figure things out for herself. She's trapped, and she's just now beginning to realize she's trapped.

Obstacles

For Mariane, panic now becomes her *inner* obstacle, along with gender expectations and lack of experience. Valère's stubbornness, along with his insistence that she declare herself by refusing to marry Tartuffe, is her *outer* obstacle. She can't be happy until he agrees to rescue her and prove his love for her.

The 180

If, in preparing to play this scene, we look to Molière's Act V, to the moment when Mariane publicly denounces Tartuffe, Mariane finds her "punchline," the moment when the 180 is completed. Every scene, then, moves Mariane one step closer to that inevitable end. This scene—our scene—with Mariane's timidity in full flower, is the beginning of the set-up for that punchline.

Victim?

Mariane's extreme insecurity (again, as we see it), coupled with a rampant sense of abandonment, suggests she's a victim, which is a passive and thankless role for an actor to have to play—unless we see Mariane's behavior as a deception, a ruse used to dupe others into rescuing her, which makes the playing active rather than passive.

The Ingenue Syndrome

Ergo, Mariane, like most ingenues, may be secretly wielding enormous emotional and/or psychological power over those she implores for help: her father, Orgon, her lover, Valère, and her BFF, Dorine.

Status

We now have hints of how to physically and psychologically play the character: use the classic low-status body posture we looked at earlier—indirect eye contact, all energy pulling into the center of the body—as the starting point for Mariane's transformation through all three acts of the scene. Start low, end high—it's the status transformation in action.

Valère

Just as Mariane presents as a docile young woman, helpless and dependent, Valère initially presents as the sophisticated young man about town. He's a gentleman—he's affluent and socially acceptable. He appears to play by all the rules, though Orgon does complain, in Act IV, that Valère gambles. As the action moves into Acts II and III of our scene, he reveals himself to be equally as insecure of Mariane's love as she of his.

Valère's Cover

Valère's cover: confident, secure, and always in charge. His inner: just the opposite. He's insecure—a wounded ego in need of validation. Ergo, when playing Valère, start with the high-status body—direct eye contact, energy radiating out from the center of the body—and gradually let it all collapse and implode. Inner obstacle: his insecurity. His outer obstacle: Mariane's intractability, her refusal to back down and let him win the argument.

Valère starts our Act I in full command of his faculties and the situation, and ends our Act III forlorn, vulnerable, wounded, and in need of emotional salve. Mariane starts our Act I in desperate need of rescuing, and ends our Act III strong, willful, rash, and impulsive. It's a classic status transformation.

The Argument

The argument is spelled out in our title of the scene: I want my way, you want yours—The Lover's Quarrel. In Act I, there's the statement of the immediate problem: how do I/you avoid marrying Tartuffe? In Act II, the argument devolves into an airing of insults and insecurities, and, in Act III, the scene ends with both lovers despondent, lost, and trapped by their own pride, ego and stubbornness.

Status

Seeing the structure of the scene as a classic status transformation, we can experiment with the tactics the characters use to make the other character feel the way they want them to feel so they will give them what they want so they can feel the way they want to feel—i.e., The Loop.

Also, our approach to this text requires playing with a deft touch, with lightness, with an ear attuned to *comedy of character*. Though it's many things, and can be played many ways, at its heart *Tartuffe* itself has the potential to be a light comedy with a touch of darkness or a dark drama with a touch of lightness. You just have to play it for real:

real people talking to one another, working through their relationship issues.

Part D—Playing the Text

We'll start preparing for the table read by asking a series of questions:

When?

Will you set the scene in 17th century Paris or contemporary Paris? Or in some other location and time period? What's the time of day? What season (which would affect what you wear)? What rehearsal clothes will you need? Corset? Wigs? Hard-soled shoes with heels? Will you need hats, gloves, handkerchiefs, a fan?

How?

Where did you first meet? What's your courtship been like? How long have you been engaged? What's Valère's family like? Where have you been educated (private tutors)? What's your experience of the world outside your home? How long has it been since you've seen one another? What are your religious beliefs?

Agree on a Where

The text tells us the action takes place in Orgon's house. Is this scene in a public room—a garden, a dining room, a kitchen? Or a private room, like a small salon or a private chapel? Is there furniture in the room? If so, where in the space? Where are the entrances, the exits? Windows? Where's this room in relation to the rest of the house? What do you need to give yourself (in terms of a physical environment) in order to ground the playing in a recognizable spatial reality?

The Template

Start alone, reading the entire play.
Scan the text of the scene, noting sentence length, punctuation,

alliteration, assonance, antithesis, the comparisons and contrasts, and the lists you use to win the argument.

Then read your scene *out loud*. Play both characters.

1st pass: Work through the entire text, *pinning* the operatives in each couplet. Test the operatives by speaking only the operatives aloud, as if you're dictating a text message and being charged per word.

2nd pass: Playing both characters, use the operatives to make and support your argument. Don't be afraid to exaggerate the operatives by *punching* them.

3rd pass: Focusing on your character exclusively, *personalize* the way you use the operatives to provoke and affect the other character.

Objective

What are you lacking at the start of the scene? How does that make you feel? How do you want to feel? What might you do to provoke your partner into making you feel the way you want to feel?

Table Read

1st Pass: Sit facing one another, making eye contact as often as possible. Read the entire scene once through.

2nd Pass: Play the scene as a status transformation: one of you starts high, the other low. By the end of the scene, trade positions: if you started low, you end high, and vice versa.

3rd Pass: Use the compliments and insults embedded in the text to jockey for position throughout the entire scene.

Evaluate

Share information you've discovered in the read. Use this information to inform your next rehearsal.

Part E: Working Act I

You must be off book for this rehearsal and every subsequent rehearsal.

Point of Focus

Agree on a point of focus for the 1st pass: how you greet one another or how you want to make the other character feel, or how to use changes in pitch, volume, tempo, and force in the greeting as a set-up for the action to come in Acts II and III. This agreed-upon focus gives you a starting point—a point of entry—into the scene.

1st Pass: Play the first act with direct focus: headlights facing one another. Don't break eye contact. Try reversing status positions; if you started high in the table read, start low, and vice versa. Remember, you're working on the moment-to-moment balance in the relationship, shifting and changing the gap as the scene progresses.

2nd Pass: Add the cover to the playing; don't let your partner see what you're feeling. Allow the cover to slip by the end of the act.

Move/No Move

Try a round of **No Move**—staying in one place throughout, making the language do all the work. Then, do the opposite, moving throughout the act. Let the movement be random, without pre-planning, but always in response to your partner. Try alternating Move/No Move and see what happens. Do you move before, on, or after the line?

3rd Pass: Play the act slowly. Then play it quickly. Try to feel the see-saw of status. How do you wish to be seen? What do you do to your partner to be seen that way? Is this in tandem with or at odds with how you really feel?

Take your time to receive what's coming your way. Again, crucial to the quality of play—the Q of P—stay open to receiving everything and anything being sent your way, even if it doesn't jibe with what you think you want/need from your partner.

If you're playing *at* your partner and not *with* your partner, use your own names at the start or finish of every thought until you feel you're speaking to (and being spoken to by) the person in front of you.

Evaluate

Is the relationship changing physically as it changes psychologically? Are you able to hear what your partner's saying, or are you still doing **teleprompter acting**?

Identify and be specific about the speed bumps needing more attention. Be strategic in how you use your time. Discuss the discoveries you made with each pass and what you'd like to keep, fix, cut or change once you've shown the work in class.

1st Showing

You will need someone to play Dorine. Though she doesn't speak, her presence is part of the scene. Use an actual person in rehearsal, if possible.

As always, take time for setting up the space. Remember, the set-up is part of the preparation for the scene. Before you begin, focus on what's just happened, what's just been said, what's just been done. This is the call to action at the start of the scene. Once again, set a goal for the playing of the scene. Take a moment, look at one another, take a deep breath, and begin.

Feedback

As per usual, take in each comment and post-scene observation with a "thank you." Stay open to the feedback without feeling defensive. We all want praise, we all want to know what's working, but we also need to know what's *not* working. That information can only come from someone on the outside, observing the work objectively: your instructor. Take it all in, and then take it with you back into the studio when you work on merging Acts I and II.

Part F: Acts I and II

As a Warm-Up: Read through both acts before moving into the space. Yes, have the text in front of you. Note the punctuation, the operatives, the set-ups, and the punchlines. Check that you've memorized the text accurately.

Pay special attention to the status shifts from Act I to Act II. As your esteem is lowered by your partner, try to restore your status, either by raising yourself or lowering your partner. This then becomes the structure for the see-saw of Act II.

1st Pass: Adjust the playing of Act I according to the notes given in the first showing. See if you can maintain the arc and progression of Act I, using it as the launch into Act II.

As the stakes escalate in this act, use changes in pitch, volume, tempo and force as a deliberate tactic to counteract the panic growing inside. Use the couplets as darts, meant to puncture and wound your partner. Focus on the argument, and use compliments and insults to win each round in the confrontation. Never lose face.

Evaluate

Discuss what's working and what isn't working. Identify what you want to keep, fix, cut or change. Agree on a focus for the next pass.

2nd Pass: Move before, on, or after the line. See which move has greatest impact. Change and vary the tempo with each couplet as a tactic to affect your partner.

Add a slight sound—an "aaah," an "ouch," or an "aha"—at the end of your partner's lines to vocalize and release your reaction. Then, cover your reaction with your line. Never let your partner see how you really feel.

As always, take your time working through the scene. There's no need to rush. Don't confuse speed with clarity of intent, or use it as a substitute for an authentic pursuit of the objective.

Evaluate

Discuss what's working and what isn't working. Identify what you want to keep, fix, cut or change. Agree on a focus for the next pass.

3rd Pass: The relationship is in transit. You both started on a level playing field as the scene began; by the end of the first act, the relationship changed.

Try playing the first act as a decrescendo, slowing down as you realize your partner is not going to give you what you want. Play the second act briskly, using the couplets as zingers, meant to stab, wound, or hurt your partner. Really focus on raising and lowering your partner throughout both acts rapidly, keeping your partner off-guard.

Evaluate

Discuss what's working and what isn't working. Identify what you want to keep, fix, cut or change. Agree on a focus for the 2nd showing.

2nd Showing

Use the set-up as prep for the scene. Focus on what's just happened before the start of your Act I. Take a moment to look at and make contact with one another before you take a deep breath and start the scene.

Feedback

Once again, stay open to the feedback. Say "thank you," without defensiveness, after every comment. Is there any specific feedback you'd like? What about this beat, that transition? What's playing clearly? What isn't? If, as someone watching the scene, you're invited to offer feedback, remember: your job is not to fix the scene, nor to direct it, but to simply tell the players "this worked for me," or "this didn't work for me." Let the discussion evolve from there.

Part G: Working Acts I, II, and III

Add any new insights you've gathered from the previous rehearsals and the feedback into the playing to clarify who you are, what you want, and how you want your partner to feel.

As the point of entry for this rehearsal: knowing what you now know about your partner's character, focus at first on personalizing the operatives for maximum impact.

Prep: change the floor plan of the playing space.

1st pass: Putting all three acts together, play the arc of the entire scene, from the brightness of the greetings to the slight decrescendo at the end of Act I, varying the pitch, volume, tempo, and force as you engage in combat in Act II, then use a very slow decrescendo in Act III.

Increase the tempo of the scene by 25 percent and see what happens when you must think on your feet. Make certain you're using the text, and not volume or force, to support your argument.

Evaluate

If the stakes aren't working for you, change them. If the inner obstacle isn't powerful, change it—that inner obstacle is your secret, after all. Remember: obstacles affect and condition the Q of P, the Quality of Play. See what happens to the Q of P if you add an outer obstacle, i.e., time's running out, you must be quick, someone might come into the room or overhear you.

The Moves

If you narrow the gap, i.e., make the relationship more intimate, try playing with quieter, softer effort. If you widen the gap, use more force, creating more space, more distance between you psychologically and emotionally.

2nd Pass: Increase the tempo 25 percent. Let the lines overlap, tumbling one on top of the other. Whisper the first act, go on voice for the second act, play the third act slowing down. Change pitch on the operatives, Do the opposite of whatever you've been doing and see if that opens any new ideas.

A Reminder

The status moves—played moment-to-moment, beat-to-beat, subtle or obvious—are the notes of the scene you're playing. Once you set the notes, they don't change. You always play the same notes in the same sequence. This is how you discover the structure of the scene, as determined and defined by the text. *How* you play the notes…well, that's how you develop your creative voice, your *style* of playing.

Evaluate

Discuss what's working, what isn't working. Make sure you're justifying changes in status by focusing on the objective, which is always stated as "I want you (to do _____) to me."

3rd Pass: Play the scene full out, at tempo. Play the scene with a French accent. See if the accent triggers your imagination. Repeat, without the accent. Remember, we're not talking about what to feel—we're focusing on what you do to stimulate feeling in your partner and provoking them into acting.

Evaluate

Discuss what's working and what isn't working. Identify what you want to keep, fix, cut or change. Agree on a focus for the 3rd and final showing.

Final Showing

Determine a focus as your point of entry for the run-through, then play the entire scene full-out. Use the set-up as prep for the scene. Focus on what's just happened before the start of your Act I. Take a moment to look at and make eye contact with one another before you take a deep breath and start the scene.

Play the scene as you've rehearsed it. Resist the temptation to pander to the audience for laughs. Play with passion and have fun.

Feedback

Use this feedback session as an opportunity to evaluate your growth from the first exercises and games you played at the start of this training process to where you are now, in this present moment.

Acknowledge the growth in your ability to read and speak verse (be it blank verse or in rhyming couplets), your ability to identify and play an objective, and your ability to assimilate this strange, esoteric, and experiential vocabulary we're developing as a natural part of your rehearsal process.

Take Aways

The psychological/emotional/intellectual gap between characters widens or narrows as characters jockey for dominance with one another. This is a natural process. It's instinctive behavior. It's visceral. As with all instinctive behavior, we're placing it under the microscope, studying it, becoming aware of it, examining its many facets, drilling it on a conscious level until you're able to employ it meaningfully and mindfully in the playing.

Some additional Molière scenes you might want to work to see and feel the status see-saw: Célimène/Arsinoé, Act III, *The Misanthrope,* **Orgon and Dorine, Act II of** *Tartuffe.* **For a more contemporary scene involving rapid status shifts,** *Top Dog/Under Dog* **by Suzan Lori Parks. For more contemporary plays in rhyming couplets, see** *The Liar* **by Pierre Corneille, adapted by David Ives, or** *La Bête* **by David Hirson.**

What's Next

We're still going to be doing detective work to flesh out context and subtext, we'll still be working from the outside, using all our language tools, to the inside, identifying and playing objectives, and we'll still be using status as the definitive tool in fleshing out the structure of a scene—and we'll still be using the 180 (i.e., the arc) of a scene to determine the shape of the relationship in transformation.

However, we're going to shift gears and move away from playing on the line in verse to playing on the line in prose. We'll move to playing below the line as we move from verse to prose in Chapter Ten.

Nine

CONGREVE: EXTENDED CHARACTER

Part A: The Who

Sometimes when approaching a character, you know exactly who that person is. Sometimes you haven't a clue. In this chapter, we're going to develop a simple, effective and efficient tool for identifying and playing a character outside your wheelhouse—those people for whom you "haven't a clue."

For example, these characters could be "extended characters"— such as Nonno, the 97-year-old poet in Tennessee Williams's *The Night of the Iguana*, or Queen Ester, the 285-year-old matriarch in August Wilson's *Gem of the Ocean*, or a character of the opposite gender, as in Caryl Churchill's *Cloud Nine*, or a succession of characters in a one-person show, where you need to transform from one character to another in a matter of seconds, as in Anna Deveare Smith's *Twilight: Los Angeles, 1992*, or Jane Wagner's *The Search for Signs of Intelligent Life in the Universe*.

How

In *Action: A Guide for Actors*, we find our way to these characters by using *iconic archetypes*. An icon is someone who is well known, who represents a cause or issue we identify with or against, as well as a person who is instantly recognizable: Elvis Presley and Marilyn Monroe are both icons, each conjuring up a different, yet specific, image and association. An archetype is a recognizable example of a person or character based on their behavior and/or their function in the story: the evil stepmother, the trusty/faithful side kick, the mean old ogre.

It's a Label

In the same way we've titled a scene (or acts within a scene) to identify and describe what happens in that act or scene, we'll use a character's iconic status as well as his/her *behavior* to identify and define his/her archetype. An archetype is a *generic* designation. The icon makes the archetype specific.

Masking

In working with a character, we'll work from the outside in. You'll identify an iconic archetype—a specific person you know or an actor you would ideally cast in the role who you think might correspond to the character you're about to play. You'll then develop a character **"mask"**—an **"invisible envelope"** you can slip into as you begin to play the role. Think of this mask as a model, a reference, aiding and abetting your transformation into the character. Rather than playing *yourself,* the mask—as it influences your behavior in the scene—has the power and the potential to move you away from your usual tricks and habits when acting and into something new.

The Process

Gradually, in the later stages of rehearsals, the mask—the "invisible envelope"—will become just that: invisible. We're not asking you to play a scene *imitating* the model/mask, but, rather, to use the *tool* of the mask to trigger your imagination (i.e., how would Francis McDormand or Robert De Niro play this scene?).

Focusing on the choices that Francis McDormand or Robert De Niro would make, you'll play the scene as them—*at first.* Then, as you start to become comfortable with the mask and its behavior, the mask will start to transform: you will find your way into making the character your own, playing *your* choices as *influenced* by, but not mimicking, the iconic archetypical.

In working with the mask, we'll focus not on *What* the character does (you've already determined that through your detective work), but on *How* the character goes about doing it, i.e., the character's behavior.

We'll start the iconic archetype/mask work with a scene from a

Restoration comedy of manners written—*in prose*—by William Congreve, in 1700.

Why This Play?

The Restoration plays are fiendishly difficult verbally; though they're written in prose, the language—and the thinking expressed through the language—is complex, filled with duplicity, camouflage, covers and reveals. These texts require high energy and the ability to make everything look and sound simple, easy, and effortless. You're still playing on the line, not under it.

Comedy of Manners

A comedy of manners focuses almost exclusively on *behavior*, often satirizing and exaggerating behavior to make us laugh. Cinematically, think of *Clueless, The Birdcage, Waiting for Guffman* or *Best in Show*—or classic sitcoms like *All in the Family, Fresh Prince of Bel-Air*, or *Arrested Development*. These are all prime examples of contemporary comedy of manners.

Each movie and sitcom takes a very specific point of view about the culture its characters live in, then satirizes its chosen culture and trusts the audience's ability to recognize and laugh at the characters' behavior at the expense of said culture.

Role Models

Theatrically, think: Oscar Wilde or Noel Coward, two writers considered masters of high style and comedy of manners. Their plays require exorbitant amounts of verbal dexterity, an understanding of wit, nuance, social grace, and a keen sense of humor in observing and accurately reporting human behavior.

In these plays, the lighting of a cigarette, the sipping of a cup of tea, the shooting of a cuff or the touching of a strand of pearls has as much significance as the flicking of a fan or the opening of a snuff box in a Restoration comedy, or as texting, sporting tattoos or wearing grunge clothing has in our own world.

Reflections

These writers, as well as Congreve, are *reflecting* as well as *commenting* on the social norms of their time. Your job as the actor in a contemporary or period comedy of manners is to understand the play's social and historical context, invest your character with the amount of subtext appropriate to the world you're in, then play the text with as much humor, intelligence, technical skill, compassion and dexterity as if the play were written three hours ago.

No Social Media

In approaching *The Way of the World*, please note that the characters live in an era without television, radio, movies, and internet. People *talked* to one another. One's social standing—one's *status*—was based on one's ability to converse, to parley, to banter, to ridicule, to zing, and to destroy reputations with well-chosen words. Verbal facility and dexterity, or lack thereof, are the basis of either praise or derision. The fish-out-of-water country bumpkin is as subject to ridicule in a comedy by William Congreve as is Inspector Rance in Joe Orton's *What the Butler Saw*.

If you can master both the language and the behavior in the scene from *The Way of the World*, you're well on your way to being able to play *any* form of romantic or dark comedy, leavening drama with humor, toning fluff with gravitas.

Style

As we move into comedy of manners, we'll continue to study thought in action, relationships transforming in the present, status, pitch, volume, tempo, force, and text/context/subtext. We'll also work to deepen your ability to play with style.

Let's not confuse style with stylization. Style involves a series of consistencies, based on knowing the world at the time of the play's creation as well as the world now, when the play's being performed. These two worlds synthesize to create a third world: the world of the production.

Style is organic behavior according to the rules of time and place. Thirty years from now, our current time and place will be part of an historic era; people will have to research what life was like "back then" to infuse its essence into their current production or revival.

Stylization is an appliqué, a laying on of artificial ways of moving, speaking, and being. We might consider it a concept of a world made up of selected highlights. When the choices are consistent across the board, the stylization becomes its own style, but it's not something springing from an organic understanding of the inner life of the play.

For example, most classic musicals are *stylized:* the Ascot Gavotte sequence in *My Fair Lady,* for instance, is a deliberate cartoon, done in black and white, to satirize the conformity of a particular class of people who think alike, move alike, and are, for all appearances, alike. *West Side Story*, on the other hand, asks us to believe these characters are real people, and though much of its story is told in dance, it's meant to replicate recognizable behavior and movement as it was lived in the late 1950s.

As we've said before—repeatedly—we create make believe worlds and then we live in them, fully, consciously, honestly, *as if* they're real. Now, on to *The Way of the World.*

Part B: Context

Congreve writes social and cultural verisimilitude; he's reflecting back to his audience the world in which they live. He's writing for an educated, privileged, leisured class, one that lives by and for wit, for its own amusement, its entertainment. The play pits town society against country manners, argues for survival of the fittest in an amoral world, prizes elegance of expression as disguise, and celebrates the triumph of the *most* elite over the *merely* elite.

Social Context

The social context of the play is defined by a series of laws and legal stratagems involving inheritances, trusts, and property rights of husbands and wives. Each of these concerns—familial, marital, legal—form the backdrop for the arguments, discussions and deceptions within each scene.

Combined with a very complicated history of relationships—who did what to whom *when*, who resents what was done to them *then*, who wants to avenge whatever was done to them *now*, we have a very rich, dark, clever, and complicated soufflé of a play.

The Argument

Although it's set in a culture of privilege, *The Way of the World* also addresses issues of family loyalty, family image, and preservation of the institution of family. Though the play is a comedy, it's a very dark comedy. Yet, as in all true comedies, it ends with a marriage.

In that sense, the play also examines marriage: the potentially successful marriage between the intellectual equals Mirabell and Millamant, the unhappy, arranged marriage of Fainall and Arabella Fainall, and the attempted marriage designed to ward off old age by Lady Wishfort.

What You Need to Know Before You Begin

• THE BACK STORY

Mirabell—whose name means "one who's admirable"—was born into society; it's his natural milieu. As a gentleman, his days would be filled with gaming, dining, and social interactions. He does not need to work, nor does he manage his own estate—there are people one hires for that. His sole purpose, his aim in life as a social animal, is to amuse himself by rising to the top of the heap.

Mirabell is in love with Millamant—a rich, witty, vivacious young woman, whose name means "one who has a thousand lovers." She's the niece of Lady Wishfort; Millamant would lose the majority of her inheritance if she marries without her aunt's consent.

Mirabell recently wooed Lady Wishfort in an attempt to win her favor, and thereby sway her in favor of Millamant's marrying him. Lady Wishfort now loathes and despises Mirabell for his sham affection while wooing her.

Mirabell also had an affair with Lady Wishfort's daughter, Arabella, who, at the time of the affair, was a young widow. Mirabell believed she was pregnant; he arranged for her to marry Fainall, a socially acceptable but wayward fortune hunter.

At this stage of their marriage, the Fainalls detest one another while maintaining the *mask of civility* towards one another. Mr. Fainall agreed to the marriage anticipating a huge payout when Lady Wishfort dies. He believes his wife will inherit the majority of her mother's estate and, as her husband, he assumes he'd be entitled to all of it.

Mirabell knows Fainall—whose name means "one who feigns, shams, deceives—or would feign have it all" to be a fortune hunter, yet one who's socially acceptable.

Mirabell knows of Fainall's affair with Mrs. Marwood, a friend of Lady Wishfort's and one of Millamant's rivals, and the potentially damaging effect its revelation would have on Fainall's marriage.

Mirabel needs to know how much Fainall knows about his plans to trick Lady Wishfort, once again, into a sham marriage with his disguised servant, thereby blackmailing her into agreeing to his marriage with Millamant.

Fainall's desperately strapped for money when the play begins. He's worked his way through Mrs. Marwood's financial resources and is, in some form, indebted to her.

Fainall suspects Mrs. Marwood's attraction to Mirabell, and, though his own attraction has cooled for her, he's jealous of her straying affection. He needs to find out what Mirabell's plans are for marrying Millamant as well as how much Mirabell knows about his affair with Mrs. Marwood.

- CLASS AND STATUS

The class differences between the two men are subtle but pervasive. Mirabell has used and duped Fainall in exactly the same manner that Fainall has used and, to some extent, duped Mrs. Marwood.

Both men are social rivals yet wear the mask of civility and congeniality in this scene. They're aware of their history; the audience is not.

In fact, one of the beauties, and mysteries, of *The Way of the World* is the way in which Congreve releases *delayed exposition* throughout the play: we're constantly being fed new information about background and history between the characters as the play moves forward.

In all of this, think high school cliques: the in-crowd, the wannabe in-crowd, the leaders of the pack, those who're content to be followers, and those who revel in merely being in the orbit of "the stars."

Text

One of the most challenging and rewarding aspects of this play is the use of formality and civility in its language. Language here is designed to reveal and conceal, at times simultaneously. Nary a harsh word is spoken, especially in this first scene. The relationship appears to be congenial, yet utterly formal. As tension grows, the language becomes increasingly *more* formal; anger and hostility are expressed in icy tones, forced smiles, and veiled insinuations, in ever expansive displays of wit, using epigrams and metaphors. The external surface is always manicured, while the inner world is roiling with tension and turmoil.

Throughout, the length of thought is extremely daunting. These characters know how to talk in complex rhetorical figures. Therefore, being able to play to the end of the thought—to the punch-line—becomes crucial in activating the language and identifying objectives.

The Cuts

For the purposes of time constraints, we've cut the small exchange with Betty and the brief scene between Mirabell and the servant; have someone read in the servant scene if you so desire, but you must play Act III of our scene as if the exchange has happened (if you choose not to include the exchange).

The scene is 161 lines long, including the aforementioned excised scenes.

The Way of the World: "Recognizance"

"Gaming"

When **Act I** opens, Mirabell and Fainall have been playing cards all night. This first exchange, seemingly off-hand, happens at the end of a card game. Mirabell has lost the game—and a great deal of money—to Fainall. Mirabell's distracted—he's awaiting news about his scheme to have his servant, Waitwell, impersonate "Sir Rowland," a would-be sham suitor to Lady Wishfort.

Mirabell is called out by Fainall for being distracted and "indifferent." Mirabell counters with a subtle insinuation that Fainall has cheated—that he has a "taste extremely delicate." Fainall deflects by going on the offensive: "why so reserved?" The game is off and running. We might assume this thrust and parry repartee has been going on throughout the entire game; now, we're privy to it.

Nine. Congreve: Extended Character

Fainall presses the point, bringing up Millamant's behavior the previous evening. Fainall has the upper hand—he has (potentially socially embarrassing) information about Mirabell's behavior at the "cabal." Mirabell tilts the balance back again by making light of the situation in his response/reaction to Millamant. Mirabell, adept at social situations, played the encounter at the cabal ever so gracefully, tactically, with Millamant.

Mirabel uses the recollection to score points with Fainall, basically saying, "I'm in charge, always, and know how to handle myself with women; I know Millamant's game and can play along." Again, Mirabell trumps Fainall, who wants to discover where Mirabel's relationship stands with Millamant.

Mirabell's too clever to be deceived by Fainall; he evades every trap, showing himself to be a shrewd player. The surface remains jovial and light-hearted, yet there's tension lurking just under the surface.

Mirabell and Fainall [rising from cards]. Betty waiting.

MIRABELL
You are a fortunate man, Mr. Fainall.

FAINALL
Have we done?

MIRABELL
What you please. I'll play on to entertain you.

FAINALL
No, I'll give you your revenge another time, when you are not so indifferent; you are thinking of something else now, and play too negligently; the coldness of a losing gamester lessens the pleasure of the winner. I'd no more play with a man that slighted his ill fortune than I'd make love to a woman who undervalued the loss of her reputation.

MIRABELL
You have a taste extremely delicate, and are for refining on your pleasures.

FAINALL
Prithee, why so reserved? Something has put you out of humor.

MIRABELL
Not at all; I happen to be grave today, and you are gay: that's all.

FAINALL
Confess, Millamant and you quarreled last night after I left you. My fair cousin has some humors that would tempt the patience of a

Stoic. What, some coxcomb came in, and was well received by her, while you were by.

MIRABELL

Witwoud and Petulant; and what was worse, her aunt, your wife's mother, my evil genius; or to sum up all in her own name, my old Lady Wishfort came in.

FAINALL

Oh, there it is then! She has a lasting passion for you, and with reason. What, was my wife there?

MIRABELL

Yes, and Mrs. Marwood and three or four more, whom I never saw before. Seeing me, they all put on their grave faces, whispered one another, then complained aloud of the vapors, and after fell into a profound silence.

FAINALL

They had a mind to be rid of you.

MIRABELL

For which reason I resolved not to stir. At last the good old lady broke through her painful taciturnity, with some invective against long visits. I would not have understood her, but Millamant joining in the argument, I rose and with a constrained smile told her, I thought nothing was so easy as to know when a visit began to be troublesome. She reddened and I withdrew, without expecting her reply.

FAINALL

You were to blame to resent what she spoke only in compliance with her aunt.

MIRABELL

She is more mistress of herself than to be under the necessity of such a resignation.

FAINALL

What? Though half her fortune depends upon her marrying with my lady's approbation?

MIRABELL

I was then in such a humor that I should have been better pleased if she had been less discreet.

FAINALL

Now I remember, I wonder not they were weary of you; last night was one of their cabal-nights. They have 'em three times a week, and meet by turns at one another's apartments, where they come together like the coroner's inquest, to sit upon the murdered reputations of the week. You and I are excluded, and it was once proposed that all the male sex should be excepted; but somebody moved that, to avoid scandal, there might be one man of the community; upon which motion Witwoud and Petulant were enrolled members.

The Hunt

The tension increases throughout **Act II**. Fainall addresses Mirabell directly: "The discovery of your sham addresses to her, to conceal your love to her niece, has provoked this separation." In essence, Fainall reprimands Mirabell, implying Mirabell's game was off—all this under the guise of friendly advice about how he could have played a better game. Mirabell manages to turn the table, ignoring this advice; he begins to hunt for information about Fainall's relationship with Mrs. Marwood. Fainall proves to be a canny player, turning the inquiry back onto Mirabell's relationship with Mrs. Marwood. Fainall's jealous—we might even assume he always has been. His jealousy almost boils to the surface as they discuss Mrs. Marwood.

The act reaches its climax as Fainall accuses Mirabell of "speaking with an indifference." Mirabell counters by accusing Fainall of "pursuing the argument with a distrust." This is the most naked exchange in the entire scene. It would be bad manners for either man to reveal too much. Though it might have the appearance of a friendly exchange, etiquette intact, the under-belly of this exchange is one of mutual distrust, dislike, and antipathy.

Remember, too, that Mirabell's still awaiting word about Waitwell, and Fainall is still in need of money. He needs to find a way to secure his future without the inconvenience of a mistress while married to Arabella.

MIRABELL
And who may have been the foundress of this sect? My Lady Wishfort, I warrant, who publishes her detestation of mankind; and full of the vigor of fifty-five, declares for a friend and ratafia, and let posterity shift for itself, she'll breed no more.

FAINALL
The discovery of your sham addresses to her, to conceal your love to her niece, has provoked this separation. Had you dissembled better, things might have continued in the state of nature.

MIRABELL

I did as much as man could, with any reasonable conscience. I proceeded to the very last act of flattery with her, and was guilty of a song in her commendation; nay, I got a friend to put her into a lampoon, and complimented her with the imputation of an affair with a young fellow, which I carried so far that I told her the malicious town took notice that she was grown fat of a sudden; and when she lay in of a dropsy, persuaded her she was reported to be in labor. The devil's in't, if an old woman is to be flattered further, unless a man should endeavor downright personally to debauch her: and that my virtue forbade me. But for the discovery of this amour, I am indebted to your friend, or your wife's friend, Mrs. Marwood.

FAINALL

What should provoke her to be your enemy, without she has made you advances which you have slighted? Women do not easily forgive omissions of that nature.

MIRABELL

She was always civil to me, till of late. I confess I am not one of those coxcombs who are apt to interpret a woman's good manners of her prejudice, and think that she who does not refuse 'em everything, can refuse 'em nothing,

FAINALL

You are a gallant man, Mirabel; and though you may have cruelty enough not to satisfy a lady's longing, you have much generosity not to be tender of her honor. Yet you speak with an indifference which seems to be affected, and confesses you are conscious of a negligence.

MIRABELL

You pursue the argument with a distrust that seems to be unaffected, and confesses you are conscious of a concern, for which the lady is more indebted to you than your wife.

FAINALL

Fie, fie, friend! If you grow censorious, I must leave you. I'll look upon the gamesters in the next room.

MIRABELL

Who are they?

FAINALL

Petulant and Witwoud.

Fair Trade

*While Fainall's been gone, **Act III** starts with Mirabell learning his plan to blackmail Lady Wishfort has been set in motion: Waitwell's now married and therefore cannot marry Lady Wishfort, though he could and will woo her. Mirabell's elated—it's working out precisely as he desires.*

The conversation shifts once again to marriage—the central issue of the play—and all that marriage entails at this level of society, i.e., the distribution of property (Millamant's inheritance) and, with it, the continuance of the family line.

Fainall feigns indifference to the consequences of the ladies' cabal nights. Mirabell contradicts him and they're off and running once again, this time debating Millamant.

Fainall probes, ever so gently, once again for information about Mirabell's feelings for Millamant, reproaching him for being "somewhat too discerning in the failings of your mistress." Mirabell shifts the playing field, flipping Fainall's critique into praise for Millamant; he sees her clearly and is comfortable with her exactly as she is.

This scene ends with a brief sally about marriage—Fainall's utter contempt for the institution countered by Mirabell's delight at its prospect.

[cut from Fainall's exit to his re-entrance]

FAINALL
Joy of your success, Mirabell; you look pleased.

MIRABELL
Ay, I have been engaged in a matter of some sort of mirth which is not yet ripe for discovery. I am glad this is not a cabal-night. I wonder, Fainall, that you who are married, and of consequence should be discreet, will suffer your wife to be of such a party.

FAINALL
Faith, I am not jealous. Besides, most who are engaged are women and relations; and for the men, they are a kind too contemptible to give scandal.

MIRABELL
I am of another opinion. The greater the coxcomb, always the more scandal; for a woman who is not a fool can have but one reason for associating with a man that is.

FAINALL
Are you jealous as often as you see Witwoud entertained by Millamant?

MIRABELL
Of her understanding I am, if not of her person.

FAINALL
You do her wrong; for to give her due, she has wit.

MIRABELL
She has beauty enough to make any man think so, and complaisance enough not to contradict him who shall tell her so.

FAINALL
For a passionate lover, methinks you are a man somewhat too discerning in the failings of your mistress.

MIRABELL
And for a discerning man, somewhat too passionate a lover; for I like her with all her faults, nay, like her for her faults. Her follies are so natural, or so artful, that they become her; and those affectations, which in another woman would be odious, serve but to make her more agreeable. I'll tell thee Fainall, she once used me with that insolence, that in revenge I took her to pieces, sifted her, and separated her failings; I studied 'em, and got 'em by rote. The catalogue was so large, that I was not without hopes, one day or other to hate her heartily; to which end I so used myself to think of 'em, that at length, contrary to my design and expectation, they gave me every hour less and less disturbance, till in a few days it became habitual to me to remember 'em without being displeased. They are now grown so familiar to me as my own frailties; and in all probability in a little time longer I shall like 'em as well.

FAINALL
Marry her, marry her! Be half as well acquainted with her charms as you are with her defects, and my life on't, you are your own man again.

MIRABELL
Say you so?

FAINALL
Ay, ay, I have experience: I have a wife, and so forth.

Objectives

Once decoded, what at first glance appears to be a scene of pure exposition—conveying information to the audience about who is who,

who did what to whom when—reveals itself to be a scene about two rivals with similar objectives: to gather the information they each need for their social survival without revealing their plans.

They each have strong, similar obstacles: the other character refuses to reveal the information they need to fulfill their plans. Both men are, in one important sense, masked: the outer does not reveal the inner. They're adept at wearing the social mask, yet skillful enough to know how to outfox one another—or to try to do so.

RTN

The key to this scene, as with all scenes, is to concentrate on the relationship and the objectives: what they need from each other and their tactics, and how they subtly shift, adjust and adapt from beat to beat as their status rises and falls in the process. Deception is part of the daily diet, the way of the world. In short, we're watching a relationship transform before our eyes.

Part C: Real People

Remember, these characters were accurate mirrors of the audience watching them; they're written and designed as recognizable people, as satires, lampooning known personalities. Approach them as such. They were not, and are not, cartoons.

Keith Johnstone Again

The following games were *inspired* by Keith Johnstone's work with masks; we've adapted the mask principles and are working with them to fit the specific needs of you playing characters of another time and place, characters outside your comfort zone or range of experience, or characters of another gender, if you're playing this scene cross-gendered.

The following games are designed to help you become familiar with the masking process. After we've worked with them, we'll move on to preparing and wearing the actual model/mask for your scene.

Putty Masks

In this game, you will be working with imaginary Silly Putty and an imaginary mirror—devices we'll use to stimulate your imagination. Ultimately, the mask determines its own formation; checking in the mirror only reinforces the image.

As you start to play, don't look at the mask in the mirror for more than fifteen seconds. You only want to hold an impression of the mask rather than a specific, detailed portrait. Later, in the autobiographical interview section of the game, concentrate on facts that'll lead you to strong physical choices: age, occupation, injuries, allergies, disabilities, etc.

Finally, the voice is the most difficult aspect of the mask to locate. Play with pitch, volume, tempo and force until you find it. You'll know the moment the voice feels right.

Take your time with this game—at least ten minutes, if not longer.

1. Scatter around the playing space.
2. Create a mask for a new you by molding the features of your face with imaginary Silly Putty.
3. Start with your forehead, then move to your eyebrows, eyes, cheekbones, nose, lips, chin, jaw, neck, and hairline.
4. When you're finished, turn and observe the mask in an imaginary mirror.
5. Leave the mirror. Begin walking in the playing space. Retain the image of the mask. Let the mask dictate your walking tempo and rhythm.
6. As the mask begins to take over, give an interview to an imaginary interviewer. Reveal all the secrets of your mask's story.
7. Shift your tone and pitch until you discover the mask's voice. Once you find the voice, always speak in that voice.
8. Freeze. Remove the mask.

Variation No. 1: Work in teams of two, alternately molding a mask onto one another.

Variation No. 2: Mold a specific mask for the character you're working on for your scene. Mold the mask for that character at a particular time in the character's life, either younger or older than the time of your scene.

Nine. Congreve: Extended Character

Variation No. 3: Body Masks: This is an extension of mask molding. Once the facial mask is molded, continue to develop and mold the body mask with the imaginary Silly Putty. Work with specificity to create all parts of the body. When you've molded the body, examine your image briefly in an imaginary mirror. Turn to an imaginary closet, dress yourself in imaginary clothing. When dressed, reexamine your fully clothed image in the mirror.

Move about the playing space, allowing the character image to suggest the walk. Complete the physical transformation by finding the voice. Once you've established the voice, develop relationships with one another. Play a scene, scripted or improvised.

The Second Game: Grab-Bag Characters

In order for this game to work, you will need to bring in five pieces of clothing. All clothing will be displayed on the floor. Everyone must have access to all the garments.

In the game, you'll be creating a new imaginary mask and using the clothing to trigger your imagination into creating who—and how—you are. The mask will develop in response to how you move in the clothing. The mask may not be imposed or manipulated to conform to a predetermined concept. It must arise spontaneously from your movements in the garments. The instructor will call out directions. Start by selecting three to five pieces of clothing, at random. Put them on.

1. Once you're dressed, begin to walk. Let the clothing tell you how you should walk.
2. Once you've clearly established the image for the body, move on to the facial mask. Use imaginary Silly Putty to form the facial mask.
3. After you've formed the facial mask, find the voice for the mask.
4. Give an autobiographical interview to an imaginary interviewer. Be sure to name the mask.
5. All masks are in a public space—for instance, a waiting room.
6. Develop relationships with one another.
7. Make an entrance into the waiting room. Make an exit

out of the waiting room. Know where you're coming from, where you're going to.
8. Freeze.
9. Take off the clothing, walk in your own tempo, rhythm, and body.

When approaching mask work, it's crucial to let the mask have its own voice, its own say. You can't impose your biases or prejudices upon the mask. It must speak for itself.

Variation: Work with clothing from the opposite gender. Play the character for real. Make as many physical adjustments as you need until you find your key into the mask.

The voice will be difficult, but justify the quality of the voice by autobiographical details, i.e., age, medical history, occupation, etc. See what happens should the mask take over.

The Third Game: Cloning

Play with a partner. The instructor will call out directions as the game progresses. You'll play the first round for one minute, and the second round for three minutes.

In this game, you'll be creating a duplicate of yourself by "cloning" your body onto your partner. This game involves touch as a primary element in playing. Therefore, before you begin, one partner (the clone) shows the other (the cloner) where they feel comfortable being touched. The clone takes the cloner's hands and guides them through all areas; the cloner repeats verbally what they understand to be areas that are okay for physical contact. If you're the cloner, you need to respect your partner's boundaries.

Before you start to play, you'll need to take a bit of time to determine how you habitually stand. You'll then use either your hands or verbal instructions to physically move and manipulate your partner into your customary and habitual posture. If you're the clone, use the body to trigger your imagination about who and how you are.

Cloner: start at the feet and work up the body. Be specific in molding the way you stand, how you hold your weight, tension, the placement of your arms, hands, the expression on your face. At the end of the minute, you should be able to stand back and see yourself. Once the clone accepts the mask and begins to make it their own, the image will evolve.

Nine. Congreve: Extended Character

The impact of the activity becomes more immediate when you transcend your everyday knowledge of one another and surrender to the impulses, the images, triggered by the mask.
Agree on boundaries for touching before you begin.

1. Decide who will be A, the cloner, and B, the clone.
2. Clone, stand in a neutral position and allow yourself to be molded, i.e., physically—or verbally—shaped by your partner. Stay alert.
3. The cloner has one minute to mold their body and stance onto the clone. Time will be announced every fifteen seconds.
4. Start at the feet and work up the body.
5. Be specific in molding the way you stand, how you hold your weight, tension, the placement of your arms, hands, the expression on your face.
6. Cloner, at the end of the minute, stand back and walk around your partner. Examine the body from all angles.
7. If you're the clone, you're frozen in time, in the midst of an action. Respond to the impulse your body sends you about your frozen action. When you're ready, complete the action.
8. Trade roles. Repeat.
9. Work in silence.

At the end of the second round, take a minute to talk to one another. What felt right? What didn't? What did you see? What did you experience?

Return to your original roles of cloner and clone.

You'll have three minutes to clone your walk onto your partner. The time will be announced every fifteen seconds. You may talk to one another.

1. Clone your walk onto your partner. You may move around the playing space. Do whatever you need to do to clone your walk. Be sure to focus on the gait, the tempo, the rhythm, and the direction of your focus in space when you walk.
2. At the end of three minutes, stand to the side of the room. Watch your partner walk around the room. **Watch in**

silence. Avoid the temptation to comment on your partner's walking, or to side coach your partner.

3. If you're the clone, make the walk your own. Use the physical life of the walk to trigger your imagination. Try to capture the spirit of the person you're cloning. Don't worry about the precision of every movement.
4. You're late for an appointment. Move around the room, preparing for the appointment.
5. Stop. Make an inventory of every object in the room. As the clone, count shoes, bags, books, chairs, tiles in the ceiling. Be as thorough as you can be as you complete your inventory. Freeze. Release.
6. Reverse roles. Repeat the entire process.

Take a moment. Talk about the process. See if there was there ever a moment, even if only for a second, when you saw yourself moving. Or if there was ever a moment when you felt you "got" the other person while you were moving. How did that happen?

Part D: Model/Clone the Character Mask

We're now going to apply these mask games as preparation for playing your character in *The Way of the World,* or whichever comedy of manners scene you've selected to work on, classic or contemporary.

If you set the scene in 1700, the date of our play's première, research paintings of the period for posture, ways of sitting, and clothing. Clothing was as much a social signifier then as it is now.

Identify—or "Pin"—the Icon

Select a well-known actor as an iconic archetype for your character, be it Daniel Day Lewis, Michael B. Jordan, John Cho, Javier Bardem, or Audrey Hepburn, Viola Davis, Salma Hayek, Zendaya, i.e., someone you can imagine as being fascinating in your role. Watch movies or clips on YouTube of your iconic actor, so your playing can be as accurate as possible. Also, watch YouTube clips of movies for social research—*Les Liaisons Dangereuses*, *The Favourite*, and *The Libertine*, for example, for a sense of time and place.

Also, watch *The Manchurian Candidate* or *The Spy Who Came in from the Cold*—any spy thriller involving double, even triple crosses, to spark your curiosity and imagination about how to play this scene.

Exaggerate—or "Punch"—the Image

Build the mask using an image of the archetype. Mold the mask physically by cloning it onto your body.

1. Start with an image—a picture you can capture on your phone or a clip from YouTube. Study the image. Imitate it.
2. Create a putty mask of your role model. You don't have to copy the body exactly, but when you move, you'll want to capture the essence and spirit of the character.
3. When you're comfortable physically, start to talk, giving autobiographical information about your family history and how you spend a typical day.

Let the mask do the talking. If you lose the image, stop, take a breath, focus on the picture or video, start again. Make it your own: ***personalize the image.*** Wear the mask whilst rehearsing the scene until it triggers your imagination. Once you know who you are, drop the mask and move into your own skin as the character. Of course, you can return to it whenever you're in need of an imaginative jolt about how to play a beat in the scene.

Parallels

Since our goal is to make the playing immediate, you have to be able to invest in the situation. Find a *parallel* context—something familiar and accessible to you, something you've actually experienced or witnessed. The more personal, the better, i.e., you suspect you're the subject of a surprise party and you want to know if this is true, or your "friend" may be spreading false rumors about you but you can't accuse them directly yet. Perhaps you're in a private, roped-off gaming room in Las Vegas, or in an exclusive members-only club in the most exclusive part of town.

One Final Game as a Parallel: Spies

1. Decide who is A and who is B.
2. Agree on a Where. It must be a public space, i.e., a park, a café, a waiting room, or in that private gaming room in Las Vegas.
3. Agree on a situation—it may be political, social, or familial.
4. Each of you has, or knows, a secret about the other.
5. Both of you are spies.
6. Gather as much information as possible from your partner, without being detected.
7. Conceal as much information from your partner as possible, without being detected.
8. You may use decoy language to move your partner *away* from the truth.

Play with life and death consequences: if you can't gather the information you need, or if you reveal information you're charged with concealing, consider the consequences for those you love and those who depend on you for their survival.

Last but not Least: Consider the Sound Mask.

Dialects are extremely useful for *class distinction*. Listen to your character model and imitate the dialect. You don't have to be perfect with it, but dialect is a necessary and vital part of the mask.

Part E: Rehearsing the Rehearsal

The Template without Scansion

Prepare the text of your scene by identifying the *operatives*: underline verbs and nouns, couple them together with adjectives and adverbs.

Consider how you can use pitch, volume, tempo and force to personalize the operatives, speaking to amuse, delight, pierce, or humiliate your partner.

Identify the proofs you'll use to win the argument.

As necessary, identify those places in the text where you'll want to pause—either for breath or for emphasis, or to score a point.

Consider how you want the other player to feel, what you'll do to achieve your goal, and what information you need and what information you wish to conceal.

Together, decide on the specifics of the physical context: the Where (a pub? A private club? A salon, a saloon?), the time of morning, how long you've been playing, the exact card game, how much money's changed hands, what you're wearing. Also discuss what will you'll need as rehearsal props and rehearsal clothing.

Table Read

Use the table read to reinforce and clarify the What and the Why, i.e., what you're doing and why you're doing it. The structure of your scene must be clear and specific before we introduce the model/mask into the playing.

1st Pass: Sit facing one another. Find a comfortable position in your chair.

Tap the table every time you hear your partner use an operative.

If the table isn't tapped while you're speaking, *repeat the line* until the operative's perfectly clear.

Don't be afraid to punch it at first to highlight what you're saying; in other words, don't be afraid of being obvious—it's only the table read.

2nd Pass: Let the language carry the action. Therefore, make sure the thought drives through the entire line so you understand the points you're making.

Try playing the entire scene *without* down endings, yet don't make it sound as if you're exiles from the San Fernando Valley doing uptalk, with each line ending in a quasi-question.

3rd Pass: Read your entire scene looking directly into one another's eyes. Read the scene as if everything you have to say is true. Repeat, never looking at one another. Shift position in the chair whenever the thought changes—yours or your partner's.

Since this is the opening scene, pay special attention to the names of all the other characters. Identify them by changing pitch or volume, revealing your feelings about them at the same time.

Evaluate

Evaluate what worked, what didn't work, and what you'd like to keep, fix, cut or change. Build on "the keeps" in your rehearsal for Act I.

Act I

We're going to introduce the model/mask in this round to help you settle into the How of Who you are. To play this first game, you must know your lines inside and out.

1st Pass: To reinforce the clarity of the structure of your scene, play the scene arm wrestling, *without dialogue.* (Do the same with the scene of your choice.) Parallel and mirror the ebb and flow of the action of the scene by how you use physical force. Play with tactics and play to win. Then, play another round, still arm wrestling. *Add* the dialogue. Play a third round without arm wrestling, but keep that sense of the ebb and flow when you speak.

2nd Pass: Keep the sense of the ebb and flow, and play the act in your model/mask. *Blatantly* imitate the model throughout the scene.

3rd Pass: Still wearing the model/mask, play your scene as if you're in a film. This scene is being shot in close-up. Focus on subtlety and intimacy in your playing.

Evaluate

Evaluate what worked, what didn't work, and what you'd like to keep, cut, fix or change. You'll build on "the keeps" when you move on to Acts I and II.

The Showing

Play the scene wearing the model/mask. Give yourself a specific focus before you start to play the scene. Use the set-up as part of your prep for the scene. Focus on what's happened, what's just been said. Take a moment before you begin to visually connect with one another, then take a deep breath and begin.

Feedback

Be open to your instructor's feedback. Ask questions and engage in a dialogue with your instructor. Absorb what's useful, shelve what isn't. Who knows—it may become *very* helpful later.

Part F: Acts I and II

Incorporate suggestions and feedback from Act I into this rehearsal.

1st Pass: Wearing the model/mask of your iconic archetype, play your entire scene *overacting*: be obvious, devious, melodramatic, spell it all out, without subtly or shame, as if you're playing for an audience not speaking your language.

2nd Pass: Still in the model/mask, use a cover to hide everything you don't want your partner to see, hear or know. Use *politeness* as your weapon of choice.

Play the entire scene in your model/mask until you're comfortable enough with it to start working without it. Don't be shy about moving in and out of the mask, especially as you're putting these two acts together.

3rd Pass: Use the model/mask *only* when you feel you're losing the sense of who you are, i.e., if your attention wanders, if you break your focus or if you're thrown by a new idea in the course of the scene.

Evaluate

Evaluate the progression in the relationship from Act I to Act II. If the relationship isn't changing, even subtly, go back and deliberately use either pitch, volume, tempo, or force to mark out the shifts in status. Incorporate those changes into your playing.

The Showing

Play the scene moving in and out of the model/mask as needed. Give yourself a specific focus before you start to play your scene. Use the set-up as part of your prep. Focus on what's happened, what's just been said. Take a moment, before you begin, to connect with one another visually, then take a deep breath and begin.

Feedback

Ask questions. Make sure you understand the feedback and what you should focus on during the next set of rehearsals.

Part G: Acts I, I, and III

Incorporate suggestions from the last showing as you put all three acts together.

1st Pass: With*out* the mask, put all three acts together, incorporating the behavior you discovered wearing the model/mask. Don't predetermine how you'll play the third act. Discover it once you get there.

Evaluate

Evaluate and discuss what's working and what isn't working, how playing Act III may change what and how you play the set-ups of Acts I and II.

2nd Pass: Work the adjustments into your playing of your scene. Adjust your behavior accordingly. Work any "speed bumps" you've encountered in the scene. Focus on what came before, what came after, and how this beat is the bridge between the two.

Go directly to:

3rd Pass: Put your scene back together as if playing a piece of music, i.e., attend to the crescendos, the pauses, the changes in tempo and tactics. It's as if you're improvising within a fixed structure; you have the freedom to listen, to respond, to play AS IF you're playing a newly written contemporary play for the first time.

Incorporate the sense of the arm wrestling from the early rehearsals. If playing the scene as two pithy stand-up comics worked, retain elements of that relationship, and if the scene worked playing it as two spies, make sure that sensibility is still in the playing. Let the sensibility of the model/mask inform who you are and how you are, but now, make it your own.

Showing the Scene

Play the scene without the mask. Give yourself a specific focus before you start to play the scene. Use the set-up as part of your prep for the scene. Focus on what's happened, what's just been said. Take a moment before you begin to visually connect with one another, then take a deep breath and begin.

Feedback

Ask questions and engage in a dialogue with your instructor.

In a Word:

Identify the model for the mask, find a contemporary parallel, clone and model the behavior of the model/mask to trigger your imagination, keep what works, cut what doesn't, make it your own.

Note: **The see-saw of this scene from** ***The Way of the World*** **is akin to the Gwendolyn/Cecily tea scene OR the Jack/Algernon muffin scene in** ***The Importance of Being Earnest,*** **either of which would be good ancillary exercises for playing in extended character masks.**

For more contemporary scene work involving character masks, transformation and physical archetypes, consider *Latin History for Morons* **by John Leguizamo,** *Buyer and Cellar* **by Jonathan Tolins,** *Irma Vep* **by Charles Ludlam, or** *The Laramie Project* **by Moisés Kaufman.**

What's Next

We're going to shift gears and move into the "modern era" of theatre—if what we deem "modern" is defined by the infusion of psychology and the desire to portray life as it's truly, intimately recognized and experienced by today's audiences.

As our model, we'll be working a scene from Act II of Henrik Ibsen's *Hedda Gabler* (translated by William Archer), the first between Hedda and her former confidante, Eilort Løvborg.

Ten

Ibsen: Opposites

Part A: Modern Realism

In the plays of Henrik Ibsen and Anton Chekhov, considered the fathers of modern realism, what's *not* being said is equally as important as what *is* being said. In their plays, the focus is on the idiosyncratic, the unique, the eccentric—the individual rather than the recognizable archetype.

In *Hedda Gabler*, we'll leave the world of playing "on the line," where thought and speech occur simultaneously. From this point forward, the texts are written in prose, and you'll be working "below the line," where language is used to conceal (more than reveal) thought, intent, and motive. In *Hedda Gabler*—indeed, in all "modern plays"—note the number of stage directions appearing in the script. Not actual "this is what the character's thinking" directions, but hints and clues as to motivation and subtext as revealed through the character's behavior as they pursue their objective.

As subtext becomes increasingly important, punctuation—the comma, the semi-colon, the dash, the full stop, ellipses—functions not just as musical notation (i.e., pause here, downward inflection there), but is given equal weight in the text itself. The punctuation allows us to witness not just what's being thought but the thought process itself, with all of its stops, starts, and hesitations. Therefore, the soon-to-be prevalent *pause* indicates active silence—a space being lived through, thought through, acted through—without words. This silent space is as alive, as engaging—indeed, at times even more engaging—than spoken text. Make no mistake: silent space is not dead space. It's to be filled with life, thought, and action at every turn. Just ask Samuel Beckett or Harold Pinter.

Approaching Prose

You'll still be reading the text to discover what happens, but since the psychology motivating speech is now obfuscated, you will have to rely more on the rules of operative speech as well as stage directions and punctuation to ferret out the intent and meaning of every sentence you'll use to transform a relationship.

How We're Going to Work

As always, you'll first map out the *structure* of the scene, defining what you do, then *speculate* about why you do it while looking for clues about how to go about playing the action—and not the feeling—in the passionate pursuit of the objective.

In rehearsals, we're going to focus on the *tension* between the characters, and we'll make this tension a visceral presence in the playing of the scene by *opposing and resisting* the offers made by the other character.

As the final step in the rehearsal process, we'll add stronger *obstacles* to deepen the stakes and to make the playing of the scene more vigorous and dangerous.

Obstacles

Obstacles are always present in every text, context and subtext. There are *internal* obstacles, which the character has to overcome in order to successfully get what they want, there are *external* obstacles, often found in cultural, gender or social expectations, which the character has to overcome, and there are the interpersonal obstacles the character confronts in the people standing in the way of them getting what they want.

As a working *tool*, obstacles demand greater energy in playing because you must increase your effort to overcome them. Obstacles affect *how* and *what* you play from moment to moment since, as the obstacles change, you must vary your tactics to meet each individual challenge coming your way.

Let's test this principle before we work on our scene from *Hedda Gabler* by playing a new game: **The Obstacle Course.**

This is a high impact, high intensity game. Even though you'll be talking simultaneously, speak in a normal voice and with normal volume. Do not yell. As the obstacles increase, take your time and don't become frustrated. If, for any reason, you lose contact with your partner, or if your partner can't hear you, stop and wait until you reestablish contact with one another before resuming play. Play for three minutes. The instructor will call out the time every 15 seconds.

1. Divide into two teams, A and B. Select a partner in the opposite team.
2. Stand opposite your partner at either end of the playing space. If you are on Team A, turn your back to Team B and close your eyes.
3. Everyone on Team B: silently scatter any objects you find in the room—chairs, shoes, bags, books—around the playing space, and then return to your position opposite your partner.
4. Team A: Keep your eyes closed throughout the entire game.
5. Team A: Move across the room to your partner. If you touch any other player, or if any other player touches you, or if you touch any object on the floor, open your eyes and return to your starting position and begin again.
6. Team B: Guide your partner across the room by calling out directions to them. Never refer to your partner by name. All directions must be communicated strictly by tone of voice.
7. Team A: Move through the center of the playing space.
8. Team B: Coach your partner to avoid contact with any other players or objects. Coach your partner through the center of the playing space.
9. Play within a fixed time period.
10. Once you make it across the room, open your eyes and watch the other players.
11. At the end of the time period, repeat the activity, reversing roles. Change the position of the objects within the obstacle course.

Notice how the stakes exponentially increase every time you come in contact with the obstacles. This is as true for any character in any scene as it is in this game.

Two New Tools

In our work with *Hedda Gabler*, we'll be working with two new tools to increase and deepen the intensity of obstacles: **opposition** and **resistance**.

You'll use both in different ways: to deepen your need to oppose and resist your own internal obstacles by *refusing* to surrender to them; to oppose and resist the external obstacles presented by your cultural and social environment by *fighting* for your independence; and finally, to deepen your need to oppose and resist the interpersonal tactics your partner will use to sway you to their point of view by *digging in,* not relenting in your pursuit of your own objectives.

Part B: Preparing for Hedda

Find the Text

With *Hedda*—indeed, with any play in translation—it's helpful to compare several different versions of the text, looking for nuance, variation, and subtlety in wording and, therefore, meaning.

Interpretation

Because *Hedda Gabler* is intentionally ambiguous, our interpretation of the scene is based on our understanding of the world at the time the play was written, our understanding of the world we live in *now,* and our careful reading of our chosen translation by William Archer.

The following information will help you determine *your* interpretation of our scene and the scene you've chosen to play:

About the World Then

Nineteenth century Norwegian culture was gender biased—a man was expected to provide for a woman financially, and a woman was expected to provide for a man by creating a pleasant home, having children, and then fading into the background. In essence, women had the same legal rights as children; they were not allowed to vote, participate in politics, or control their own money. In this primarily Lutheran culture, divorce *did* exist, but it was a rarity.

Women of Hedda's class did not work. Thea Elvsted (Hedda's former schoolmate) is an anomaly: she's had to work to survive, and is, therefore, considered by Hedda to be of a lower social class.

George Tesman, Hedda's husband, is an academic, and is therefore considered one of the elites. As a rule, Nordic men were not emotionally demonstrative.

Sidebar: Ibsen was interested in the science of mental illness as well as the plight of women who, like Hedda, felt they had to fulfill the social obligations expected of them, whether they liked it or not.

Moving On

As you read *Hedda Gabler,* focus on the *tension* between *opposites:* the seen and the unseen, the direct and the indirect, and especially, between what's said and what's left unsaid. These opposites are the basis of your obstacles.

Clues in the Text

Assuming you've read the entire play, here are some important clues to keep in mind as you look for the *obstacles* you can use to create tension in the scene: the title of the play is *Hedda Gabler,* not Hedda *Tesman.*

In the opening stage directions, Ibsen has a large portrait of General Gabler, Hedda's father, in a place of honor in the sitting room. The General is, therefore, a constant presence in all four acts of the play. General Gabler bequeathed his pistols to Hedda. She knows how to use them.

There is never a mention of Hedda's mother. Hedda is used to a life of luxury. Hedda is being pressured by Tesman's Aunt Julie to have a baby, a prospect Hedda detests.

Tesman is financially overstretched—as a wedding gift, he bought Hedda the house she said she wanted, and he's now waiting to hear about a promotion at the university to help finance his wife's lifestyle.

Hedda wants Løvborg to die beautifully, with "vine leaves in his hair."

Hedda is afraid of scandal. And she's bored.

Speculation

Let's start with a simple question: what happens to Hedda at the end of the play, i.e., what's her punchline? Simple answer: she commits suicide.

As we see it, every beat within the play has to lead her, slowly, inevitably, to the conclusion that there's no other way out for her. At the same time, in every beat within the play, Hedda has to struggle to find life, to find a reason to live.

Everything Hedda engages in has a *positive* intent—for her; it has to be there in how she breathes, how she fights for life. In Hedda's mind, she's doing what needs to be done to preserve her sanity in a time of crisis.

The Characters

With a careful reading of the text, and a bit of interpretive leeway, we learn:

Hedda is an only child. She lived a vicarious life, free of gender restrictions, through Løvborg. She felt time was running out when she agreed to marry Tesman. She'd never married before because there was never anyone suitable or good enough—nor was she rich enough to attract a husband of high rank. She settled on Tesman for economic reasons as well as social security. For her, it's an inconvenient marriage of convenience. Hedda's highly territorial: when confronted with Thea Elvsted, she renews her claim on, and possession of, Løvborg's attention and affection.

In analyzing her patterns of action, we see Hedda as a woman addicted to control, yet she lives in a world in which she has no control. Her way of navigating in this world is to manipulate others, trying to bend them to her will, to dominate, and in the process, feel more powerful, more alive.

Her Obstacles:

Hedda's *inner* obstacles: her boredom, her jealousy of Thea, her disdain for love, her cowardice, and her desire for freedom and adventure. Her *external* obstacles: society's dictates—maintaining a suitable image by not causing a scandal. *Interpersonal* obstacles: Løvborg's presence, his insistence on infidelity, his sobriety, his relationship with Thea, and Tesman's dependence on her.

Eilert Løvborg is brilliant but lost. He comes from a background of social rank and privilege—enough to attract Hedda when they were younger. He led a wild, dissolute life, experiencing and enjoying the freedom of his rank and privilege. Hedda thrived on hearing about his exploits; he lived the life she craved but was incapable of claiming for herself. Hedda tried to shoot him. Having been hopelessly, helplessly in love with Hedda, Løvborg exiled himself from her life when her attempt failed.

In analyzing his pattern of action, we know he is addicted to self-destruction. He's now a recovering alcoholic. In his encounter with Hedda in Act II, he professes his sobriety and his desire to start a new life.

Upon reuniting with her, he falls back into the Hedda trap almost immediately. He uses almost every trick in his book of tricks to seduce her: he conjures their past, he challenges her directly, he questions her about her perception of their prior relationship, and he grapples with understanding and accepting the terms, limits, boundaries of who they are to one another now.

His Obstacles:

Løvborg's *inner* obstacles: his proclivity for self-destruction, his drinking, and his need for female connection and support. His *external* obstacles: having to respect Hedda's marriage, rehabilitating his image as a respectable member of society, and his need to prove himself intellectually. His *interpersonal* obstacles: Hedda's insistence on respectability, her refusal to submit to him sexually, and his relationship with Thea.

George Tesman is devoted to his Aunt Julie and his Aunt Rina. Though he says he loves Hedda, he spent his honeymoon working. He's unaware of Hedda's past relationship with Løvborg. He recognizes Løvborg as his intellectual superior.

A reminder: your job, as always, is to discover the structure of the scene, play the objectives encoded in the text, overcome the internal and external obstacles—and do all this in service of transforming the relationship.

Part C: Hedda Gabler, Act II (translated by William Archer)

Context: The Story Thus Far

As the scene begins, Tesman is relieved to find he won't be competing with Løvborg for the same academic position. Løvborg is interested in restoring his good name and reputation, not in securing an academic post. Løvborg has written one well received book about social history and has just finished a second one about the future. He is, quite literally, suspended between the past and the future.

When Hedda broke off their relationship—a relationship threatening to become sexual—Løvborg left Hedda to become the tutor to Thea Elvsted's two sons. He's now sober and has become, with Thea's help, a free-thinking writer.

This is the first time Hedda and Løvborg have met since Hedda's marriage. Tesman and Brack are visible in an "inner room" while Hedda and Løvborg talk quietly together.

Subtext

As we see it, this first encounter between Hedda and Løvborg is a cat-and-mouse game, as the two seek to establish their positions in the new relationship: Løvborg wants to lure Hedda into a new relationship by any means possible. He calls her "Hedda," rather than the more formal, and socially acceptable, "Mrs. Tesman." Insisting on propriety, Hedda sets the ground rules for the relationship ASAP.

Hedda needs Løvborg to bend to her will. She is used to control and needs the challenge of Løvborg in order to feel that she has some control over her life. She's in a marriage already threatening to suffocate her. This scene is built on the secret they share: the intimacy of their past relationship. They'll each use the past to negotiate the present.

Title for Scene: "Negotiation"

- NEW OPPOSITES

As you read this scene, see if you can you sense/feel the tension in the conflict of *these* opposites. Think in terms of space for a moment: one character, whom we'll call the **pusher,** pushes space out—the energy emanates from the center of the body, moving to fill the physical or psychological space with its presence. Think of a politician or performer who embraces their audience, making them feel as one. The polar opposite, the **puller,** pulls the energy into the body. Think of the politician or performer who makes you lean forward and to go to them rather than the other way around. An easy way to identify the two opposites is to think introvert/extrovert—but, in using pusher/puller, we'll eliminate the psychological inferences of those titles.

We'll be returning to these opposites as we prepare for and then engage in "rehearsing the rehearsal." As you'll see, we'll use them as tools to increase the dynamic tension in the relationship between Hedda and Løvborg.

The Present

In **Act I**, *the newly reformed Løvborg begins his campaign to seduce Hedda by challenging her marriage to Tesman. For her part, Hedda evades direct confrontation, preferring to set the ground rules for their conversation herself. Løvborg's future as a respectable citizen is at stake. Every time they begin to negotiate seriously, Tesman enters, disrupting and suspending the action.*

HEDDA.
[*Raising her voice a little.*] Do you care to look at some photographs, Mr. Løvborg? You know Tesman and I made a tour in the Tyrol on our way home?
[*She takes up an album, and places it on the table beside the sofa, in the further corner of which she seats herself. EILERT LØVBORG approaches, stops, and looks at her. Then he takes a chair and seats himself to her left.*]

HEDDA.
[*Opening the album.*] Do you see this range of mountains, Mr. Løvborg? It's the Ortler group. Tesman has written the name underneath. Here it is: "The Ortler group near Meran."

LØVBORG.
[*Who has never taken his eyes off her, says softly and slowly:*] Hedda—Gabler!

HEDDA.
[*Glancing hastily at him.*] Ah! Hush!

LØVBORG.
[*Repeats softly.*] Hedda Gabler!

HEDDA.
[*Looking at the album.*] That was my name in the old days—when we two knew each other.

LØVBORG.
And I must teach myself never to say Hedda Gabler again—never, as long as I live.

HEDDA.
[*Still turning over the pages.*] Yes, you must. And I think you ought to practice in time. The sooner the better, I should say.

LØVBORG.
[*In a tone of indignation.*] Hedda Gabler married? And married to—George Tesman!

HEDDA.
Yes—so the world goes.

LØVBORG.
Oh, Hedda, Hedda—how could you throw yourself away!

HEDDA.
[*Looks sharply at him.*] What? I can't allow this!

LØVBORG.
What do you mean?
[*TESMAN comes into the room and goes towards the sofa.*]

HEDDA.
[*Hears him coming and says in an indifferent tone.*] And this is a view from the Val d'Ampezzo, Mr. Løvborg. Just look at these peaks! [*Looks affectionately up at TESMAN.*] What's the name of these curious peaks, dear?

TESMAN.
Let me see. Oh, those are the Dolomites.

HEDDA.
Yes, that's it!—Those are the Dolomites, Mr. Løvborg.

TESMAN.
Hedda, dear—I only wanted to ask whether I shouldn't bring you a little punch after all? For yourself at any rate—eh?

HEDDA.
Yes, do, please; and perhaps a few biscuits.

TESMAN.
No cigarettes?

HEDDA.
No.

TESMAN.
Very well.

[*He goes into the inner room and out to the right. BRACK sits in the inner room, and keeps an eye from time to time on HEDDA and LØVBORG.*]

LØVBORG.
[*Softly, as before.*] Answer me, Hedda—how could you go and do this?

HEDDA.
[*Apparently absorbed in the album.*] If you continue to say Hedda to me I won't talk to you.

LØVBORG.
May I not say Hedda even when we are alone?

HEDDA.
No. You may think it; but you mustn't say it.

LØVBORG
Ah, I understand. It is an offence against George Tesman, whom you—love.

HEDDA.
[*Glances at him and smiles.*] Love? What an idea!

LØVBORG.
You don't love him then!

HEDDA.
But I won't hear of any sort of unfaithfulness! Remember that.

LØVBORG.
Hedda—answer me one thing—

HEDDA.
Hush! [*TESMAN enters with a small tray from the inner room.*]

TESMAN.
Here you are! Isn't this tempting? [*He puts the tray on the table.*]

HEDDA.
Why do you bring it yourself?

TESMAN.
[*Filling the glasses.*] Because I think it's such fun to wait upon you, Hedda.

HEDDA.
But you have poured out two glasses. Mr. Lóvborg said he wouldn't have any—

TESMAN.
No, but Mrs. Elvsted will soon be here, won't she?

HEDDA.
Yes, by-the-by—Mrs. Elvsted—

TESMAN.
Had you forgotten her? Eh?

HEDDA.
We were so absorbed in these photographs. [*Shows him a picture.*] Do you remember this little village?
Oh, it's that one just below the Brenner Pass. It was there we passed the night—

HEDDA.
—and met that lively party of tourists.

TESMAN.
Yes, that was the place. Fancy—if we could only have had you with us, Eilert! Eh?
[*He returns to the inner room and sits beside BRACK.*]

The Past

Act II is composed of a series of feints, parries, and counter-parries. As Løvborg presses his case—his previous submission and surrender to Hedda—she exercises her ability to fascinate and hold him in thrall. He wants explanations. She gives just enough to satisfy him. Tesman's presence is a constant reminder to Hedda of the stalemate she's created for herself.

Because Løvborg has resisted surrendering to her, the stakes ratchet up. She has to work harder to get what she wants. Because Hedda has not acquiesced to Løvborg, he has to oppose her tactics, working harder to win her over.

This is the longest of the three acts—the "meat" of the scene. Here the "argument" comes most alive—freedom vs. inhibition, convention vs. bohemian dissolution.

This is, quite literally, a psychological tango of desire—his for her, her for his sense of adventure and experience. Each has their own agenda, yet they're managing to engage in a very dangerous duel of conflicting desires. The stakes escalate as they continue to oppose and resist one another.

LØVBORG.
Answer me one thing, Hedda—

HEDDA.
Well?

LØVBORG.
Was there no love in your friendship for me either? Not a spark—not a tinge of love in it?

HEDDA.
I wonder if there was? To me it seems as though we were two good comrades—two thoroughly intimate friends. [*Smilingly.*] You especially were frankness itself.

LØVBORG.
It was you that made me so.

HEDDA.
As I look back upon it all, I think there was really something beautiful, something fascinating—something daring—in—in that secret intimacy—that comradeship which no living creature so much as dreamed of.

LØVBORG.
Yes, yes, Hedda! Was there not?—When I used to come to your father's in the afternoon—and the General sat over at the window reading his papers—with his back towards us—

HEDDA.
And we two on the corner sofa—

LØVBORG.
Always with the same illustrated paper before us—

HEDDA.
For want of an album, yes.

LØVBORG.
Yes, Hedda, and when I made my confessions to you—told you about myself, things that at that time no one else knew! There I would sit and tell you of my escapades—my days and nights of devilment. Oh, Hedda—what was the power in you that forced me to confess these things?

HEDDA.
Do you think it was any power in me?

LØVBORG.
How else can I explain it? And all those—those roundabout questions you used to put to me—

HEDDA.
Which you understood so particularly well—

LØVBORG.
How could you sit and question me like that? Question me quite frankly—

HEDDA.
In roundabout terms, please observe.

LØVBORG.
Yes, but frankly nevertheless. Cross-question me about—all that sort of thing?

HEDDA.
And how could you answer, Mr. Løvborg?

LØVBORG.
Yes, that is just what I can't understand—in looking back upon it. But tell me now, Hedda—was there not love at the bottom of our friendship? On your side, did you not feel as though you might purge my stains away—if I made you my confessor? Was it not so?

HEDDA.
No, not quite.

LØVBORG.
What was your motive, then?

HEDDA.
Do you think it quite incomprehensible that a young girl—when it can be done—without any one knowing—

LØVBORG.
Well?

HEDDA.
—should be glad to have a peep, now and then, into a world which—?

LØVBORG.
Which—?

HEDDA.
—which she is forbidden to know anything about?

LØVBORG.
So that was it?

HEDDA.
Partly. Partly—I almost think.

LØVBORG.
Comradeship in the thirst for life. But why should not that, at any rate, have continued?

HEDDA.
The fault was yours.

LØVBORG.
It was you that broke with me.

HEDDA.
Yes, when our friendship threatened to develop into something more serious. Shame upon you, Eilert Løvborg! How could you think of wronging your—your frank comrade.

The Understanding

Hedda and Løvborg almost come to an understanding about the past—and with it, the present in **Act III**. She confesses that she didn't shoot him that singular night because she "was a coward." He senses within her an even deeper connection: they both were and are hungering for life.

Neither Hedda nor Løvborg relent. They have to either break down the other's defenses or surrender, and there's very little time left to complete the negotiation before Thea arrives.

LØVBORG.
[*Clenches his hands.*] Oh, why did you not carry out your threat? Why did you not shoot me down?

HEDDA.
Because I have such a dread of scandal.

LØVBORG.
Yes, Hedda, you are a coward at heart.

HEDDA.
A terrible coward. [*Changing her tone.*] But it was a lucky thing for you. And now you have found ample consolation at the Elvsteds'.

LØVBORG.
I know what Thea has confided to you.

HEDDA.
And perhaps you have confided to her something about us?

LØVBORG.
Not a word. She is too stupid to understand anything of that sort.

HEDDA.
Stupid?

LØVBORG.
She is stupid about matters of that sort.

HEDDA.
And I am cowardly. [*Bends over towards him, without looking him in the face, and says more softly:*] But now I will confide something to you.

LØVBORG.
[*Eagerly.*] Well?

HEDDA.
The fact that I dared not shoot you down—

LOVBORG.
Yes!

HEDDA.
—that was not my arrant cowardice—that evening.

LØVBORG.
[*Looks at her a moment, understands, and whispers passionately.*] Oh, Hedda! Hedda Gabler! Now I begin to see a hidden reason beneath our comradeship! You and I—! After all, then, it was your craving for life—

HEDDA.
[*Softly, with a sharp glance.*] Take care! Believe nothing of the sort!

[*Twilight has begun to fall. The hall door is opened from without by BERTA.*]

HEDDA.

[*Closes the album with a bang and calls smilingly:*] Ah, at last! My darling Thea, come along!

As we see it, the scene is a negotiation for control based on *opposition* and *resistance*: he wants closeness, she wants distance; he wants illicit passion, she wants respectability.

The Transformation

The transformation of the relationship in the scene is simple: the characters start apart—in our vocabulary, in a maxi-gap, and in the course of the negotiation, move psychologically and emotionally closer to one another—towards a mini-gap.

The tension in the scene lies in each character's refusal to relent or submit to the other—they're each other's obstacle. The more they resist, the harder they have to work to overcome the obstacle, and the stronger the resistance and the longer it takes, the deeper/higher the stakes become.

Though there exists a prior relationship between these two based on their history together, this conversation is tempered by the conventions of haute bourgeois society: they each desperately want something from the other—a purpose in life—but they can never *reveal* what they're actually thinking or feeling. They must maintain the *mask of polite society:* smiling, gentle head nods, and a gentle turning of the page of the photo album might be appropriate behavior.

As the negotiation becomes more dangerous—and the stakes higher—each must play their cards closer to their chests, aware their conversation could easily be overheard by Tesman and Brack.

Part D: A Note about Rehearsing the Rehearsal

We keep repeating The Template, and with each new scene we're adding new tools to increase the breadth, depth and quality of play, the Q of P. If we're not talking about The Loop or the punchline or deepening personalization, it's because we assume these steps are becoming part and parcel of your work process.

As usual, we'll start by working this scene from the outside in, and then using opposition and resistance as our major tools, we'll work on raising/deepening the stakes to work from the inside out. Note: we've chosen this scene as our focus because it *appeals to us*; follow the same steps, wherever applicable (and they are *all* applicable) with the scene you've chosen to rehearse because it *appeals to you*.

As Preparation for First Read

As always, use The Template. Take the time to underline every operative, especially the verbs and nouns, adverbs and adjectives, and note comparisons and contrasts as the "argument" develops. The contradictions are as important as the agreements, and vice versa.

Ask yourself, with every line: What do I *need* from the other character? How do I have to make the other character feel in order to get what I need from them?

Highlight the stage directions; note what your character actually physically does in the course of the scene.

Note the changes in volume, from loud to whispered, as indicated by the text.

Highlight the punctuation. If you ask a question, actually ask the question; if you make a statement, actually make a statement.

Really talk *to* one another, not *at* one another.

Now, We're Going to Look for Opposites

Study the scene in terms of the *status*: even though this scene is a conversation between equals (*a mini-gap*), you'll still move from high to low or low to high in small increments as the scene progresses. Identify the tactics—compliments and insults (implied or actual)—that you'll use as you jockey for position. Add:

Consider the *Who*: you're either the *pusher*, enveloping your partner in space (as we see it, Løvborg) or the *puller*, drawing your partner in to you (Hedda).

And consider the *How*: since the scene is a game of cat-and-mouse, consider developing an "invisible envelope" or model/mask of an actual cat for your character—a jaguar, a puma, a lion or tiger.

The mask would be your secret, yet it would inform all the choices you make in terms of how you play the scene, i.e., sitting back and waiting and watching, with feline grace, or growing agitation, stalking, and ready to pounce.

And Finally

Consider the internal and external obstacles and how they'll impact the playing of the scene. If the scene, in our interpretation, really is about control, you have to play the game to get what you want without tipping your hand or revealing your tactics. Løvborg: if you're embarrassed or ashamed of your former dissolute ways, you have to make Hedda believe you're now clean and sober. Hedda: if you're terrified of breaking the rules of social convention, you have to insist on good behavior at all times. And if you're both concerned about Tesman's possible re-entry, or of being overheard by Brack or interrupted by Thea's imminent arrival, you'll have to play the scene with increasing urgency as the discussion becomes more and more personal and potentially uncomfortable.

Table Read

We're going to read and then work the scene, looking to define and increase the tension by *exaggerating all the opposites* at play, paying especial attention to the following: when you're intimate and when formal, when you're rigid and when flexible, when you push, when you pull, when you're higher in status and when you're lower, when you pursue and when you allow yourself to be pursued.

1st Pass: Read the entire scene for the operatives and punctuation, following the stage directions exactly. Emphasize changes in tactics by changing your pitch, volume, tempo or force.

Take your time establishing the relationship, making eye contact with one another. Once eye contact has been made (and with it the attendant sense of connection), you don't have to maintain visual contact all the time in order to feel connected. In fact, playing indirect, with your face turned away from your partner, may be the perfect tactic to entice your partner into coming to you.

2nd Pass: Change your partner's status throughout, focusing on the tactics you use in the see-saw. Be overt and obvious. Then, do the opposite.

3rd Pass: Add a social cover to this reading: you're always smiling, always polite, never increasing or changing your pitch, volume, tempo, or force, no matter how maddening your partner is in not responding directly, overtly, to you.

Evaluate

Discuss the quality of play after each pass: what worked, what didn't work, what you'd like to do more (or less) of once you move from page to stage.

Then, Attend to This

Discuss the ground plan and how you'll set-up and arrange furniture in the space. Even though most of the action of the scene happens around a sofa, a chair and a table, create the sense of the entire room: agree on the placement of windows and what's on the imaginary fourth wall of the room. Be sure to locate, precisely, the "inner room where Tesman and Brack are seated." Make as much sense of the geography of the room as possible. It's far too easy to play the scene with just a couch center stage and a chair alongside it. To quote Hedda: "boring."

Moving on.

Part D: Act I

As a Warm-Up: We'll use a new game to help personalize the relationship:

You Always, You Never

To play, you must accept every offer, amplify it, build upon it and accept every aspect of the relationship it offers. Once you have the feel of the game, play as Hedda and Løvborg.

Use the clues in the script—what you say, what's said about you— to describe previous encounters between the two of you. Be bold in telling the other character what you cherish and what you despise about them.

You Always

1. Agree on a Where. Play an All Offer/All Accept scene.
2. Begin every sentence with "You always…."
3. Tell your partner what they always do, or how they always make you feel.
4. Be specific. Keep the scene active, physical, and alive.

You Never

1. Agree on a Where.
2. Play an All Offer/All Accept scene.
3. Begin every sentence with "You never…."
4. Tell your partner what they never do or say to you, or how they never make you feel.
5. Be specific. Keep the scene active, physical, and alive.
6. Try playing "You never…" as a love scene.

Move directly from this game to:

1st Pass: Following the stage directions precisely, use the information you've gathered in *You Always, You Never* to inform how you look at, or avoid, one another and how you'll use that special tone of voice—the one reserved just for your partner—to either pull in or push away the other character.

Evaluate

Tell your partner what worked for you and what didn't work for you. Help your partner by offering practical information as they tailor their playing to affect you.

2nd Pass: Remembering the givens and the danger of being overheard by Tesman or Brack, play the start of the act leisurely, as if you had all the time in the world. Then, in the middle of the act, as it becomes clear you're not getting what you want, add a moderate crescendo. One of you wants to build the crescendo, the other *resists*. Move directly to:

3rd Pass: Focus on the stage directions and the *opposition of direct and indirect physical focus*. Hedda has the album—a perfect opportunity to be looking away from Løvborg, giving him access to look at and peruse her directly. Hedda: decide when you want to flip through the pages and when to stop all movement and just listen. Løvborg: experiment with tactics to grab Hedda's attention and make her look at you.

Remember, one's stable, the other mobile, one direct, the other indirect, one the pusher, the other the puller, one higher, one lower. Try to keep these opposites in balance throughout all three acts, i.e., for every move there's a counter-move, for every adjustment there's a counter-adjustment.

Evaluate

Discuss what worked and what didn't work. Talk about what you'd like to keep, fix, cut or change in the playing of the scene. Talk about the status transformation and The Loop, and if or how you might need to change your tactics as you move from Act I to Act II.

1st Showing

Agree on the focus before you begin the act, recognizing that each moment in this first act might appear leisurely and spontaneous, but must be carefully designed and thought through to create the *illusion* of a casual discussion.

Use the setting up of the space as part of your preparation. Take a moment to connect visually with one another before you take an easy breath and begin to play the scene.

Feedback

As always, stay open to the feedback from your instructor. Gather information about how the impact and effect of what you just played affected the observer. Store the information to help you shape the next round of rehearsals.

Part E: Acts I and II

As a warm-up: Start with a line run-through of both acts. One of you starts loud, the other quietly, or one slow, the other fast, or one strong, the other light. Whichever tactic your partner is using, play the opposite and change tactics from line to line, so you always keep your partner off-guard.

1st Pass: *Play both acts once through with an exercise devised by Michael Cobb, Head of Voice, Speech and Text at the National Theatre Conservatory: It's a competition, so play to win. Keep your focus on your partner, and see if you can make your partner drop the book. Play the combined acts with a book balanced on your head. Try to stay perfectly still. Whoever drops the book loses the game. See if you can get better* and better at being still. Movement is now your obstacle. Make your partner respond to you without raising your volume. Let your voice do all the work. Move directly to:

2nd Pass: Focus on shaping the two acts, i.e., on the jockeying for position in Act I and the gradual coming together—the move towards a mini-gap—in Act II.

Play the acts slowly, carefully, almost daring your partner to make the next move. Speed is now the obstacle. Repeat, doing the opposite: overlap the ends of the lines. Build the tempo and force as you overlap, but be aware of Tesman and Brack's presence and the fact you might be overheard. Slowness is now the obstacle. Move directly to:

3rd Pass: Play the scene as you've just scored it, but exaggerate and play the scene as if you're in a football stadium. You want everyone in the top tier to see and hear what you're doing. Justify the size of the playing. Subtlety is your obstacle.

Now do the opposite, and play the scene as if you're in a movie: play the scene in close-up; barely whisper the dialogue. Justify whispering. Bigness is your obstacle.

Countering

As we mentioned earlier, you must continually *counter* your partner, always keeping them in check. Resist your partner's advances, in either a bold and blatant manner, or with barely perceptible grace and finesse. It's all about how you want to make your partner feel, and whether or not you succeed in doing so.

Evaluate

Discuss what worked and what didn't work, and what you'd like to keep, fix, cut or change.

Talk about the shape of both acts and how they fit together: set-up, climax of Act I, then another set-up, another climax at the end of Act II, and driving towards the punchline at the end of Act III.

Use external obstacles—Brack and Tesman, Thea's imminent arrival—to color, condition and influence the quality of play by either speeding up the tempo of the scene overall or deliberately slowing it down to torment or entice your partner.

2nd Showing

Agree on the focus before you begin the showing. Use the setting-up as your prep. Connect with one another before you begin to play, and stay open to insights you may have about the scene as you play it through.

Feedback

As always, stay open to the feedback from your instructor. Gather information about whether or not the impact and effect of what you just played is what you intended. Store the information to help shape the next round of rehearsals.

Build the Resistance

Obstacles are there for you to work *against*. Your need to overcome the obstacle—in yourself or in your partner—deepens as you meet *resistance*. And as the need deepens, the stakes are elevated.

Part F: Acts I, II, and III

1st Pass: *We're going to use a game devised by Viola Spolin to examine power and control in playing. In this game, you're utterly dependent on your partner in order to play the game, which is a wonderful metaphor for the playing of our scene. Learn to play this game first, then play it within the context of your scene.*

Touch and Talk

You must touch in order to talk. At the same time, you must integrate the touch into the natural fabric of the scene. It cannot stand out as a gimmick or a device. It's best when the touch goes unnoticed by the audience.

Decide on the givens of the situation, including a Where and a When.

Play an All Offer/All Accept scene with a status transformation.

You can talk only when you touch your partner. Justify the touching.

Try not using your hands to touch. Touch only when necessary.

Variation: You can only talk when your partner touches you.

This variation changes the quality of the play. You're no longer in control of the action. You truly need your partner in order to speak. You must play the scene together, from moment-to-moment, beat-to-beat. There's absolutely no way to predict what will happen. Allow the unspoken tension of the scene to emerge. Make the changes work for *you rather than* against *you.*

2nd Pass: Play Touch and Talk again, using eye contact as your only form of touching/not touching. Løvborg: focus on Hedda, making her react to what you're saying and doing. Hedda: do not give Løvborg the reaction you know he wants. Make him react to you the way you want him to. Focus on your own agenda. Løvborg: do not give Hedda what she wants. Focus on your own agenda. Move directly to:

3rd Pass: Connecting all three acts, focus on the arc, the transformation of the relationship from Act I to II to III. Build Act III to *almost* arrive at an agreement, and let it end on a suspended, unresolved note. Use the information you've just gathered from Touch and Talk to adjust the playing of the entire scene.

Keep working to affect your partner, especially as time is running out. The more your partner tries to change you, the more you cannot yield or surrender—i.e., don't give in. As you deepen your inner obstacle—your fear of impropriety, your revulsion of conformity—focus more and more on using your partner as your moment-to-moment external obstacle.

Evaluate

Discuss what worked and what didn't work. Talk about what you'd like to keep, fix, cut or change in the overall playing of the scene.

Talk about the shape of the entire scene and whether or not you're able to use your partner's not giving you (i.e., the character) what you want as an ongoing obstacle throughout the scene.

3rd Showing

Decide on a focus for the showing. Take your time in setting up the environment, and as always, use this time as preparation for playing the scene.

Focus on the texture of the furniture, the photo album, and the chairs as a way to release into the moment and the playing of the scene. Take a moment to make eye contact with one another, then take a deep breath and begin the scene.

Feedback

As always, ask questions if you're unsure about the feedback, or if you need clarification about how to deepen obstacles to raise the stakes and how to use opposition and resistance as rehearsal tools.

Thus Far

We've analyzed and looked at a scene—the process of transforming a relationship—from the point of view of *acting*; we've focused on the What and the Why: objectives, obstacles, given circumstances, and the psychological needs compelling your character to speak and take action. We've also been examining the *playing* of a scene by using different tools: The Loop, status, masks/models, obstacles/opposites and resistance to create ever deepening stakes.

You're now using operative speech to make and support "the argument," and you're following the stage directions and punctuation as guides for playing specific, moment-to-moment actions as you passionately pursue your objective.

All these tools take us back to the *visceral* experience of doing *what* we do to get what we want, and help take us deeper into *why* we do it, and *how* we do it.

For more contemporary plays dealing with social issues, consider: *Fires in the Mirror* by Anna Deveare Smith, *Vietgone* by Qui Nguyen, *Slave Play* by Jeremy O. Harris, or *Funny House of a Negro* by Adrienne Kennedy.

What's Next

We're going to continue to focus on the Who and the How—on the *playing* of action—by working a scene from *Heartbreak House* by George Bernard Shaw. In addition to working with status, model/masks and obstacles, we'll focus on discovering the inner core—or in Stanislavski's vocabulary, the spine of a character—by analyzing the character's *patterns* of action.

Eleven

SHAW: THE BASIC 8

Part A: No Talking Heads

George Bernard Shaw's characters are passionate about thinking and passionate in expressing their thoughts. Ergo, it's easy to think of Shavian characters as talking heads, spouting philosophy and opinions at the drop of the hat. To counteract this perception, we're going to use a new tool—the **Basic 8**—in tandem with pitch, volume, tempo, and force—to animate, activate and accentuate the moment-to-moment tactics we'll employ in working our scene from *Heartbreak House*.

Follow the Text

In this scene, the characters don't move unless a move is indicated by the text. Shaw keeps his characters still because he wants the audience *to listen* to the argument. He uses language to provoke as well as entertain, and, in our view, he wants his audience to think, but not at the expense of being bored by polemics. Your job is to fulfill that intent by engaging in the most lively, high-stakes argument possible. Ellie Dunn and Alfred "Boss" Mangan are quite literally playing for their lives.

Disappearing Act

To help you disappear into the life of your character, we're going to use a new tool—the Basic 8—as a way to articulate the "spine" of your character.

The Basic 8 is a practical, text-based approach to action based on the work of Rudolf Laban, an Austro-Hungarian movement analyst and dancer. We've adapted Laban's work as a tool to analyze, define and "organize" how you do what you do.

The iconic mask/model and the Basic 8 are the primary tools you'll need to achieve your disappearing act, i.e., your transformation into the character. One tool—the mask/model—works from the outside in, while this new tool—the Basic 8—works from the inside out.

Inside Out

With the Basic 8, the focus moves even deeper into the What and Why, and especially the How of what you do to get what you want. We'll identify the *habitual patterns of action* the character uses to navigate the world, then burrow more deeply into the psychology informing those patterns, and finally, focus on the visceral impact that playing those patterns—and variations of those patterns—might have on other characters.

Visceral Action

In the same way we've been using pitch, volume, tempo and force to describe the technical aspects of *vocal* action, we're now going to use time, weight, focus-in-space and flow—the prime components of the Basic 8—to describe the technical aspects of *visceral* action, i.e., the non-verbal patterns which are always present, felt and experienced in addition to those patterns of speech and rhetoric contained in words alone.

Stillness

Granted, these four "aspects" of visceral action—time, weight, focus-in-space and flow—are best understood in terms of physical action, but they can also be used to describe action played in stillness: inner actions, i.e., the psychological movement towards or away from someone or something. Inner action can be felt without necessarily having to be seen.

As we've seen with our scene from *The Way of the World,* and as we'll soon see in our scene from *Heartbreak House,* two characters can be still, physically, yet deeply engaged in a highly *active* exchange of ideas, thoughts, and energy.

Stereo and Beyond

Working from the inside out, by simply varying *one* of these four aspects of action—time, weight, focus-in-space, and flow—you will be able to move out of mono-action (i.e., repeating the same tactic and action over and over again) and into stereo and then quadraphonic action, where your tactics are unexpected and ever changing.

To be clear, when we focus on these aspects of action, we're going to be talking—*technically*—about the **effort** used to do something. For instance, closing a steel door requires a different use of effort—a different use of *energetic weight*—than you'd use blowing a feather off your finger.

Three out of Four

We're concentrating on three of these elements—time, weight, and focus-in-space—because when combined, these three elements create the fourth element: flow. We'll work with the Basic 8 as examples of *flow patterns of action* and see how these patterns, when tied to a central core, form what Stanislavski called "the spine" of a character.

The Spectrum

Let's think of time, weight, and focus-in-space as existing on a spectrum. When we talk about *time* and the effort it takes to do something, think of time as moving anywhere on a spectrum from quick (running a 100-yard dash) to sustained (stirring batter for a cake); when we talk about the *weight* of an effort, the weight can move anywhere from strong (closing that steel door) to light (blowing that feather); and when we talk of effort in terms of *focus-in-space*, the focus could be anywhere on the spectrum from direct (single focus) to indirect (multiple foci, changing in quick succession).

The Basic 8—as a Verb

Here are the **Basic 8**—combinations of effort first described and codified by Laban. First, we'll list them as verbs:

To press, to punch, to flick, to dab, to slash, to wring, to float, and to glide.

Let's think of these Basic 8 actions in the same way we think of Dr. Richo's 5 A's (attention, affection, acceptance, allowance and appreciation): they're *generic* descriptors that become increasingly more specific as you work with them, from moment-to-moment, in a scene.

The Basic 8 as a Noun

If you, the character, habitually use one of these patterns of action more than any other, we can identify you, the character, by using that central action as a noun: you're either a presser, puncher, flicker, dabber, slasher, wringer, floater or glider. That doesn't mean you, the character, will only play one action. Oh, no. You, the character, can play the full spectrum of actions—but you'll play each individual action in the manner of your core or spine (i.e., you, as a presser, might flick or slash, but you'd do so as a presser flicking or slashing). For example, think of **Viola Davis** in *Ma Rainey's Black Bottom*—as Ma, she was a **presser**: she was *direct*, *strong* and used a *sustained* rather than quick sense of time.

Or think of **Chadwick Boseman** as Levee Green, also in *Ma Rainey*—he was a **puncher**: the weight of his effort was *strong*, his focus-in-space *direct*, but his timing was *quick*, not sustained.

Then there's **Eddie Murphy** as Axel Foley in *Beverly Hills Cop*—he was a **flicker**: his use of time was *quick*, his effort *light*, but his focus-in-space was *indirect* rather than direct.

Or think of **Meryl Streep** as Miranda Priestly in *The Devil Wears Prada*—everything she did sprang from her core as a **dabber**: her focus-in-space was *direct*, her use of time was *quick*, but the weight of the effort was *strong* rather than light.

Elizabeth Taylor, as Martha in *Who's Afraid of Virginia Woolf,* **slashed** her way to an Academy Award: her use of time was *quick*, her focus-in-space *indirect*, but the weight of her effort was *strong* rather than light.

Sharon Stone was a **wringer** as Ginger in Martin Scorsese's *Casino*: her focus-in-space was *indirect*, her weight *strong*, but she used *sustained* rather than quick effort.

By keeping his focus-in-space *indirect* and his use of time *sustained* rather than quick, and by just changing the weight of his effort to *light* rather than strong, **Sean Penn** as Spicoli in *Fast Times at Ridgemont High* played a **floater**.

And, finally, think of **Audrey Hepburn** in any role she played—she was a **glider**, through and through: the weight of her effort was *light*, the timing of her effort *sustained*, and her focus-in-space was always *direct* rather than indirect.

Just One

Note: each of these examples involves a shift in just *one element* to change the core—the noun—and the way the core plays other actions—the verb. The point is: with this new tool, you don't have to be trapped into playing the same actions the same way in scene after scene.

Now, You Try

Your instructor will guide you through the following exercise, and, to make this first experience working with the Basic 8 more visceral and immediate, try adding music to underscore the playing.

1. Walk around the room.
2. Exaggerate your use of time, weight, and focus-in-space. Determine whether you personally are a presser, a puncher, a flicker, a dabber, a slasher, a wringer, a floater, or a glider.
3. Focus on the other players, and decide what their core action is.
4. Clone them whilst they're moving.
5. Return to your core action.
6. Exaggerate your core action.
7. Still exaggerating, play its opposite.
8. Play your basic action one more time, and
9. Minimalize the external action, making it invisible.

Discuss the experience as a group. Consider what you discovered about yourself by using the Basic 8 and what you discovered about someone else by using the Basic 8.

Also, note how each individual action you played, as either yourself or as another (using the Basic 8 as verbs) was informed by your central core action (your noun).

We'll use the Basic 8 in tandem with all our other tools to shock, provoke, amaze, and stun your partner by transforming into Ellie Dunn and Boss Mangan, as well as transforming the relationship between Ellie and Boss Mangan.

Part B: Heartbreak House

As we see it, in *Heartbreak House*, everyone is not who they appear to be; this jolly, carefree lot are lost, lonely, confused, and paralyzed. They're also humane, contradictory, clever, and hungry for life, and secretly filled with despair.

There is, after all, a reason why the play is called *Heartbreak House*: anyone who enters this house—a house resembling a ship—the ship of state—has their heart broken at some point in the play's three acts. Disillusion is as rampant as the wit, humor, and humanity inherent in each and every character's DNA.

The Story Thus Far

Ellie Dunn, a romantic young woman, her father, Mazzini Dunn, and Ellie's fiancé (and Mazzini's employer) Alfred "Boss" Mangan have been invited to spend a weekend in the country with Hesione Hushabye, an unconventional, eccentric, free-thinking daughter of Captain Shotover, an inventor of weapons of mass destruction.

Earlier, Ellie confessed to Hesione that she has fallen in love with a dashing, mysterious adventurer, Marcus Darnley, whom she met one afternoon at the National Gallery. In Act I of the play, Ellie has learned the true identity of Darnley: he's Hector Hushabye, Hesione's philandering husband.

The Characters

Young and middle-class **Ellie Dunn** is the practical, poetic, romantic, realistic, and adoring daughter of Mazzini Dunn, the aforementioned failed businessman now working for "Boss" Mangan. Having just had her heart broken, Ellie's more determined than ever to "keep her gloves clean" by marrying her much older suitor, Mangan. She wants economic security and a house in the country near Hesione. As a model/mask, we think of a young Emily Blunt.

Alfred "Boss" Mangan is a blustering, bombastic, and ruthless bully who believes he can fool the world and keep his true nature hidden. He self-identifies as a titan of business yet, in reality, he's as poor as a church mouse, living on commissions from his business backers. He plays "the Boss," yet is revealed to be a sad, weepy little boy when truth comes calling. He enters *Heartbreak House* a confident tycoon, clothed and shod in success, and ends semi-naked, dying in a gravel pit, blown to bits by Shotover's dynamite. As a model/mask, we think of Anthony Hopkins having a particularly bad day.

The Relationship, Part I

*In **Act I** of our scene, which is at the start of Shaw's Act II, Mangan is the pusher; he seemingly owns every inch of space he occupies. If Mangan is the pusher, then Ellie is the puller; her composure, her seeming inscrutability is magnetic, seducing Mangan into confessing the real object of his attraction: Hesione.*

He thinks he's in control until he realizes he's not and never has been in control with Ellie. She's willing to listen and learn as Mangan tries to wheedle out of their engagement, and her education in disillusion grows exponentially, along with her strength.

As Mangan tries to resist heartbreak and ultimately descends into it, Ellie begins with acceptance—her heart having already been broken—to rise above the situation into true power through self-knowledge.

The Relationship, Part II

The status positions are very clear: Mangan assumes the higher position—or rather, Ellie lets him think he has the higher position. She does so by listening, giving the floor to Mangan, who pushes and punches, hoping to find a way to weasel out of their engagement. Ellie just has to sit, watch, wait, let Mangan huff, puff, do all the heavy lifting until he tires himself out.

The balance in Act I shifts with Ellie's "Do you like this part of the country?" She's direct; her directness throws Mangan off guard. He's unprepared for her opposition and resiliency, her sense of equality, and most of all, her directness. She's logical and sensible as she negotiates, whereas Mangan is emotional, hot tempered, and unprepared for what Ellie has to offer.

The Gaps

Keep in mind the structure of the relationship transformation: as their understanding of their engagement transforms, the relationship transforms from a mini to a maxi-gap.

Working the Text

A reminder: heed Shaw's stage directions. He knows precisely what he wants his characters to do and when he wants them to do it—the how is up to you. Follow the directions as accurately and as faithfully as possible. Shaw gives you a starting point; there's a reason and logic to it—your job will be to discover what that is and then, embody it.

Our title for our scene from Shaw's Act II is "**The Arrangement.**" **Act I** of our scene starts with *Ellie and Mangan returning from dinner.*

The Cards Are on the Table

MANGAN. What a dinner! I don't call that a dinner: I call it a meal.

ELLIE. I am accustomed to meals, Mr. Mangan, and very lucky to get them. Besides, the captain cooked some macaroni for me.

MANGAN. [*shuddering liverishly*] Too rich: I can't eat such things. I supposed it's because I have to work so much with my brain. That's the worst of being a man of business: you are always thinking, thinking, thinking, By the way, now that we are alone, may I take the opportunity to come to a little understanding with you?

ELLIE. [*settling into the draughtsman's seat*] Certainly. I should like to.

MANGAN. [*taken aback*] Should you? That surprised me; for I thought I noticed this afternoon that you avoided me all you could. Not for the first time, either.

ELLIE. I was very tired and upset. I wasn't used to the ways of this extraordinary house. Please forgive me.

MANGAN. Oh, that's all right: I don't mind. But Captain Shotover has been talking to me about you. You and me, you know.

ELLIE. [*interested*] The Captain! What did he say?

MANGAN. Well, he noticed the difference between our ages.

ELLIE. He notices everything.

MANGAN. You don't mind then?

ELLIE. Of course I know quite well that our engagement—

MANGAN. Oh! You call it an engagement.

ELLIE. Well, isn't it?

MANGAN. Oh, yes, yes: no doubt it is if you hold to it. This is the first time you've used the word; and I didn't quite know where we stood: that's all. [*He sits down in the wicker chair; and resigns himself to allow her to lead the conversation*]. You were saying—?

ELLIE. Was I? I forget. Tell me. Do you like this part of the country? I heard you ask Mr. Hushabye at dinner whether there are any nice houses to let down here.

MANGAN. I like the place. The air suits me. I shouldn't be surprised if I settle down here.

ELLIE. Nothing would please me better. The air suits me too. And I want to be near Hesione.

MANGAN. [*with growing uneasiness*] The air may suit us; but the question is, should we suit one another? Have you thought about that?

ELLIE. Mr. Mangan: we must be sensible, mustn't we? It's no use pretending that we are Romeo and Juliet. But we can get on very well together if we choose to make the best of it. Your kindness of heart will make it easy for me.

MANGAN. [*leaning forward, with the beginning of something like deliberate unpleasantness in his voice*] Kindness of heart, eh? I ruined your father, didn't I?

ELLIE. Oh, not intentionally.

MANGAN. Yes I did! Ruined him on purpose.

ELLIE. On purpose!

MANGAN. Not out of ill-nature, you know. And you'll admit that I kept a job for him when I had finished with him. But business is business; and I ruined him as a matter of business.

ELLIE. I don't understand how that can be. Are you trying to make me feel that I need not be grateful to you, so that I may choose differently?

MANGAN. [*rising aggressively*] No. I mean what I say.

ELLIE. But how could it possibly do you any good to ruin my father? The money he lost was yours.

MANGAN. [*with a sour laugh*] Was mine! It is mine, Miss Ellie, and all the money, the other fellows lost too. [*He shoves his hands into his pockets and shows his teeth*] I just smoked them out like a hive of bees. What do you say to that? A bit of a shock, eh?

ELLIE. It would have been this morning. Now! I can't think how little it matters. But it's quite interesting. Only, you must explain it to me. I don't understand it. [*Propping her elbows on the drawing-board and her chin on her hands, she composes herself to listen with a combination of conscious curiosity with unconscious contempt which provokes him to more and more unpleasantness, and an attempt at patronage of her ignorance.*]

The Lessons

*In **Act II**, Mangan recovers his sense of self as he describes his business philosophy: let the others sweat it out, then swoop in for the kill once the businesses have been established. Mangan's self-regard seems to blossom and triumph: he's the tycoon instructing, impressing the neophyte. As we see it, he's looking for that look of surrender signaling Ellie's capitulation. He's relentless in laying it on, denigrating her father, boasting of his own prowess. Think: cutthroat businessman.*

Ellie doesn't flinch. She sits, she listens, she genuinely takes it all in. If she gives too much away in reacting to Mangan during his diatribe, the scene's over. She keeps her cards close to her chest; the more implacable she is, the harder Mangan has to work. When she finally does speak, she remains calm, direct, and centered.

As we see it, whereas Mangan has been hurling grenades, Elle throws darts, piercing and puncturing, without breaking a sweat. Notice the stage directions: "very calmly" for Ellie, "rising aghast" for Mangan, and again, for Ellie, "patiently," after Mangan's "quite at a loss."

Here are more opposites: Ellie remains cool whereas Mangan becomes hotter and hotter, more and more desperate, as the act progresses. We witness Ellie's transformation in the course of Act II and Mangan's gradual disintegration. A clean status transformation. He tries to play the "age card"; it doesn't work.

He finally confesses his attraction and interest in Hesione; she counters with her attraction, her interest in Hector. While he tries to press and pressure her, she stays fixed, true to her core. She has nothing to lose; she has the stronger hand and she knows it. Mangan realizes he's met his match; there's almost no way he can win.

MANGAN. Of course you don't understand: what do you know about business? You just listen and learn. Your father's business was a new business; and I don't start new businesses: I let other fellows start them. They're what you call enthusiasts. In a year or so they have either to let the whole show go bust, or sell out to a new lot of fellows for a few deferred ordinary shares. As likely as not the very same thing happens to the new lot. And that's where the real business man comes in: where I come in. But I'm cleverer than some: I don't mind dropping a little money to start the process. I took your father's measure. I saw that he was a child in business, and was dead certain to outrun his expenses and be in too great a hurry to wait for his market. I knew that the surest way to ruin a man who doesn't know how to handle money is to give him some. I explained my idea to some friends in the city, and they found the money; for I take no risks in ideas, even when they're my own ideas. You've been wasting your gratitude: my kind heart is all rot. I'm sick of it. When I see your father beaming gratitude, I sometimes feel I must tell him the truth or burst. He'd think anything rather than the truth, which is that he's a blamed fool, and I am a man that knows how to take care of himself. [*He throws himself back into the big chair with large self-approval*]. Now what do you think of me, Miss Ellie?

ELLIE. [*gripping her hands*] How strange! That my mother, who knew nothing at all about business, should have been quite right about you! She always said—not before papa, of course, but to us children—that you were just that sort of man.

MANGAN. [*sitting up and hurt*] Oh! Did she? And yet she'd have let you marry me.

ELLIE. Well, you see, Mr. Mangan, my mother married a very good man—for whatever you may think of my father as a man of business, he is the soul of goodness—and she is not at all keen on my doing the same.

MANGAN. Anyhow, you don't want to marry me now, do you?

ELLIE. [*very calmly*] Oh, I think so. Why not?

MANGAN. [*rising aghast*] Why not!

ELLIE. I don't see why we shouldn't get on very well together.

MANGAN. Well, but look here, you know—[*he stops, quite at a loss*].

ELLIE. [*pointedly*] Well?

MANGAN. Well, I thought you were rather particular about people's characters.

ELLIE. If we women were particular about men's characters, we should never get married at all, Mr. Mangan.

MANGAN. A child like you talking of "we women"! What next! You're not in earnest?

ELLIE. Yes I am. Aren't you?

MANGAN. Do you mean to hold me to it?

ELLIE. Do you wish to back out of it?

MANGAN. Oh no. Not exactly back out of it.

ELLIE. Well?

[*He has nothing to say. With a long whispered whistle, he drops into the wicker chair and stares before him like a beggared gambler. But a cunning look soon comes into his face. He leans towards her on his right elbow, and speaks in a low steady voice.*]

MANGAN. Suppose I told you I was in love with another woman!

ELLIE. [*echoing him*] Suppose I told you I was in love with another man!

MANGAN. [*bouncing angrily out of his chair*] I'm not joking.

ELLIE. Who told you I was?

MANGAN. I tell you I'm serious. You're too young to be serious; but you'll have to believe me. I want to be near your friend Mrs. Hushabye. I'm in love with her. Now the murder's out.

ELLIE. I want to be near our friend Mr. Hushabye. I'm in love with him. [*She rises and adds with a frank air*] Now we are in one another's confidence, we shall be real friends. Thank you for telling me.

MANGAN. [*almost beside himself*] Do you think I'll be made a convenience of like this?

ELLIE. Come, Mr. Mangan! You made a business convenience of my father. Well, a woman's business is marriage. Why shouldn't I make a domestic convenience of you?

MANGAN. Because I don't choose, see? Because I'm not a silly gull like your father. That's why.

ELLIE. [*with serene contempt*] You are not good enough to clean my father's boots, Mr. Mangan; and I am paying you a great compliment in condescending to make a convenience of you, as you call it. Of course you are free to throw over our engagement if you like; but, if you do, you'll never enter Hesione's house again: I will take care of that.

MANGAN. [*gasping*] You little devil, you've done me. [*On the point of collapsing into the big chair again he recovers himself*] Wait a bit, though: you're not so cute as you think. You can't beat Boss Mangan as easy as that. Suppose I go straight to Mrs. Hushabye and tell her that you're in love with her husband.

ELLIE. She knows it.

MANGAN. You told her!!!

ELLIE. She told me.

And the Winner Is?

Act III is really a coda to the scene. Mangan has been broken—if not his heart, then at least his spirit, whereas Ellie has found strength in her broken heart, her disillusion.

Mangan is, quite literally, in pain; his head's about to explode. He has degenerated from the puffed-up, overfed businessman into a little boy in need of Mummy's help. Shaw describes Ellie as "steady," Mangan as "humble" as the battle ends.

Note: *As we see it, this is a classic status reversal, a moment-to-moment transformation for both characters, each dependent on the other in order to inch forward in the transformation. The action, for Mangan, has the shape of an extended crescendo, becoming more and more agitated and bombastic as the scene progresses. Ellie's transformation is more internal, gathering strength and force from beginning to end.*

> **MANGAN.** [*clutching at his bursting temples*] Oh, this is a crazy house. Or else I'm going clean off my chump. Is she making a swop with you—she to have your husband and you to have hers?
>
> **ELLIE.** Well, you don't want us both, do you?
>
> **MANGAN.** [*throwing himself into the chair distractedly*] My brain won't stand it. My head's going to split. Help! Help me to hold it. Quick: hold it: squeeze it. Save me. [*Ellie comes behind his chair; clasps his head hard for a moment; then begins to draw her hands from his forehead back to his ears.*] Thank you. [*Drowsily*] That's very refreshing. [*Waking a little*] Don't you hypnotize me, though. I've seen men made fools of by hypnotism.
>
> **ELLIE.** [*steadily*] Be quiet. I've seen men made fools of without hypnotism.
>
> **MANGAN.** [*humbly*] You don't dislike touching me, I hope. You never touched me before, I noticed.
>
> **ELLIE.** Not since you fell in love naturally with a grown-up nice woman, who will never expect you to make love to her. And I will never expect him to make love to me.
>
> **MANGAN.** He may, though.
>
> **ELLIE.** [*making her passes rhythmically*] Hush. Go to sleep. Do you hear? You are to go to sleep, go to sleep, go to sleep; be quiet, deeply quiet; sleep, sleep, sleep, sleep, sleep.
>
> [*He falls asleep. Ellie steals away; turns the light out; and goes into the garden.*]

Part C: Rehearsing/Working the Text

Follow The Template

As we've said before, we're working our interpretation of this scene as a model for implementing and using *all* the tools at hand. Follow the steps of The Template and use them as a guide for your own Shavian scene.

Preparation

Read the entire play. Then reread your scene in the play. Underline the operatives and analyze sentence structure to identify the rhetorical devices you use in making your case and winning the argument.

Gather information and begin to speculate about the subtext, working from outside—the text—to the inside, focusing on the psychology motivating you to say these particular words in that particular order to affect the other character—in other words, the objectives.

Consider the context, especially the inner obstacles—the fears, doubts and insecurity that you'll have to overcome to get what you want; research and consider the social, economic and gender obstacles—the external obstacles—that you will have to overcome to get what you want as you play within the rules of the game, and consider the obstacles/resistance that you'll encounter in the other character.

Next, read the text one last time looking for clues about opposites: who's the pusher, who the puller, who's high and who's low on the status ladder in this scene and in this world.

What's New?

As we add the Basic 8, look for patterns involving the elements of visceral effort (i.e., the use of time, weight, and focus-in-space) to determine *how* the character goes about doing what they do (verbs) and to locate the action core/spine of the character (noun), be it presser, puncher, flicker, dabber, slasher wringer, floater or glider.

If you're a presser in your own life, playing a floater will be challenging, but not impossible: you now have tools to help you make that transformation.

Compressing the Steps

As you've adapted to our way of working, the process should start to feel a little easier. So, we're going to compress the steps in the process to move it along a bit more efficiently.

Part D: Table Read

1st Pass: Read the entire scene. As always, focus on using pitch, volume, tempo and force to activate the operatives. Especially with Shaw, play the action through to the end of the line. As with Shakespeare, beware the internal pause. During the read, score your point, don't linger, move on.

Pay attention to the obstacles—internal and external—and how they *intensify* as the scene progresses. Focus on your tactics to overcome those obstacles.

Most critically: talk *to* each other, not *at* each other.

2nd Pass: Working the entire scene, play it quick and light. Get a sense of the forwardness of the scene, the arc of the transformation as it moves from mini to maxi-gap.

To get the thoughts into your body, mark out each beat by changing the way you sit. Eventually you might want to remain still, but for now, get a feel for how you can use all of the Basic 8—the verbs—to disarm your opposition.

Most critically: talk *to* each other, not *at* each other.

3rd Pass: Read the scene, focusing on changing the aspects of time, weight and focus-in-space in tandem with pitch, volume, tempo, and force from line to line, speech to speech. Don't plan out a strategy; use the changes as tactics to respond to whatever's coming your way.

Most critically: talk *to* each other, not *at* each other.

Evaluate

Evaluate the table read: what worked, what didn't work, what you'd like to keep, fix, cut or change as you move from page to stage.

Also, in preparation for that shift, talk about class distinctions, which will always be reflected in dialect. Perhaps Mangan is a bit of a Cockney, while Ellie moves toward standard British. Perhaps. Even if you're not proficient in dialects, attempt one in some form to feel the separation and opposition in social status.

Rehearsal Prompts

Map out the *floor plan* for the house. Know where the garden is, what's behind the doors, what you can see through the windows. Place the furniture to create a real room, not a presentational/theatrical depiction of a room. Once again, *rehearsal clothes* are important. As scripted, Mangan is in evening dress—a tuxedo with a stiff shirt, cufflinks, button studs, and hard soled shoes, and Ellie, as a proper middle-class girl, is also in evening dress, but corseted (while Hesione, as the Bohemian, is uncorseted). Approximate the clothing as best you can to feel what it's like to work within these restrictions.

Consider props: It might be helpful for Mangan to work with a cigar—he is, after all, a successful businessman, and nothing impresses like a cigar after dinner. And Mangan wants to impress all the time; he continually self-references, boasting and bragging about his successes, desperate for attention. Ellie needs to maintain her white-gloved dignity, her integrity. Perhaps she has a small evening bag along with those gloves, which she can remove or keep in hand as the scene progresses.

Part E: Rehearsing the Rehearsal: Acts I and II

As a Warm-Up: *You must know the text verbatim to play this game.*

Stand back-to-back, linking arms. Speaking the text *aloud*, run through the text for Acts I and II. Press into or pull away from your partner's back from line to line.

Speak in tandem with the physical pressure—i.e., make the speaking strong, direct and quick if you're punching, then change the effort slightly—*just one aspect of it*—to punch, or tap, or caress, or wound your partner as the beat changes. Change the action in reaction to what your partner is saying, even if the change feels arbitrary at first. Really play the scene from moment to moment. Repeat, reversing your tactics; play the opposite of what you just played in the warm-up.

1st Pass: Follow the stage directions faithfully.

Resist the temptation to speed through because you think Shaw should be played quickly. Do just the opposite: go slowly from thought to thought. Allow yourself to pause; take in what's been said. You'll eliminate the pauses later.

The script gives you information about *who* you are; experiment with the Basic 8 to discover *how* you are. Mangan, if you believe you're a puncher, start Act I as a puncher by flicking or dabbing; Ellie, if you believe you're a glider, start the act as a glider by flicking or lightly pressing.

Remember, these are the opening salvos in the debate; they will *intensify*—through the use of weight and force—as the scene progresses, depending on whether or not you feel you're winning or losing the "argument."

2nd Pass: Focus on the progression of your argument from Act I to Act II, keeping in mind the punchline at the end of each act, building the argument from Act I to Act II.

Intensify the impact of the operatives by changing the pitch, volume, tempo or force in tandem with changing the Basic 8 as the argument progresses. Mangan: use all elements of the Basic 8 as well as pitch, volume, tempo and force as your control begins to spiral *out* of control. Ellie: use all elements of the Basic 8 as well as pitch, volume, tempo and force to penetrate deeply into Mangan without obvious hostility or open warfare.

3rd Pass: As the objectives, obstacles, and action become clearer to you, focus on *covering* them. Mangan: keep the *mask of success* alive until it starts to crumble by the end of Act II. Ellie: see what happens if you use the *mask of respectability* to resist reacting to Mangan; make him work hard to get a response. Mangan: persist in trying to make Ellie respond.

Evaluate

Evaluate the progress you've made in this rehearsal: what worked, what didn't work, what you'd you like to keep, fix, cut or change.

Showing Acts I and II

As always, use the setting-up of the space as a way to focus your attention physically as well as mentally. Have a specific focus in mind for this run-through—what you'd like to accomplish. Before you start, take a moment to make eye contact with one another, take a deep breath and then begin to play the scene.

Feedback

As you build the score of action, speed bumps are inevitable; you think you know what you're doing but sometimes, alas, it just doesn't read the way you'd like it to. Stay open to feedback about what *isn't* working; that's really more helpful at this stage of the game than feedback about what is working.

Part F: Rehearsing Acts I, II, and III

In this rehearsal, you cannot remain neutral; you must engage viscerally as well as vocally if you want to change emotionally as well as intellectually.

As a Warm-Up: Standing back-to-back, linking arms, and *without* speaking the text aloud, play the entire scene maintaining physical contact with your partner's back; use changes in effort—the Basic 8—rather than the dialogue to make your partner react.

1st Pass: As a lark, clone a model/mask for your character, an iconic actor you'd cast in the role. Play the scene as that iconic mask/model, focusing on the *external* behavior of the character: pressing, punching, flicking, dabbing, slashing, wringing, floating, or gliding (i.e., use the Basic 8 as verbs).

As you play the verbs, use them to take you into the *internal* organizing principle of the character, i.e., the Basic 8 of the noun, be it a presser, puncher, flicker, dabber, slasher, wringer, floater or glider.

Use these two opposing ways of gathering information to strengthen and intensify your ability to play from inside out as well as from the outside in.

2nd Pass: Incorporate your new discoveries into the playing of the scene, and see what happens if you never play the scene *exactly* the same way twice. Yes, even if it's arbitrary or contradictory—*at first*—force yourself to adjust and adapt to your partner with slight changes physically via the use of time, weight, focus-in-space, as well as with pitch, volume, tempo, and force. Keep intensifying all these aspects as the scene progresses by using more force and weight. If your partner reacts in the same way twice, stop, go back, reverse physical positions (changing the relationship in space), begin anew.

Also, play opposites as much as possible. As Mangan loses control and becomes louder, Ellie digs in and becomes quieter. As Mangan flails, Ellie remains still. When Mangan slashes, punches or wrings, Ellie dabs, glides or floats, if necessary.

Again, you're changing just *one aspect* of the effort factors to change the nature of the action (the verb) you're playing. Endow the action with these energetic qualities, and see what happens to the Q of P, the Quality of Play.

Evaluate

Discuss what works, what isn't working—yet—and what you want to keep, fix, cut or change.

3rd Pass: Attend to the speed bumps—those moments when you feel lost, unclear, or unfocused. Work those moments first, then play the entire scene.

As the scene starts to fall into place from moment to moment, eliminate the pauses. This is Shaw, after all, not Chekhov. Shaw's characters, even when lost, confused, adrift or at sea, still want to talk.

Tipping Point

To intensify the playing, think of starting the action in the fourth act of the character's life; this scene is the tipping point in the character's arc and transformation. Then play Act I of the scene already balancing on the cusp of change.

Progression

Remember, you're going to gradually increase either the time—speeding up or slowing down—or the weight—becoming stronger or lighter—as well as increasing or decreasing pitch, volume, tempo, and force—to physicalize the progression of the internal action from Act I to Act II to Act III of the scene.

I'm Right

Use this pass to continue to find proof that you're right. Rather than defending your point of view, *change* your *partner's* point of view: I'm right, you're wrong, I can prove it. Use "I'm right" to expose the flaws and weaken your partner's position in the argument.

Evaluate

Decide what you want to adjust or change when you show the scene. Perhaps it's increasing the impact of what you're saying/doing, or continuing to investigate the core/spine of the character and how it influences the playing of action, or how to deepen the stakes and intensify the playing of the objective while the relationship is transforming. Whatever you decide, individually and collectively, use it to focus your playing as you show the work for the final time.

Showing Acts I, II, and III

As always, take your time setting up the space.

To focus your attention even further, feel the texture of the fabric of your rehearsal clothing, or look around the space and imagine it as the Shotover ship of state, or imagine the meal you've just had and the walk from the dining room to this room.

Take a deep breath, look at one another before you start to play, and when ready, begin the scene.

Feedback

Focus this feedback session on how the scene transformed from rehearsal to rehearsal, and your progress in using the old and the new tools to discover the text, inform the playing, intensify the quality of play and disappear into a character, all while passionately pursuing an objective.

Additional scenes for examination and exercise: with Shaw, Ellie and Hesione, opening of Act I, *Heartbreak House*; Hesione and Mazzini, Act II, *Heartbreak House*; Jack Tanner and Ann Whitefield, Act IV, *Man and Superman*; Tanner and Stryker, Act II, *Man and Superman*, or, for more contemporary plays, *The Normal Heart*

by Larry Kramer, *Ruined* by Lynn Nottage, *Single Asian Female* by Michelle Law, *A Raisin in the Sun* by Lorraine Hansberry, or *Chinglish* by David Henry Hwang, all plays infused with political and social consciousness. as well as heightened language.

What's Next

We'll capitalize on the information you've gathered from the feedback as we move from Shaw to Lynn Nottage and a scene from her Pulitzer Prize winning play, *Sweat*.

We'll use the scene to focus on **releasing** as a tool to increase and encourage spontaneity while exponentially increasing the joy of playing in your playing of a scene.

Twelve

NOTTAGE: RELEASES

Part A: Free Flowing Velocity

Lynn Nottage notes, in her stage directions of *Sweat*: "In general the dialogue should have the free-flowing velocity of a bar conversation, where people step on each other's thoughts, but also occasionally find moments of silence and introspection."

How do we approach this play and infuse Ms. Nottage's language with the same honesty, care, consideration and respect we've shown the plays and language of Shakespeare, Molière, Congreve, Ibsen, and Shaw?

The Steps

By using The Template, adapting it to the needs of the text and the intent of the playwright (as we understand it), you will:

- pinpoint, punch and personalize the operatives;
- identify the punchline, work backwards, then forwards, to craft the set-up and create the arc of the scene—its 180;
- divide the scene into three acts and work each act with a focus on The Loop;
- investigate status shifts and physicalize them by focusing on relationships in space;
- continue to explore pitch, volume, tempo, force and the Basic 8 to deepen and heighten the quality of play, the Q of P, and
- continue to focus, as we've done throughout, on talking *to* rather than *at* one another, and playing action rather than emotion.

We're now going to add into this mix three new tools to heighten spontaneity and increase the sense of The Bounce in rehearsal and performance. In short, you're going to be using *all* the tools at your disposal to continue focusing on relationships transforming in the now—the RTN in *Sweat*.

The New Tools

We're introducing these new tools now because we think they're appropriate for the playing of a very contemporary scene, one requiring vocal and visceral *release* from moment to moment rather than stillness and concentration on speech.

In rehearsals for *Sweat*, we'll be focusing on your ability to listen and respond to your partner with the head nod to signal "I got it, go on with what you're saying," or a long sigh in exasperation, or a little laugh, or an eye roll—in short, the visceral and vocal behavior we use to *fill the silences and pauses*, the unspoken (but always present) subtext, saying without words what you're really thinking and feeling.

We'll develop three "releases," using games inspired by Keith Johnstone, as rehearsal tools, and then apply them to elevate the moment-to-moment quality of playing in our scene.

Here are the tools:

Over-Accepting Offers

As you've discovered, an offer triggers your partner's imagination. Your acceptance of the offer completes the basic unit of play. This game deliberately shifts the focus from one side of the pattern—offering or accepting—to the other. You'll exaggerate to change the dynamics of the playing.

There'll be a high release of energy in this game if you're willing to play an entire range of responses. If you feel trapped responding in one manner, change the pattern dramatically to its opposite end of the spectrum and see what happens.

As an example of over-accepting an offer, watch how Elaine and Kramer react to offers made to them on Seinfeld.

1. Agree on a Where, who will be A, and who will be B.
2. Play a scene in which you over-accept every offer. Scream, yell, shout, laugh, cry—whatever you want, as long as you exaggerate your response to the offer.

3. Once you've reacted and accepted the offer, make an offer of your own to your partner, who'll over-accept the new offer.
4. Play the scene back and forth, over-accepting each offer.
5. Vary the pattern by "over-offering"—making the offer as dynamic, vibrant, and urgent as you can.
6. Accept the offer simply, then over-offer to your partner.
7. Play the scene to its conclusion by either over-offering or over-accepting.

Now, let's add specific "fillers," what we'll call **leads**, into the mix as our second new tool:

When mind and body are in sync, gesturing happens simultaneously with speech. Each reinforces the other; both illustrate the thought as it develops. For example, we all know people who "speak with their hands," i.e., they over-gesture, but the gesture works in conjunction with speech and thought.

Unlike over-accepts, which are played with synchrony, leads deliberately break the synchrony. They literally lead you by either physical or vocal reaction into finding the pathway to the thought of your next line. If you're truly engaged and using the leads, you won't be able to predict how you'll say the line.

Physical and sound leads can be used to trigger spontaneous reactions at the beginning of a line, or they can be used internally within a line to keep the thoughts active and alive. The more non-verbal the lead—using open vowel sounds like oooh! Aha! Ha! Eow!—the better. The more active the physical lead—using arms, hands, torso, even legs to gesture—the better.

1. Play an all offer/all accept scene with your partner. Make as many offers as possible.
2. React physically to every offer. Jump up and down or fall on the floor or run around the room in excitement, despair, exhilaration—whatever your reaction may be.
3. Don't speak when you physicalize. Speak *after* you physicalize.
4. Let the physical response lead you directly *out* of the emotion you're experiencing and *into* speaking.
5. Don't anticipate what you'll say. Let it grow out of the physical lead.

6. Change the pattern: respond vocally, with sound, to each offer. Scream, yell, laugh, cry—whatever emotion arises in response to your partner's line.
7. Use an open vowel sound, if you can, to release the emotion.
8. Let the sound lead you *into* responding.
9. Don't anticipate what you'll say. Let it grow out of the sound lead.
10. Alternate between physical and sound leads.
11. Bring the scene to its logical conclusion.

Both over-offers and leads sound easy. They aren't. If your tendency is to get caught in your head, these tools are designed to scramble that impulse. Once again: the more physical or vocal the lead, the better.

We'll use both over-offers and leads in rehearsal. Once you're familiar with the releases—and the surprises they trigger—you'll be able to either integrate them into your playing of the scene, or tuck them inside as unvoiced or unexpressed internal triggers as you play the scene.

And finally, one more game—our third new tool—a group game about synchrony: **The Squeeze.**

The Squeeze is an advanced game for advanced players. You'll need four players and four chairs to play the game. Johnstone devised this game as a friendship game—the initial premise stresses good humor and mutual respect, with everyone liking one another, which is a prerequisite for playing.

We'll use this game with a different focus: you'll have to fight to stay in the game, and, at times, you will have to resist *your natural impulse to save or rescue someone when they're on the verge of being squeezed out. It will become obvious fairly quickly who's high and who's low within the group, although that will change in the course of the playing. This game will be particularly helpful in establishing the pecking order and hierarchy of dominance in the relationships in the scene from* Sweat.

Learn to play the game first, and then adapt it as you play as your character in the scene from Sweat.

1. Play an all offer/all accept scene.
2. Play seated, with the chairs lined up next to one another,

facing front. Once you sit, you may turn the chairs to face one another.
3. Give each other character names as soon as possible.
4. You are colleagues, working in the same office.
5. First player enters, sits.
6. Second player enters, sits.
7. Third player, also a colleague working in the same office, enters and sits.
8. Fourth player, another colleague, enters and sits.
9. In the course of the scene, try to squeeze, i.e., ignore or eliminate—one person out of the scene.
10. *Really* try to eliminate one player while staying in the scene yourself.
11. Do not talk about who you'll squeeze out. See if it's possible to agree with one another, tacitly, in the course of the playing.
12. If you feel you're being squeezed out, do whatever it takes to stay in the scene.
13. You may move your chair or change your physical position at any time in the course of the scene. Fight to stay in the game.
14. The game ends when someone is eliminated. Just make sure it isn't you!

Keep The Squeeze in mind as you read the *Sweat* scene and track The Squeeze as it progresses throughout the action. As a rehearsal warm-up, we'll play The Squeeze as the characters in the scene.

Using the Rehearsal Tools

Remember that these releases, as well as the Basic 8 and pitch, volume, tempo, force, obstacles, opposition, resistance, operatives and masks, are all tools to make the playing of the scene alive, dynamic, and *fun*—serious fun, but fun all the same. You don't have to be dutiful and check them off a list with *every* scene in every rehearsal. Use them when necessary, discard them when they're not. After all, you're still rehearsing.

Part B: Lynn Nottage, Sweat—Origins

Sweat was commissioned by the Oregon Shakespeare Festival. Lynn Nottage began her writing process for *Sweat* by interviewing citizens in Reading, Pennsylvania, a town of interest to her, she has said, because she wanted to find out what was happening in the country outside of New York. She interviewed Pennsylvanians for a year and a half, then put her research away and began writing.

After its premiere in Ashland, Oregon, the production moved to The Public Theatre in New York, then to Broadway in 2017. The play won the Pulitzer Prize for Drama that year, making Ms. Nottage the only woman in history to win two Pulitzers (she was awarded her first in 2008 for her play *Ruined*).

Points of View

Once again, we're using our interpretation of the text to model the analytical skills you need when you read a play—any play. As you're discovering, these skills—actually, all the skills and tools we've been developing—become easier with time and practice. The goal is for you to approach a play and a role from *your* point of view, not ours.

The Argument

With *Sweat*, Nottage takes a stand against corporate greed and the devastating price paid by American workers and their families in response to it.

Sweat straddles two contrasting eras, pre–2008 recession and post–2008 recession America. The characters themselves exist in a state of contradiction, balancing their loyalty to the factory (and their employer) with loyalty to family and friends. They're united in an abiding belief in the promise of the American Dream.

The long suppressed racial prejudices, rages over economic disparities, and the seemingly distant threat of the NAFTA deal (the North American Free Trade Agreement, which would move American jobs overseas) live under the surface, creating an inflammatory, toxic environment of emotional and psychic violence.

Painting in both broad and detailed strokes, Nottage parallels two stories: the historic decline of blue collar/rust belt America in the first decade of the 21st century, and the more personal stories of those whose lives are quietly being shattered by economic upheaval.

Context

"August 4th, 2000—Outside it's 80 F. Partly cloudy and pleasant. In the news: Republican presidential candidate George W. Bush begins a post-convention train blitz across the Midwest."

Tracey, Cynthia, and Jessie, all in their mid–40s, worked the line at Olstead's, a steel tubing factory in Reading, PA. Cynthia, who is African American, applied for and was awarded a position in management, bypassing Tracey, who is Caucasian.

Management is in the process of downsizing its work force by moving manufacturing to Mexico as part of the NAFTA trade deal. Tracey and Jessie have been laid off; Cynthia continues to work.

These three women have been drinking companions for years. While Cynthia ascends in management, Tracey's been left behind. Deep resentments have gradually risen to the surface in the course of this year, as the workers try to save their livelihoods and their identities.

The Setting

The three women celebrate birthdays at Loco's bar. Stan, the bartender, once worked on the line until an accident forced him to quit. Tonight is Cynthia's birthday. She's hoping her friends will show up to help her celebrate. Relationships are strained, to say the very least.

Nottage frames each act of her play with scenes set in 2008. In essence, the bulk of the play happens in flashback. We know at the top of Act II that Cynthia no longer works for Olstead's—she has two jobs, as a university maintenance worker and at a nursing home on weekends. Tracey, no longer working, is strung out on drugs.

The Characters

Whereas Congreve's and Shaw's characters speak in aristocratic, well-educated prose, Nottage's characters speak from the heart, as people educated in the school of hard knocks. Stan and Jessica's characters have lines here that have been left in for continuity, but this exercise only needs two actors.

- **CYNTHIA**

    Having worked at Olstead's since she was 19, Cynthia is a self-proclaimed "worker" who wants more for herself than working on the line. She's someone who plays by the company's rules and is trying to remain loyal to her friends. She now suspects that she was a token hire by Olstead's—hired to do the dirty work of terminating workers while the higher-ups sit in their air-conditioned offices finding ways to cut costs while boosting profit margins.

    ### The Stakes for Cynthia

    Cynthia wants to help Tracey, Jessie, and the others, yet she needs to hold on to her job and the income it provides. Brucie, her estranged husband, has pretty much given up; he's abandoned the family, returning to Cynthia for handouts when he's in desperate need of cash. Cynthia hopes her friends will remember and help her celebrate her birthday—at least that's the excuse she makes to justify her return to the bar.

- **TRACEY**

    Tracey has worked at Olstead's for over 20 years, in keeping with family tradition (her father was also a worker at the factory). For both women, work is all they've ever known. When they were able to provide for their families, both women enjoyed the camaraderie of the bar community. Along with Jessie, they'd gather at Loco's for a few laughs, or to commiserate, or to celebrate the end of the day or the end of the work week.

    Tracey is a widow and a Caucasian of German descent. She's outspoken, fierce in her opinions, and not afraid of a fight. She feels betrayed by Cynthia; she believes that she, Jessie and the other workers are now victims of Olstead's disloyalty to its workers. She also feels abandoned by her union.

    ### The Stakes for Tracey

    Money is running out, and she's watching her life crash and burn. While she would still like to honor her friendship with

Cynthia, Tracey has to push her away as someone disloyal to her cause. Twenty-five years of friendship is now on the line, and that line is rapidly evaporating.

Tracey also resents Oscar, the Colombian-American bar-back who has crossed the picket line to pick up extra cash. Tracey is unabashed in her dislike of Oscar, as her racist comments make clear. She's not afraid to speak her mind, political correctness be damned.

The Contrasts

Tracey's the slasher and the wringer; she comes out swinging, continuing in like manner throughout the scene. Her sound—her pitch and force—grows in intensity as the argument develops. She switches gears in our Act II, then downshifts once again in our Act III to hit home, hard and deep.

Cynthia, in contrast, is too strong to be a glider, too fierce not to punch, when necessary, yet is primarily someone who presses, consistently, to clear the path in front of her, forging her own way.

Tracey makes a lot of noise. She seems to drive the confrontation, while Cynthia's the calm presence in the center of the storm. The status see-saw is constant throughout, and the force of the argument veers from one side to the other.

Text

This scene is a quartet; Jessie and Stan, crucial for our Act II of the scene, are not the major focus of the conflict. They comment and reinforce, but they don't drive the action. You will need two additional actors to rehearse the scene in the latter stages of the rehearsal process.

Sweat, Act II, scene 3

The title of our scene: "**The Break-Up**"

Tracey wants Cynthia to help her win the stalemate with management, but Cynthia is like the rock of Gibraltar: she can only go so far, no further. Cynthia seemingly has the high position, in terms of status, yet she cedes the floor to Tracey. Tracey makes all the noise, yet needs Cynthia to show some compassion, some empathy.

The argument dominates **Act I**; *there's no small talk, no prelude. Cynthia and Tracey see-saw from line to line. Point/counterpoint. Tracey's the pusher, Cynthia the puller. The action moves directly into "you abandoned us/what am I supposed to do?"*

This first act builds in intensity to its climax with Tracey's lament of being housebound. In fury, she asks Cynthia: "Why'd you come in here? Huh? What do you want?" Cynthia's quiet response, "It's my birthday. And this is where we always celebrated," acts as the denouement, bringing things back to a quiet balance.

The Stand-Off

Tracey and Jessica enter. They stop short upon seeing Cynthia. The tension is palpable.

TRACEY. [*Under her breath.*] Fucking traitor.

CYNTHIA. What did you say?

TRACEY. I said you fucking traitor.

JESSIE. How does it feel to shit on your friends?

Cynthia stands up.

CYNTHIA. [*To Stan.*] I'm gonna go.

TRACEY. That's right. Walk away.

CYNTHIA. I'm not walking away, I'm leaving. There's a difference, don't get it confused. You know, you coulda taken the deal.

TRACEY. What deal? I'd rather get locked out, and take handouts from the union than let go of everything I worked for. That's the truth.

JESSIE. What you did wasn't right!

TRACEY. They didn't even give us a fucking choice! After all of those years.

CYNTHIA. I just delivered the news, babe. I didn't make the policy.

JESSIE. [*Shouts.*] You're supposed to be on our side!

CYNTHIA. [*Shouts back.*] I am!

TRACEY. Do you know what it felt like to walk up to that plant, and be told after all them years I can't go in? I can't even go into my locker and get my stuff. I have photos of my husband in there. I have my grandfather's toolbox.

CYNTHIA. I'll get it for you, babe.

TRACEY. I don't want you to touch anything in that locker! They didn't even have the decency to let us clear out with dignity. A note taped to the door, what is that? And then to see you just standing there. I thought I was gonna lose my shit.

CYNTHIA. I tried to warn you. I hated it.

TRACEY. I looked for your eyes. Just gimme something Cynth. A little look, to let me know its's okay, but you wouldn't even fucking look at me.

CYNTHIA. I'm in a tough-ass position, babe. I got enough attitude from folks to give me a heart attack. I'm trying to hold things together as best I can.

TRACEY. What the fuck am I supposed to do? Huh? You coulda called me. Given me a heads up. I mean come on. What am I supposed to do? Who's gonna hire me?

CYNTHIA. I know it hurts, babe. Take the deal.

TRACEY. NO! You hear yourself?

JESSIE. Can I have a beer, Stan?

STAN. Sure.

TRACEY. The other day, I walked over to the union office. Do you know what they offered me? A bag of groceries and some vouchers to the supermarket. They asked us to hold out, they're gonna help. Yeah, pay my fucking bills, that's how you can help. But, you know how many people were there for handouts? I looked for your eyes. Gimme something, Cynth. It was fucking humiliating.

CYNTHIA. Look, I'm sorry.

TRACEY. What am I supposed to do with that? Huh? What do you want me to do with that? You know what? This is my first time outta my house in one solid week. Do you know what it's like to get up and have no place to go? I ain't had the feeling ever. I'm a worker. I have worked since I could count money. That's me. And I think I'm not gonna go out, you know why? Because I don't wanna spend money, because when my unemployment runs out I'll have nothing. So, I don't go anywhere. And if Jessie hadn't called me, I'd still be sitting on my couch feeling sorry for myself, picking at my fucking cuticles. Why'd you come in here? Huh? What do you want?

CYNTHIA. It's my birthday. And this is where we've always celebrated.

Atlantic City

Tracey shifts tactics in this act by telling the story of the two-family vacation to Atlantic City she made with Cynthia, their husbands, Brucie and Hank, and their sons, Jordan and Chris.

Rather than play the action directly, Tracey tells the story to Jessie and Stan, avoiding contact with Cynthia, though the story is aimed directly at Cynthia and is being told for her benefit. She talks about the past to make a point in the present, softening Cynthia up by recalling happier times with their younger selves. Cynthia goes along with it. Tracey ends the act by bringing them back to the present: "That's my friend, and I miss the Cynthia who understood that."

*Equilibrium has been established in **Act II**: Tracey takes the lead; Cynthia provides color commentary. The entire tone of the scene has shifted; the animosity has dissipated and a balance has been reestablished. There appears to be a truce. Common ground. The status seesaw has slowed down.*

There's a performative aspect to what Tracey says and does; after all, she's in a bar, talking and telling stories as we've seen her do at the top of the play's Act I. Now, however, there's a deeper meaning to her story: Tracey wants to woo Cynthia, to bring her in as an advocate, a compatriot in the cause. She uses personal history, indirectly, to score points, to win the round. She almost does.

[*A moment. Tracey lights a cigarette.*]

TRACEY. Do you remember that time we went to Atlantic City for your twenty-fifth?

CYNTHIA. Yeah, it was before Hank got sick.

TRACEY. The boys Jason and Chris were little. It was the four of us. You, Brucie, me, and Hank. We splurged, got a suite.

CYNTHIA. Of course I remember.... It was for the fight. Larry Holmes.

TRACEY. That's right. Hank had a friend, a high roller, and after the fight he invited us to one of those back-room clubs, you know very fancy, Champagne, buffet, seafood fountain, everything, really classy stuff.

CYNTHIA. Why are you bringing this up, Tracey?

TRACEY. Brucie was at the craps table rolling like a pro. Drenched in luck. It was just dripping off of him. The chips were leaping into his hands. And if I recall, he was also looking sorta fine that evening.

CYNTHIA. Yes, he was.

TRACEY. And then this chick.

CYNTHIA. C'mon, stop—

TRACEY. Yes, this chick. Legs, ass, boobs, weave. She was giving a full service vibe, "walks" up and settles in next to Brucie—

JESSIE. Settles?

TRACEY. Her breasts were enormous, epic. Her dress, barely visible. I'm not a lesbian, but I couldn't take my eyes off of her boobs.

CYNTHIA. Why are you telling this story?

TRACEY. This chick was in heat, and she ever so gently places her hand on Brucie's shoulder, like this. I look over to Cynthia—

CYNTHIA. Don't—

TRACEY. And—

CYNTHIA. No—

TRACEY. She—

CYNTHIA. Lord, help me—

TRACEY. Is wearing the look. Stone age. Prehistoric. T. rex. And I know what it means, Brucie knows what it means, but this bitch doesn't. Boobs leans over and whispers something into Brucie's ear. That's it. You just grab this chick's tits, and dig your fingernails in as hard as you can.

CYNTHIA. Yes, I did.

STAN. Whoa.

CYNTHIA. I'd had a couple tequilas. I wanted to deflate those fake tits. Puncture them with my fingernails.

TRACEY. Next thing I know, Cynthia's on the floor rolling around. Two grown women. It was sick. You put up a fight like a pro wrestler.

STAN. Jesus. Atlantic City. That's why I avoid it.

TRACEY. But, I remember thinking: That's my friend. She's tough as hell. Don't mess with her. She'll fight for what she loves, even if it means getting scrappy and looking ugly. That's my friend, and I miss the Cynthia who understood that.

The Show Down

Act III is a short act, just eight lines. In those eight lines, the conflict is both resolved and deepened. This act has its own distinctive dynamic: it's much quieter than the previous two, much more intimate. The first act was explosive, direct; the second, lighter in tone, more indirect, working through Jessie and Stan; this third act returns to direct contact, but with a newer, more resolved, more resolute tone.

> **CYNTHIA.** What do you want from me, Tracey?
> **TRACEY.** Walk with us. C'mon.
> **CYNTHIA.** I can't.
> **JESSIE.** C'mon.
> **CYNTHIA.** I've stood on that line same line since I was nineteen. I've taken orders from idiots who were dangerous, or even worse, racist. But I stood on the line, patiently waiting for a break. I don't think you get it, but if I walk away, I'm giving up more than a job, I'm giving up all that time I spent, standing on line waiting for one damn opportunity.
> **TRACEY.** You want us to feel sorry for you?
> **CYNTHIA.** … I didn't expect you to understand, babe. You don't know what it's been like to walk in my shoes. I've absorbed a lotta shit over the years, but I worked hard to get off that floor. Call me selfish, I don't care, call me whatever you need to call me, but remember, one of us has to be left standing to fight.

Part C: Preparation

Follow the steps in The Template as closely and as accurately as possible for whichever contemporary scene—preferably from *Sweat*—you choose to work on.

Context

This is blue collar country; the characters deserve to be played with the same dignity Nottage accords them. You can't judge them based on their socio-economic conditions, education, or life choices. You have to empathize with them, give them the full humanity they deserve.

Just as you have to know the world you're going to live in if you're doing Congreve, Shaw or Ibsen, now you must know the world of Reading, PA, in 2000 and 2008: look for photographs taken before and after the 2008 recession in Reading. Watch *Mare of Easttown*, *Norma Rae*, *Frozen River*, or *The Fighter*. Immerse yourself in the history of the labor movement and the politics informing the 2008 presidential election.

Biographies

Group biographies are vital in developing the life of this community, as are *individual biographies*. Think of these group biographies as a history of a *relationship*. Play "You Always, You Never" to build the shared history between Tracey and Cynthia. Expand it to include the ancillary relationships with Jessie and Stan.

Rehearsal Prompts

Know the layout of the bar. Since we're pack animals, we all have our favorite watering holes, our traditional—or habitual—spots to mark our territories, our personal queen/kingdoms. Decide who sits where at Loco's, and what it means to cross the line, i.e., to sit at someone else's table.

Gauge the emotional temperature just before last call, that hour of frustration and desperation right before the lights come on, when reality descends and the night ends.

Every object, every garment, especially in contemporary theatre, is an instantly recognizable artifact giving us socio-economic information. Therefore, consider what you'd wear for a night out, after so many nights of confinement. Do you dress up or wear your work clothes? Hard or soft soled shoes? Shoulder bags with straps or small purses?

The Dialect

You're not playing aristocrats or the haute bourgeoisie—you're playing working class Americans, yet accents and dialects are as important as British accents and dialects in English plays: they give us information about character, education, background, and life experience. Use them.

Preparing the Text

As a reminder, even though the text is deliberately written to have a working-class veneer, as you did with Shakespeare, Molière, Congreve, Ibsen and Shaw, *pin*, *punch* and *personalize* the operatives; heed the length of the sentences; play through to the end of the thoughts. Beware the off-glide/downward inflection; if you're going off voice before the end of the line, chances are you're not playing the objective through the entire line.

Compression

As we did with *Heartbreak House,* we're compressing the rehearsal process to take you further faster.

1st Read: Read this scene, Act II, scene 3 of *Sweat*, in its entirety. Start at the top of the scene with the exchange between Stan and Cynthia.

Remember, every scene starts with a reaction to what's just been said and/or done. Build the memory of this first scene into your muscle memory at the start of our scene.

1st Pass: As always, sit with headlights facing one another, even if, in our Act II, you might be playing indirectly rather than directly. Establish contact.

Concentrate on how you want your partner to feel and what you do to provoke them into making you feel the way you want to feel. Build into this foundation of the scene specific, moment-to-moment shifts in tactics by changing physically and vocally every time the thought changes. Use pitch, volume, tempo, and force as well as the Basic 8 to make the changes.

Even as you sit reading, overlap the dialogue and keep the cues tight. As in life, if you're truly listening, you'll have something to say in response to what's being said, for, in life, halfway through someone's thought we're already anticipating where the thought's going and we're ready to break in and move the conversation along.

2nd Pass: To help clarify the "argument" of the scene and your character's point of view, *switch roles.* Argue the other character's point of view. Understanding what they want from you—by you having to pursue it from *their* point of view—will help you clarify *your* character's point of view and what you want from your partner. Remember, the want—the objective—is always stated as: "I want you to … (do something) … to me."

Evaluate

Talk about what's working, what isn't working, and how you'll adjust the playing next time to keep it fresh.

Part D: Acts I and II

1st Pass: In this rehearsal, develop a visceral feel for the interaction between the characters by focusing on variations with the Basic 8 as both noun and verb: to press, punch, flick, dab, slash, wring, float or glide.

Once again, don't be afraid to exaggerate the Basic 8: go over the top, do too much, anything to clarify the action by making it specific. If you need an image of the character, build a body mask or clone a friend, one who you think corresponds to your character. Play in that "invisible envelope" to see what it feels like to live in that character's world.

Since Act II is built on strong opposition, be mindful of who is sitting, who is standing and when you change position. Stan, Jessie: experiment with how near or how far you are from Cynthia and Tracey. You'll have to decide if you sit at the bar or at "your usual," and how that affects your comfort or discomfort in the scene.

Cynthia and Tracey: the person with the highest status usually moves least, holding their space. No extraneous arm movements or over-gesturing. Physical stillness equates with power. Use both extremes—stillness and movement—to define and clarify your status.

Evaluate

Discuss what worked, what isn't working, and what you'd like to keep, fix, cut or change for the next pass.

2nd Pass: Use The Squeeze in conjunction with the text. Decide, at any given moment, who's your Number 1 (the person at the top of your status pyramid), and who you want to squeeze out of the game. If you feel you're being squeezed, fight to stay in viscerally and vocally.

Attend to the changing physical and emotional dynamics in this specific Squeeze and incorporate that new information into your playing of the score of action.

Evaluate

Discuss what worked, what didn't work, what you'd like to keep, fix, cut or change based on the information you gathered during The Squeeze. Incorporate that information into the next pass.

3rd Pass: Try to *never* repeat yourself each time you work a moment in either act. Make small adjustments from moment to moment; surprise yourself and your partners.

Then, concentrate on the shape of both acts: as you're adjusting your playing, build a crescendo into Act I by *topping* one another, letting the action crest from line to line with pitch, volume, tempo and force.

Change tactics for Act II and play with a lighter energy throughout most of the act until it deepens at the end of the act. Focus on discovering the forwardness in the playing. If the forwardness is happening, chances are there's a bounce happening as well.

Evaluate

Talk about what's working, what isn't working, and what you'd like to keep, fix, cut or change when you show the scene.

The Showing

Have a specific focus for this run-though. Use the physical setting-up of the space as part of your preparation for the scene. Take a moment to look at one another before you start to play, take a deep breath and then play the scene.

Feedback

As always, stay open to the feedback from your instructor. If you have specific questions about any moment in the scene, ask.

Discuss the feedback with your partner after you've finished showing the scene. Talk about your plan of attack for the next rehearsals.

Part E: Acts I, II, and III

1st Pass: To further test, enhance, and improve the Quality of Play: play the entire scene as if you're in a movie; play full out, speaking and gesturing as normal. Now: imagine someone pushed the mute button on a remote control—you're still playing the scene, speaking and moving, but there's no sound. Don't whisper; simply eliminate all sound from the scene. Move directly to:

2nd Pass: Restoring sound to the scene, run through all three acts using either *physical and/or sound leads*, or alternate them. Don't plan how or when you'll use them; let them arise spontaneously in reaction to what's being said to you.

Use the physical leads to keep your body alive before you speak. Do the same with sound leads; use them to keep your playing alive and spontaneous before you speak. Allow your emotional reactions to lead you into your next line. You're not playing emotion; you're playing *action* triggered by emotion.

You don't have to use sound leads all the time. Move directly to:

3rd Pass: Without *having* to use the actual leads, run through the entire scene again. If the leads arise spontaneously, use them to change how you react to what's being said or sent your way. If they don't arise spontaneously this time through, continue to stay alert and alive to the changes they provoked in the 2nd pass. They're a tool to help keep you present by focusing on reacting before you leap into action. Let them lead you. *That's the point: spontaneous reaction leading to spontaneous action.* Continue to overlap the lines, and remember: the scene is a quartet, not a duet.

Evaluate

If the playing isn't specific from moment to moment, i.e., if the thought isn't alive and changing, if you're not listening and responding as if for the first time, if you're playing by rote or constantly judging and critiquing what you're doing from moment to moment, you aren't really present, you aren't really playing, and you're short-changing the audience, your scene partner, and yourself.

The Showing

Have a specific focus for this run-though. Use the physical setting-up of the space as part of your preparation for the scene. Take a moment to look at one another, then take a deep breath before you start to play.

Feedback

Your instructor and your colleagues have witnessed your growth from the beginning of this process to the moment you've finished playing your scene. Share the changes and transformation you've experienced in yourself and in your fellow players.

Take in and recognize your growth, your ability to play, your ability to respond *in* the moment *to* the moments of darkness and the moments of light throughout the process.

For other contemporary plays combining heightened language, social issues, and a realistic context, see *Marisol* by José Rivera, *Anna in the Tropics* by Nilo Cruz, or *Zoot Suit* by Luis Valdez.

We'll End Where We Began

There aren't any shortcuts in this process. No easy outs. No instant fixes. You have to put in the work to reap the benefits of the work. Yes, this is very old school thinking, but *it works*.

Gradually, over time, the process becomes easier. You don't have to think as much about what you're doing. You're free to play more, to be spontaneous as you respond to your partner.

With patience, practice and persistence, you'll gradually feel secure in your ability to work: it's no longer hit-or-miss, and there's a method to the madness. It serves you. How you use The Template—the steps in the process—may vary from scene to scene, but The Template always works.

With this knowledge, you're able to build confidence in your ability to play any text, anywhere. You know how to work, and there's joy, release, pleasure in the playing. It's not about the homework;

no one wants to see your preparation. It's about how you play in the moment.

As you play more freely, more openly, with a deeper sense of creativity, a deeper connection to yourself, and a deeper connection to the material, you will begin to discover your own creative voice and, with it, the joy of playing action on the line or below the line, playing action through words and movement, in stillness and in motion. Action is theatrical life itself, living and breathing within the text, context and subtext of every play. As you master the technique of acting, you can begin to play with style.

Appendix

Additional Plays and Playwrights

Baraka, Amiri—*Dutchman*
Behn, Aphra—*The Rover*
Brecht, Berthold—*Mother Courage and Her Children, The Caucasian Chaulk Circle*
Calderón—*Life is a Dream*
Chin, Frank—*The Chickencoop Chinaman*
Churchill, Caryl—*Cloud Nine, Top Girls, Serious Money, Far Away*
Corneille, Pierre—*Le Cid*
de Vega, Lope—*Fuente Ovejuna*
Ford, John—*T'is Pity She's a Whore*
Fornés, María Irene—*Fefu and Her Friends, Abingdon Square*
Fugard, Athol—*"MASTER HAROLD" … and the Boys*
Goldoni, Carlo—*Servant of Two Masters*
Gotanda, Philip Kan—*Yankee Dawg You Die*
Hansberry, Lorraine—*A Raisin in the Sun, The Sign in Sidney Brustein's Window*
Harris, Jeremy O.—*Slave Play*
Huang, David Henry—*M. Butterfly*
Ionesco, Eugène—*Rhinoceros, The Bald Soprano*
Jonson, Ben—*Volpone, The Alchemist*
Joseph, Rajiv—*Dirty Rotten Playground Tricks*
Kalidasa—*Shakuntala*
Kennedy, Adrienne—*Funnyhouse of the Negro*

Leguizamo, John—*Latin History for Morons*

Marlowe, Christopher—*Doctor Faustus, Tamburlaine, The Jew of Malta*

Middleton, Thomas, and Benjamin Rowley—*The Changeling*

Parks, Suzan-Lori—*Topdog/Underdog, The Death of the Last Black Man in the Whole Entire World*

Racine, Jean—*Phaedra*

Sartre, Jean-Paul—*Antigone*

Smith, Anna Deveare—*Twilight: Los Angeles, Fires in the Mirror*

Soyinka, Wole—*Death and the King's Horseman, The Lion and the Jewel, The Strong Breed*

Treadwell, Sophie—*Machinal*

Vogel, Paula—*How I Learned to Drive*

Webster, John—*The Duchess of Malfi*

Wilde, Oscar—*The Importance of Being Earnest, Salomé*

Wilson, August—*Ma Rainey's Black Bottom, Joe Turner's Come and Gone, Jitney*

Wolfe, George C.—*The Colored Museum*

Yew, Chay—*A Language of their Own, Red*

Glossary

Action: what you do to provoke a response

Antithesis: comparing opposites

As If: engaging the imagination

Beat: a unit of action

Blank Verse: groups of words with an unequal balance of length of syllables

Bounce: the exchange of energy between players

Cognitive pauses: time used to plan what to say in silence

Congruency: matching gesture with gesture

Cover: using an action to disguise or divert attention from what's really happening

End Stop: when a thought ends in verse, usually signaled by a period (.)

Filled Pauses: oh, um ... sounds filling silences in verbal communication

Five A's: Attention, Affection, Acceptance, Allowance, Approval

Flow: the sensation of connected head/heart/body playing

Forwardness: the sensation of action moving in a specific direction

Hinge: the moment a speech or scene turns from one action to another

Idling: marking time, not engaging in forward action

Incongruency: when gestures don't match

Indicating: representing an emotion or action, not experiencing or playing it

Jumps: intellectualizing the progression from M2M rather than allowing it to evolve on its own

KFCC: Keep, Fix, Cut, Change

Maxi-Gap: the widest distance possible in a status gap between two players in a master/servant relationship

Mini-Gap: the narrowest distance possible in a status gap between two equal players

M2M: moment-to-moment

Mono-Active: Playing one action over and over and over again

Offer & Accept: offering a provocation, accepting the provocation

Operative Words: words carrying the most important information in a sentence or phrase

Pin, Punch, Personalize: identifying, stressing and exaggerating, then individuating operative words

Playing: how you do what you do, involving flow, forwardness, and bounce

Point of Entry: the focus used at the beginning of a scene in rehearsal

Pusher: people who fill and inhabit space, moving out to the listener

Puller: people who draw the listener into them

RTN: Relationships Transforming Now

Run-ons: a thought so filled, in verse, it elides directly from the end of one line into the next

Score of Action: a repeatable sequence of actions making up a scene

Speed Bumps: problem moments in the score of action, needing special attention in rehearsal

Status: patterns and positions of dominance

Super-Objective: the punchline at the end of a scene or act or play; what you want for yourself

Syncing Loops: action/reaction loops indicating stops and starts in communicating

Social Pauses: signals saying, "Don't interrupt!"

Teleprompter Acting: seeing the words on the page when you look at your partner

Tension Blocks: energy traps stopping the flow of imagination, preventing creative release

The Loop: the action/reaction/action chain between players based on how you want the other to feel

Verse: groups of words with a balancing of the felt weight and length of syllables

Sources and Resources

Alberti, Joe. *Acting: The Gister Method*. Pearson, 2013.
Bandler, Richard. *The Ultimate Introduction to NLP*. HarperCollins, 2013.
Barton, John. *Playing Shakespeare*. Methuen, 1984.
Berry, Cicely. *The Actor and the Text*. Charles Scribner's Sons, 1987.
Briggs Myers, Isabel. *Gifts Differing*. Davis Black Publishing, 1980.
Chekhov, Michael. *To the Actor: On the Technique of Acting*. Routledge, 2002.
de Bono, Edward. *Lateral Thinking*. Penguin Books, 1970.
Dell, Cecily. *A Primer for Movement Description*. Dance Notation Bureau Press, 1970.
Dudeck, Theresa. *Keith Johnstone: A Critical Biography*. Metheun Drama, 2013.
Edelstein, Barry. *Thinking Shakespeare*. Revised edition. TCG, 2018.
Elgin, Suzette Haden. *The Gentle Art of Verbal Self Defense*. Prentice-Hall, 1982.
Gist, Jan. *Shakespeare's Shapely Language*. Unpublished manuscript used with permission.
Hagen, Uta. *Respect for Acting*. Macmillan Publishing Co., 1973.
Harrop, John, and Sabin Epstein. *Acting with Style*, 3rd edition. Allyn & Bacon, 2000.
Henley, Nancy. *Body Politics*. Prentice-Hall, 1977.
Johnstone, Keith. *Impro*. Theatre Arts Books, 1979.
Jung, Carl. *Man and His Symbols*. Doubleday Windfall, 1964.
Lewis, Hedwig. *Body Language*, 3rd edition. Sage Publications, 1998.
Pease, Allan. *Signals*. Bantam Books, 1981.
Richo, David. *How to be an Adult*. Shambala Publications, 2002.
Skinner, Edith. *Speak with Distinction*. Applause Theatre Books, 1990.
Spolin, Viola. *Improvisation for the Theatre*. Northwestern University Press, 1963.
Stanislavski, Constantin. *An Actor Prepares*. Translated by Elizabeth Reynolds Hapgood. Theatre Arts, 1948.
Wheatley, Margaret. *A Simpler Way*. Berret-Koehler Publishers, Inc. 1998.

Index of Games and Exercises

Arm Wrestling 178

Back-to-Back 226
Basic 8 213
Book Balance 213

Changes of Direction 68
Changing Tempo 26
Cloning 172
Compliments 130
Count the Syllables 51
Cross Thru 27

Different Setting 110
The Dolly 95

Getting Dressed 133
Grab Bag Characters 171

How You Say What You Say 33

I'm Right 228
In Nine 27
Insults 131

Just Once 118
Just 3 Moves 90

Leads 232
Linked Arms 224
Love Poem 56

Move/No Move 148
Mute 248

Obstacle Course 83
Over Accepts 231
Over Offers 231

Parallels 110
Paraphrasing 68
Pin/Punch/Personalize 174
Playing a Sonnet 67
Pro & Con 61
Putty Masks 170

Real Names 109
Remember When 23
Rhyming Images 125

See Saw 131
Sell the Car 112
Song Exercise 48
Spies 176
Squat 10 28
The Squeeze 233
Status Bodies 129
Status Transformations 134
Stomping 68
Switch Roles 245

Tapping 17
Tell a Story 13
Tilting 121

Which Ear? 21

You Always 201
You Never 202

www.ingramcontent.com/pod-product-compliance
Ingram Content Group UK Ltd.
Pitfield, Milton Keynes, MK11 3LW, UK
UKHW041933140426
5217IPUK00014B/460